READING CHINESE FORTUNE COOKIE

READING CHINESE FORTUNE COOKIE

The Making of Chinese American Rhetoric

LUMING MAO

UTAH STATE UNIVERSITY PRESS
Logan, UT

Utah State University Press
Logan, Utah 84322-7800

Manufactured in the United States of America
Cover design by Barbara Yale-Read

Library of Congress Cataloging-in-Publication Data

Mao, LuMing, 1957-
  Reading Chinese fortune cookie : the making of Chinese American rhetoric / LuMing Mao.
    p. cm.
  Includes bibliographical references and index.
  ISBN 0-87421-640-0 (pbk. : acid-free paper)
  1. English language–United States–Rhetoric. 2. Chinese Americans–Languages. 3. Chinese lan-
guage–Influence on English. 4.
Language and culture–United States. 5. Intercultural communication–United States. 6.
Sociolinguistics. I. Title.
  PE3102.C45M36 2006
  808'.04208951073–dc22
                          2006004974

To my parents

CONTENTS

ACKNOWLEDGMENTS

In early July 2001, I participated, at the invitation of Professor Keith Gilyard of Pennsylvania State University, in the Biennial Penn State Conference on Rhetoric and Composition, and the theme of the conference was "American Ethnic Rhetorics." By that time I had just begun to conceptualize the role of rhetorical borderlands in the formation of Asian American and Chinese American rhetoric. I was therefore anxious to share with my colleagues and other conference participants some of these initial, mostly unsettled, thoughts on the subject. Not only did the audience who came to my session respond to my talk quite warmly, but also they offered many thoughtful and constructive comments. The fact that this short talk has now turned into a book has a lot to do with them, and with what went on at that conference in the summer of 2001. In particular, I thank Professor Gilyard for his invitation, for organizing the conference, and for, above all, his support of this project and of all other work I do.

In the intervening years, I have accumulated many debts from friends and colleagues. To write a book of this kind is never a solitary undertaking, but one that calls on the kindness and generosity of many others. While it is perhaps a futile exercise to mention here all the people who have had a hand in helping me to bring this project to fruition, I would be remiss indeed should I fail to acknowledge these individuals.

My friends and colleagues in the Department of English at my own institution have always been quite supportive of my work. Their generosity and their capacity for understanding are what I treasure and depend on day in and day out. For their encouragement and many productive conversations, I thank Donald Daiker, Mary Fuller, Britton Harwood, Jean Lutz, Max Morenberg (who is now at Boca Raton, retired only in name), Susan Morgan, Kate Ronald, Jerome Rosenberg, Dianne Sadoff, David Schloss, Kay Sloan, Edward Tomarken, and Morris Young. My chair, Keith Tuma, was particularly supportive as the project moved into its final phase. And William Wortman, our humanities librarian, is always willing and able to assist me whenever I need him, and often without any advance notice. I am very thankful to the Department and the University for providing me with research time and funding, which have made it possible for me to complete this project in a timely fashion.

I have learned much from my students, with whom I have engaged in many fruitful discussions both in and outside class. These discussions have propelled me to ask tougher questions and to search for more satisfying answers. I simply could not have asked for more engaging interlocutors.

I am also in debt to many friends and colleagues beyond my own institution—individuals who have listened to my ideas with understanding and who have inspired my work with their own exemplary contributions to the field. I thank Patricia Bizzell, Marilyn Cooper, Lisa Ede, Helen Fox, Mary Garrett, Lawrence Green, Xiao-Ming Li, Xing Lu, Andrea Lunsford, Marilyn Moller, Charles Schuster, and Jan Swearingen. And I am grateful to members of Asian/Asian American Caucus at the annual Conference of College Composition and Communication for the kind of community that they help to nurture, and that in turn has helped to nurture and sustain my work. I am equally grateful to my Cincinnati Chinese American community for their unwavering support of this project. As a matter of fact, it is my association with this community that has in part led me to develop and practice a different rhetoric—a different way of speaking for ourselves and for the world.

In late October 2004, Professor Susan Jarratt at University of California, Irvine, organized a colloquium on comparative rhetoric titled "Rhetorical Encounters: Persuasion, Pedagogy, and Practice in Colonial and Immigrant Contexts." I was invited to be part of this colloquium, which allowed me to hear what my colleagues were saying on this important subject and to present some of my own findings that grew into part of Chapters Three and Five of this book. I am grateful to her for providing me with this opportunity, and for her continuing counsel and friendship.

In fall 2004, Professor Susan Romano at the University of New Mexico asked her graduate students in her Comparative Rhetoric class to read an earlier version of Chapter Three of this book. I was gratified to learn later that they were not only interested in the kind of argument I was developing, but also offered some very constructive comments. I am grateful to them for their interest and support. I thank Professor Romano for making my work available in her class and for her support of this project.

Michael Spooner, director of Utah State University Press, has been enthusiastic about this project throughout the entire process. His support, understanding, and professionalism have been so comforting and reassuring—especially at times when they matter most. I owe him a lasting debt of gratitude.

Two readers for Utah State University Press read my manuscript with care and insight. I thank them for their generous, thoughtful responses. Thanks to their work, my revised manuscript is a much better product now. Naturally, any errors or slippages that might still remain in the book are mine alone—and in spite of their better judgment.

I wish to thank my teacher Michael Hancher at the University of Minnesota for what he has taught me. Words are inadequate to convey how much I have learned from him, and from all those who have taught and guided me in the past.

Finally, I must express my gratitude to my wife AiPing and to my preteen daughter WeiWei—to my wife, for her unfailing trust and patience; to my daughter, for her amazing ability to understand that a book on the meaning of Chinese fortune cookie is actually worth whatever time Dad was spending on it, even at her own expense. It is their love and sacrifice that have made the completion of this book a reality.

I dedicate this book to my parents: it is to their enduring love, and to their faith in their son, in what he is doing on this side of the Pacific— though this book and whatever else he claims to have accomplished so far may not be, after all, deserving of or equal to what they have given him over these years.

INTRODUCTION
Thinking through Paradoxes

Men of the world who value the Way all turn to books. But books are
nothing more than words. Words have value; what is of value in words
is meaning. Meaning has something it is pursuing, but the thing that
it is pursuing cannot be put into words and handed down.

(Zhuangzi 152)

Lately I have been increasingly drawn to a growing paradox—one that
has produced a polarizing discourse pitting unreserved enthusiasm on
one side against downright resistance on the other. On the one hand,
we now live in this increasingly interconnected and interdependent
world, brought about in part by rapid technological advances such as
the Internet and the World Wide Web and by the spread of English as
a language of commerce and science, as a lingua franca. These developments not only make it possible to collapse time and space in ways
that have never been imagined before, but also seem to have rendered
geographical distance and cultural differences less relevant, less material. Consequently, there is almost a rush, in our media as well as in our
national discourse, to embrace such developments as validation that
globalization has now entered into a brand-new phase and that boundaries, both physical and metaphorical, can indeed be blurred and even
obliterated. Or as Carpenter and McLuhan predicted way back in 1960,
our world would turn into a "global village" where "everything happens
to everyone at the same time: everyone knows about, and therefore participates in, everything that is happening the minute it happens" (xi).[1]

On the other hand, skepticism and resistance toward integration and
uniformity abound. Different nations and communities are becoming
more and more vocal and insistent on claiming their distinctive identities and on celebrating their cultural heritages. They are determined
to reassert their rightful agency and to forge their own alliances and
affiliations. These kinds of discursive performances serve to counter this
seemingly unstoppable march toward what Barber calls "a McWorld"
(53)—a world that has been made possible by technology, ecology,

communications, and commerce. They serve to challenge this new world order that seems either to reinforce the existing relations of power or to promote different hierarchies or control structures that are no less in favor of the dominant, the powerful.

A few random examples have recently caught my attention and they speak volumes—at least to my mind—for the level or extent of this resistance. First, in former Yugoslavia since the early 1990s when the country broke up, what were considered dialects are now regarded as different national languages. This proliferation of languages is largely prompted by a growing desire among these new nations to reclaim their identity and to bring back what has been lost either through violent imposition or forced adoption. Second, while English seems to have become a de facto global language, it is now, as is stated in the 1996 South African Constitution, only one of eleven national languages in South Africa. And in Nigeria, linguistic multiculturalism seems to be replacing the use of English as a unifying language. Third, in Asia and elsewhere, local Englishes with distinctive national or regional characteristics have mushroomed to compete with British or American English. Fourth, in our own continent, Native American tribes and other ethnic communities have been actively involved in recovering their lost languages and cultures, in trying to make their voices heard and listened to with their own languages. Fifth, individuals have come out in greater numbers than ever to reclaim what has been hidden from or denied to them—be it ethnic and linguistic identity, sexual orientation, or religious affiliation. In short, there is no shortage of self-asserting discourse or counter-discourse amidst this on-going clamor for globalization or global order.

Reading Chinese Fortune Cookie: The Making of Chinese American Rhetoric is situated within this broad context and, in fact, connected to this growing paradox. The making of Chinese American rhetoric represents an example of togetherness brought about by two different rhetorical traditions coming in contact with each other, and it is a phenomenon of rhetorical borderlands or contact zones (Pratt, "Contact Zone"). As an example of togetherness, the making of Chinese American rhetoric enables me to engage, to think through this paradox in a more productive way. Indeed, it allows me to problematize and move beyond this discourse of dualism that seems to have permeated—in varying degrees of explicitness and often with significant consequences—both our national dialogue and our everyday practice, be they about globalization or war on terrorism.

That is to say, Chinese American rhetoric grows out of Chinese and European American rhetorical practices, and it is an example of hybridity born of two very different, if not entirely incongruous, traditions. As a hybrid, Chinese American rhetoric blurs the boundary and serves to challenge, to transcend this dualistic discourse or impulse. On the other hand, as a hybrid, Chinese American rhetoric, so I will argue shortly, should not then be conceived of as an example of harmony-in-difference, but one of what Professor Ien Ang calls "togetherness-in-difference" (200). In other words, while Chinese American rhetoric does blur the boundary and does provide the potential for positive change and transformation, it entails necessary perils, too—perils of misunderstanding, misrepresentation, and outright rejection (Pratt, "Contact Zone" 37). Instead of a stand-in for happy fusion or harmony, it is in fact infused with conflicts, contestations, and ambiguities. Seen in this light, the making of Chinese American rhetoric constitutes a viable response to this growing paradox and to its corresponding discourse—not so much as a harmonious hybrid that magically dissolves all the differences, but as a creative, dialectical form of communication that practices togetherness-in-difference without any "exaggerated notions of uniqueness and incommensurability" (Ang 175), and "in a way that makes the same no longer the same, the different no longer simply different" (R. Young 36).

I harbor no illusion that my project will make this paradox go away. Paradoxically, I almost feel enabled by its almost ubiquitous presence. Not only do I feel inspired to develop a discourse that is not dualistic, that refuses to draw the line between "us" and "them," but also I have been enabled to think in terms that would not have become available without confronting this paradox, without facing up to those dualist responses. More specifically, I have now come to realize the need to go beyond *just* disrupting or opposing the binary that divides Chinese and European American rhetorical practices. I no longer feel adequate enough to appeal to internal coherence and local identity to resist either globalization or fragmentation. I am more than ready to ask the question of how to hold on to Chinese American rhetoric as a hybrid, as a living example of togetherness without it being idealized or exoticized, without it being easily co-opted for reproduction. To appropriate cultural geographer Doreen Massey, I want to characterize the making of Chinese American rhetoric as "articulated moments in networks of social relations and understandings" (154)—to be created, negotiated, and experienced between "border residents" (M. Lu, "Conflict" 887) and their European American counterparts. And such articulations can be motivated by Chinese and European American rhetorical experiences at the borderlands as well as by our critical reflections of Chinese rhetorical experiences transported, as it were, to the borderlands for dialogue. What bears emphasizing is that the making of Chinese American rhetoric is not a retreat into our own discursive enclave sealed off with a boundary of its own. Rather, it is another indication that discursive experiences at rhetorical borderlands cannot help being implicated by both sides and by their own signifying practices, "with layer upon layer of different sets of linkages, both local and to the wider world" (Massey 156).

This project also owes its genesis, in no small part, to the Chinese fortune cookie—hence the first half of its title. Here is why. While it is common knowledge that a Chinese fortune cookie serves as the finale of a Chinese meal in Chinese restaurants in America, it is perhaps not as widely known that it embodies two very different traditions. Namely, on the one hand, the fortune cookie represents a centuries-old Chinese tradition of using message-stuffed pastry as a covert means of communication—a tradition that started in fourteenth-century China. On the other hand, serving dessert at the end of a meal is a European American tradition, because the Chinese traditionally do not eat dessert at the end of a meal. That is why one does not find fortune cookies in restaurants in mainland China, Hong Kong, Taiwan, or Europe at all—and one doesn't feel cheated either for not eating them at the end of such meal over there.

In a sense, the Chinese fortune cookie becomes a product of contradictions: it is born of two very different traditions and made viable—not to mention, for some at least, its tastiness—in a border zone where two cultures come into contact with each other, and where rhetorical experiences intermingle with gastronomical narratives. Further, the reading of a Chinese fortune cookie embodies a joint meaning-making activity: we share each other's "fortunes" either with comforting laughs when there is a "good fit" or with loud protestations when the encoded message is deemed to be "inauspicious" to the recipient.

I argue that the making of Chinese American rhetoric bears an unmistakable resemblance to the birth of the Chinese fortune cookie and to its underlying dynamics. Such resemblance does not stem, obviously, from any shared essence or identity between the Chinese fortune cookie and Chinese American rhetoric. Rather, their resemblance is predicated upon the kinds of associations they invoke with both Chinese and European American traditions. To be more specific, Chinese American rhetoric is also born of two rhetorical traditions at rhetorical borderlands, and it becomes viable and transformative not by securing a logical or unified order, but by participating in a process of becoming where meanings are situated and where significations are contingent upon each and every particular experience. Further, in this process of becoming, Chinese American rhetoric is not to be had either by abstraction or by us searching for fixed features of harmony or seamless blending. Rather, the making of Chinese American rhetoric lies in the process of contestation, interrogation, and reflection—or in what I call "heterogeneous resonance."[2] That is to say, while there is no shared essence between these two traditions, there is a great deal of proximity-induced interaction, realignment, and unsettled association. Further, heterogeneous voices at rhetorical borderlands are being heard and listened to through competing expressions and situated experiences—both of which are inextricably connected to a particular past and both of which are necessarily indicative of a shifting subject position.

As you might have noticed already, I have left, in the title of this book, the noun phrase "Chinese Fortune Cookie" in the singular without the definite article modifying it. Omitting the definite article before this noun phrase is a considered choice, though I know, in the back of my mind, that it risks vexing some of my readers, who might view, with good reason, this omission as a grammatical infelicity, as simply too jarring or disruptive. However, by flouting, as it were, the proper English usage in the title, I am gesturing toward Chinese syntax, toward the fact that it is quite proper not to use the definite article before such a noun phrase in Chinese, because the article as a grammatical category is nonexistent in Chinese. In other words, this flouting enables me to encode this noun phrase in English lexicon, but with Chinese syntax. In a way, I am almost yoking English and Chinese or their two very different syntactic preferences together in a new, creole-like form. In so doing, I want to effect an instance of togetherness-in-difference at the very outset, and to initiate the process of inviting my readers to join me in experiencing the kind of heterogeneous resonance that will inform and permeate the rest of this book.

By dubbing, as I am doing in this project, an emergent hybrid discourse *Chinese American* rhetoric, I have also become quite mindful of the complications or dangers involved. For starters, I have no intention of suggesting that this rhetoric is necessarily and sufficiently unique; nor am I suggesting that it is unified or unchanging. What I do want to suggest is that Chinese American rhetoric should be conceived of as a process of becoming, as unsettled associations infused with heterogeneous resonance. Further, this process of becoming unfolds in spaces where Chinese and European American rhetorical practices meet face to face and where they engage in the *making* of Chinese American rhetoric—hence the second half of the title for this project. Or to put the matter another way, this process takes place "in the travel between cultural sites and in the multivocality of heterogeneous and conflicting positions" (Lowe 39).

So, what is the making of Chinese American rhetoric? How can this process of becoming, which takes place at rhetorical borderlands, be most effectively articulated and promoted? I answer these central questions in Chapter One, where I theorize and situate my work within the context of emergent ethnic and borderland rhetorics. I then focus on four specific examples—each of which constitutes a chapter—to illustrate how Chinese and European American rhetorical experiences have come to be in contact and in conflict with each other, and how their reflective encounters become the form and expression of Chinese American rhetoric. I conclude in Chapter Six: I return to the Chinese fortune cookie again to exert some productive pressure on its affinity to the making of Chinese American rhetoric and to stimulate more reflections on these encounters, on these emergent voices. Below is a brief outline of these six chapters.

Chapter One—"Opening Topics: Reading Chinese Fortune Cookie"—seeks to map out both the context and content for the articulation of Chinese American rhetoric as an emergent ethnic rhetoric at rhetorical borderlands, as a hybrid that offers both promises and pitfalls. In particular, I underscore the need to trace those specific contexts that have informed both the Chinese and European American rhetorical practices under discussion. And I consider it essential to be reflective in this process, to be able to interrogate where we *are* and where we want *to be* as we border residents participate in the making of Chinese American rhetoric. In the same chapter, I also begin to experiment with a style of writing that seeks to disrupt the boundary between Chinese and European American rhetorical practices and to promote a sense of togetherness-in-difference discursively.

Chapter Two—"Face to Face: Chinese and European American"—begins the first of four specific examples I engage in this book. Chapter Two focuses on how Chinese face meets with European American face, and on how such encounter enacts new sets of discursive articulations in which borders and ethnic boundaries are blurred, and "where processes of hybridization are rife inevitably because groups of different backgrounds, ethnic and otherwise, cannot help but enter into relations with each other, no matter how great the desire for separateness and the attempt to maintain cultural purity" (Ang 89–90). I draw upon classroom interactions and encounters from the real and the fictional world to illustrate moments of articulation as well as withdrawal, and to argue how such on-going, "face-to-face" experiences and reflections can contribute to the making of Chinese American rhetoric.

Chapter Three—"Indirection versus Directness: A Relation of Complementarity"—directs its attention to Chinese indirection, to how it dialogues with and indeed constitutes North American directness. I re-evaluate Chinese indirectness by placing it in its larger cultural context, and in terms of the topic-comment structure of the Chinese language. I argue that Chinese indirection should be seen not as an example of a nontransparent style of communication, but as part of an ever-expanding effort to establish a field of conditions and contingencies. For Chinese indirection, I highlight co-existence or interdependence; for European American directness, I point to the need to go directly to the marrow of a subject; and for both Chinese indirection and European American directness, I propose a "yin-yang" relationship. I use *The Woman Warrior* and other discursive examples, including my own personal narrative, to illustrate the making of Chinese American rhetoric and to demonstrate this relation of complementarity between indirection and directness.

Chapter Four—"Terms of Contact Reconfigured: 恕 ("Shu" or Reciprocity) Encountering Individualism"—is in part motivated by the need to problematize, and to move beyond, the discourse of deficiency or difference that seems to be underpinning much of our conversation at rhetorical borderlands. Drawing upon the work of Confucius and contemporary sinologists and comparative philosophers, I develop the discourse of 恕 ("shu") to focus on reciprocity and interdependence, and I use this discourse to embrace "the unity of two organismic processes which require each other as a necessary condition for being what they are" (Ames, "The Meaning" 159). The discourse of 恕, as I will soon demonstrate, not only helps recuperate some Chinese rhetorical practices, but also initiates a dialogue that interrogates the ideology of Western individualism and that productively engages "ethos" in European American rhetorical tradition. In the process, its development contributes significantly to a reflective encounter that nurtures a third voice—one that is both critical and inventive (Pratt, "Criticism" 88–89), and one that becomes the stuff that Chinese American rhetoric is made of.

Chapter Five—"From Classroom to Community: Chinese American Rhetoric on the Ground"—addresses the last of my four examples.

Specifically, Chapter Five focuses on how my fellow Chinese Americans use language to combat racism, to reclaim agency, and to effect positive changes through their participation in a particular speech event. I ask, for example, How does their language behavior implicate or signify Chinese and European American rhetorical traditions, and how does it empower them as they fight for social justice and for racial harmony? Differently stated, how is Chinese American rhetoric being born and experienced on the ground and through the speech acts of my fellow border residents? And how do these actions validate and exemplify the authenticity and effectiveness of Chinese American rhetoric? In addition, how do these actions find resonance in other ethnic or minority rhetorics, such as protest rhetoric? In short, Chapter Five takes the making of Chinese American rhetoric to the street.

Chapter Six—"Closing Comment: Chinese Fortune Cookie as a Topic Again"—serves as a concluding chapter. In this chapter I not only seek to illustrate further the importance and implications of such a study, but also I want to tease out instances of "richly vague significance" (Hall and Ames, *Anticipating China* 124) in my use of the Chinese fortune cookie as a "fitting" analogy. As a matter of fact, my return to the Chinese fortune cookie aims to signify that I have now come full circle both in content and in form. I now want to imagine my whole project as one gigantic Chinese utterance informed and indeed constituted by a topic-comment structure. That is to say, this Introduction and my next five chapters are a series of interconnected topics or frames spelling out clusters of contingent conditions or relationships, and Chapter Six functions as a closing commentary. By revisiting the Chinese fortune cookie again, I want to end where I began in order to complete, as it were, the circle. In doing so, I have no plan to "square the circle"[3] or to rationalize the "irrational." Rather, I intend to foreground those dissimilarities, which may have so far been obscured, between Chinese fortune cookies and Chinese American rhetoric, and to flush out their implications for the making of Chinese American rhetoric or of any other ethnic rhetoric for that matter.

I begin this introductory chapter with a passage by Zhuangzi (Chuang Tzu),[4] a Daoist philosopher (361–286 BCE) in ancient China. By choosing this passage as my first epigraph, I am not *just* interested in introducing Zhuangzi or his philosophical and rhetorical ideas to my interlocutors—which probably would be reason enough, at least to my mind. Rather, I want to use the epigraph both to lend a theme to this introduction and to put in motion a self-reflective process that will inform my next six chapters. That is to say, paradoxes—including this epigraph by Zhuangzi—often infect or adhere to our discursive experiences—a phenomenon that is both constraining and enabling.

Without a doubt, I want to acknowledge, in no uncertain terms, the limitation or inadequacy of language in representing ideas in general and in articulating the making of Chinese American rhetoric in particular—as Zhuangzi reminded us well over two thousand years ago through his own mind-jolting paradoxes. Having now acknowledged this inadequacy, I feel liberated. I feel anxious to get on with the business at hand and to use language to articulate the making of Chinese American rhetoric. This newly acquired sense of freedom on my part is certainly not based on the belief that I can now use language freely to mean what I choose to mean in order to transcend its inadequacy.[5] Rather, my sense of freedom comes from the realization that the use of language at any given moment in time also creates, with the participation of the audience, new meanings, new associations, and new possibilities. However inadequate, ambivalent, or inflected by their own precedents and by their attending asymmetrical relations of power, these articulated moments foster a new sense of authenticity and agency, and they enable border residents to practice togetherness-in-difference with humility, with hope for a brighter future—a future that finds echoes and resonances both in our present and in our past.

Finally, I must come to terms with my own position in the making of Chinese American rhetoric, with my own residency at rhetorical borderlands. In "Worldliness-without-World, Homelessness-as-Home," JanMohamed identifies four modes of border-crossings between the West and the Other, and they are associated, respectively, with the exile, the immigrant, the colonialist, and the anthropologist. According to JanMohamed, the exile is marked by the absence and loss of the home culture; such a subject position in turn makes the exile "indifferent to the values and characteristics of the host culture" (101) but, I might add, more loyal toward the formative culture of birth. By contrast, the immigrant is motivated by "a purposive directedness toward the host culture" and by "a voluntary desire to become a full-fledged subject of the new society" (101). Far from being troubled by "structural nostalgia," the immigrant is eager to discard the formative culture of birth and to take on the values and characteristics of the host culture (101).[6]

Like the exile, I feel this "structural nostalgia," and I secretly nurse, if only in my imagination, this longing for my ancestral culture. But unlike the exile, I also feel enabled by the fact that I am outside the home culture: the distance, both physical and metaphorical, has allowed me to gain a critical perspective, to develop what Bakhtin calls "creative understanding."[7] Again unlike the exile, I do not feel indifferent at all to the values and characteristics of my host culture. On the contrary, as I engage in these reflective encounters, I feel it all the more necessary to understand, and to dialogue with, its history and its underlying ideology. As a matter of fact, I cannot help it.

Like the immigrant, I want to be "a full-fledged subject of the new society" (JanMohamed 101). Wanting to be accepted, I have turned from a resident alien to a naturalized citizen for some time now. But in so doing, I have no desire to discard the formative influences of my culture of birth, nor do I want to embrace the subjectivity of the host culture without interrogation or reflection. And I also know full well that the change in my legal status will not prevent me from being "recognized" and that my yearnings for the ancestral home will always inflect and intrude upon the everyday reality of the host culture.

In short, as I engage in this undertaking of mine, I find myself increasingly cultivating a subjectivity that connects to and distances from (the subject position of) both the exile and the immigrant. Neither the exile nor the immigrant, I am literally situated at a crossroads, learning to deploy a mode of representation that enables me to practice togetherness-in-difference through the making of Chinese American rhetoric. While I am mindful of the challenges and setbacks ahead, I am quite excited about the transformative opportunities such practice offers and indeed constitutes. As a matter of fact, I cannot wait for this to commence.

1

OPENING TOPICS
Reading Chinese Fortune Cookie

Chineseness becomes an open signifier, which acquires its peculiar form and content in dialectical junction with the diverse local conditions in which ethnic Chinese people, wherever they are, construct new, hybrid identities and communities. Nowhere is this more vigorously evident than in everyday popular culture. Thus, we have the fortune cookie, a uniquely Chinese-American invention quite unknown elsewhere in the Chinese diaspora or, for that matter, in China itself.

(Ang 35)

As a descriptive catch-all term, "hybridity" per se fails to discriminate between the diverse modalities of hybridity, for example, forced assimilation, internalized self-rejection, political cooptation, social conformism, cultural mimicry, and creative transcendence.

(Shohat 110)

I pause and struggle already—even before I start—over how I should proceed or in what forms I should present my thesis and advance my argument. Should I situate myself right away in European American rhetorical tradition where I assume a direct, logical, and agonistic persona—so that I can stand a better chance of being recognized, understood, and eventually accepted? Or should I enact and adopt, not a minute too soon, some *other* rhetorical approaches or tropes that are not informed by, or implicated in, the directness paradigm or the ideology of individualism? More specifically, can I present my arguments, say, with indirection, in small increments over time and/or through repeated analogy and allusion? Or can I completely do away with subheadings within each of my chapters and keep other transitional signposts to a minimum so as to gesture toward high-context communication (Hall 79)? Or can I even try some other strategy, say, by throwing in some Chinese along the way, or by flouting, as I have already done in the title of this book, some grammatical convention in English in order to create togetherness-in-difference? As I reflect upon these questions, upon the opposing opportunities these questions imply,

I find myself somewhat being sucked into, or involuntarily re-inscribing, a discursive dichotomy—one that I very much want to reject, and replace with this project at hand. Can I, therefore, develop a narrative that moves away from this shadowy dichotomy and that serves as another living example of *Chinese American* rhetoric? Is it rhetorically appropriate, in other words, to try to define and articulate an object of study (i.e., the making of Chinese American rhetoric) with a narrative that is inextricably infused with and deliberately constituted by the same object?

My apprehension and my hesitation are not without merit, I am afraid. Not only because I am acutely mindful of my own space—in both its literal and metaphorical sense—where different traditions and competing voices cannot help but speak and listen to each other within some highly asymmetrical relations of power, but also because I cannot shake off the dire warning Pratt gives in her "Arts of the Contact Zone," of the indeterminate, often perilous, status that can be the fate of such narrative (37). The stakes are high, and the consequences are huge. However, like Hall and Ames (*Anticipating China* 119), I know I may never "get it right," but I also know that I cannot let this realization stop me, and that I cannot let my own apprehension or hesitation handicap my action, stifle my narrative. In short, I must "get on with it" even as I continue to pause, to reflect, and to persuade.

It is perhaps not surprising to see emergent discourses trying to define themselves in terms of their uniqueness in relation to other, already-established discourses. Such effort, to a large extent, is in response to a traditional demand for identification, for a stable system of reference that serves as signs of discrimination and distinction. Emergent discourses that secure their uniqueness from this kind of internal coherence help counter potential skepticism and remove miscomprehension or incomprehension. They create a sense of authenticity and authority when they begin to be heard and listened to as unique discourses—though, it must be stated, such discourses are not necessarily equal in discursive value to other competing or more dominant discourses. Before too long, hopefully, they could achieve stability and identity—both of which seem essential if emergent discourses want to shed the status of being "emergent" and to secure the status of an established discourse. The question, then, becomes this: Should the making of Chinese American rhetoric exhibit this idealized growth pattern or follow this uncomplicated teleological trajectory? Put in a slightly different way, should Chinese American rhetoric be expected to demonstrate, or to be constituted by, what I call "uniqueness-qua-coherence?"

Definitions of rhetoric vary relative to, for example, historical periods and social and technological contexts—not to mention rhetoricians' own ideological and ethnic commitments. In this global context of ours, rhetoric, for me at least, represents the systematic, organized use and study of discourse and discourse strategies in interpersonal, intercultural contexts, reflecting and reinforcing rhetoricians' own ideology, their own norms of discourse production and discourse consumption, and their ability to persuade, to adjust, and to realign. In light of this definition of rhetoric, one may want to devise for Chinese American rhetoric a core set of discursive features that could be viewed as internally coherent and that could be realized by different forms of enunciations or representations in particular contexts and practices. In other words, one may expect Chinese American rhetoric to be able to show its own unique characteristics—that are consistently different from other rhetorical traditions and from their corresponding manifestations—in order for it to achieve both visibility and viability. For example, Chinese American rhetoric, whatever discursive features it may end up commanding, must be Chinese American enough so that it can be coherently differentiated from, say, African American rhetoric or Native American rhetoric.

The process of differentiation, unfortunately, is never an innocent one: it always embeds a likely risk of differentiating one tradition according to or in relation to the norm of some other tradition. In light of our recent experiences, the latter regularly turns out to be more recognized, more dominant, and it is invariably aligned with the powers-that-be. It is not unusual at all, as a result, to find out that such a norm enjoys a wider circulation and a longer disciplinary canonization. In fact, to all intents and purposes, it is the widely circulated, the perennially canonized that persistently serves as the interpretive example of general applicability in spite of its apparent unmarkedness.[1] One conceivable outcome from this kind of differentiation and evaluation is a body of knowledge that, however coherently distinct, reproduces this hierarchical relationship or this existing order of discourse.[2] Ironically, of course, it is this existing order of discourse that emergent discourses are purported to challenge and transform in the first place—so much so that it can become both possible and viable to think and communicate outside such an order, outside its (largely invisible) discursive rules and categories.

My effort to conceptualize Chinese American rhetoric without reverting back to the dominant tradition as its measuring norm coincides with, and in fact draws inspiration from, a growing number of projects that aim to articulate and to conceptualize emergent ethnic rhetorics as sites of difference, as transformative practices, and as viable alternatives to the oft-invisible, but no less dominant, European American rhetoric.[3] These projects are predicated more on their own terms than on the terms of European American rhetoric, or on the terms of what Glenn calls "the male-dominated and male-documented rhetorical tradition" (10). As alternative, transformative rhetorics, they "challenge and put pressure on traditional canons of rhetorical thought" and they "give voice to those whose discursive acts have gone unrecognized within Western culture" (Gray-Rosendale and Gruber 3). By "reading it [the rhetorical tradition] crookedly and telling it slant," and by making "the unfamiliar familiar and the familiar unfamiliar" (Glenn 8), these efforts make what used to be invisible rhetorical experiences visible and consequential, and they transform what used to be at best marginalized players into legitimate, viable contenders.

A word of caution is perhaps in order here with respect to our characterization of emergent ethnic rhetorics as "alternative," as "transformative." First, the use of the term "alternative" to characterize emergent ethnic rhetorics is not without problems. Gray-Rosendale and Gruber are mindful of the fact that "no rhetoric is fully 'alternative' but always both rewrites the tradition and inevitably becomes part of it" (4). Nevertheless, they see alternative rhetorics as significant in their own right because they "advance a critical counterpoint to the tradition" and they "expand the territory of what constitutes students' and teachers' perceptions of rhetoric and rhetorical texts" (4–5).

On the other hand, there is a paradox lurking here that may have escaped Gray-Rosendale and Gruber. Given the fact that words hardly ever shake off their past (Austin, "A Plea for Excuses" 201; Gee, *Discourse Analysis* 54), the use of "alternative" acknowledges, and in fact reproduces, a hierarchical division between (the dominant) one and the (subordinate) other—because it is precisely such division that motivates the emergence of an alternative as the "disruptive" other. Such division further risks marginalizing the alternative/the other given the value differential evidenced in cultural capital[4] that each element in this division represents and delivers. The use of "alternative" may also imply, however incorrectly, that its counterpart (read as the dominant or the mainstream) is pure and stable, and that it is otherwise immune from *alternative* influences or infiltrations. As a matter of fact, though, the emergence of any rhetoric, whether it be alternative or ethnic, in part owes its genesis both to the internal divisions and instability experienced by its counterpart and to an environment where discursive differences cannot be fully dissolved and where the process of assimilation is filled with elements of resistance.

Second, to view emergent ethnic rhetorics—like Chinese American rhetoric—as transformative in relation to European American rhetoric should not be taken to suggest at all that the latter is monolithic, rigid, and unchanging. After all, rhetoric is about discourse production and discourse consumption in particular communities and environments. As I have proposed elsewhere, since European American rhetoric, like any other rhetoric, changes over time, it might be more accurate to view such (dominant) rhetoric as consisting of certain clusters of discursive features on a discursive continuum, and over time new clusters or new alliances emerge that can overlap with the old (Mao, "Re-Clustering" 114–15). Such discursive clusters are likely to give rise to codified expressions and patterns that serve as preferred, though unmarked, modes of communication for people in positions of power. It is the same group of people that have a stake in ensuring the continuity or stability of these discursive features—because the latter help encode and reinforce a pattern of assumptions, beliefs, values, and interpretations of the world by which these people operate (Foss 291). On the other hand, these "institutionalized" features may not necessarily reflect or square with ever-changing, multi-faceted practices on the ground—even though, ironically, individuals or people of lower social status might rely on these features or these discursive constructs to read or critique their own divergent behaviors, thus perpetuating the existing power imbalance. To appropriate Bizzell ("The Intellectual Work" 3), it is the privileged social position that has remained constant and that has in turn allowed such discursive constructs to count as European American rhetoric.

Effective as these alternative, transformative articulations might be in contesting the normative powers of the dominant rhetoric, their effectiveness cannot be achieved, I want to suggest, by appealing to rhetorical uniqueness, by claiming an abstract pattern of coherence. Similarly, the making of Chinese American rhetoric cannot be realized through rhetorical uniqueness-qua-coherence. Not only because there is none to be had, but also because such a move leads to at least three problems.

First, rhetorical uniqueness is evidently predicated upon the importance of being different. But the notion of "difference" deserves some critical reflection. Renato Rosaldo, in *Culture and Truth*, criticizes the methodological norms in ethnographical studies that conflate the notion of culture with the idea of differences. For him, the term "cultural difference" becomes just as redundant as that of "cultural order," because "to study a culture is to seek out its differences, and then to show how it makes sense, as they say, on its own terms" (201). In this regard, the notion of difference poses a problem because such differences can never be absolute and because they are only "relative to the cultural practices of ethnographers and their readers" (202). Further, an exclusive focus on differences risks obscuring the dynamics of power and culture. For example, there are those who are culturally less visible, but enjoy enormous power to perform this kind of cultural analysis and to evaluate differences according to a (preferred) norm. And there are those who possess rich culture but wield no power, and who are only supposed to be dissected and disseminated (201–2).

Further, any discussion of difference—be it cultural or rhetorical—has to deal with the effects of difference, too. That is to say, there is a difference—no pun intended—between those who set out to identify differences *only to* contain their effects with, say, a metaphor of "otherness," and those who perceive such differences not simply as the object of interpretation, but as "the active agent of articulation," as possessing the power "to signify, to negate, to initiate its historic desire, to establish its own institutional and oppositional discourse" (Bhabha, *Location of Culture* 31). In other words, any recognition of rhetorical differences pertaining to Chinese American rhetoric, or to any other ethnic rhetoric for that matter, does help challenge rhetorical homogeneity or the norms of European American rhetoric. However, if such recognition presupposes an insistence to maintain a boundary because of these differences, and to frame them within an overall boundary of a nation-state, we then run the risk of reduplicating a power dynamic that would probably make it quite daunting, if not impossible, for Chinese American rhetoric to be heard and listened to on its own terms.[5]

Second, internal coherence is based on an assumed boundedness, in this case on a belief that Chinese American rhetoric can be cleanly set apart from other ethnic rhetorics and that it can be interpreted or illuminated as a self-contained system of signs. Drawing upon leading cultural thinker Ien Ang's provocative work, I see our appeal to such a belief almost as analogous to claiming an essentialized Chinese identity in a postcolonial nation-state, because both—the belief and the claim—would be "tantamount to overlooking the complex, historically determined relations of power" (Ang 13). These relations of power inevitably shape and contaminate the making of Chinese American rhetoric, as the latter has come to be constructed in relation to Chinese rhetorical tradition, on the one hand, and European American rhetorical tradition, on the other. These complex interrelationships are fraught with uncertainties, ambiguities, and contradictions—so much so that Chinese American rhetoric can never be unique, not only because there is no internal coherence to speak of, but also because it is always in a state of adjusting and becoming, both in relation to its "native" (Chinese) identity and in relation to its "adopted" (American) residency. And the process of adjusting and becoming is forever infused with its own tensions, struggles, and vulnerabilities, within the context of each and every borderland speech event.

Third, if "our everyday lives are crisscrossed by border zones, pockets, and eruptions of all kinds" (Rosaldo 207), and if "we are all implicated in each other's lives" (Anzaldúa 243), the making of Chinese American rhetoric is no exception. It is hopelessly intertwined with other ethnic rhetorics, because its voices and aspirations can easily find resonance and empathy in the chambers of other people's hearts both at crossroads and across space and time. Moreover, any on-going efforts for Chinese American rhetoric to stake out rhetorical uniqueness through internal coherence may in fact betray a nagging anxiety, both distorted and revealing, to vaiidate its existence by, ironically I might add, clinging to a European American ideal of "a bounded, distinctive, and independent whole" (Geertz 59). Just as such a whole is in fact always both situated and "distributed,"[6] so the making of Chinese American rhetoric cannot be *not* situated and distributed—in the sense that it is always located in particular, specific contexts, and that it always operates at many different but interlocking levels informed or implicated by both Chinese and European American rhetorical traditions. Not only is this ideal of a "coherent whole" deeply flawed, but also any stabilized, unique characteristics could quickly become candidates for stereotyping and for easy reproduction.

How do we, then, move beyond uniqueness-qua-coherence? How can we articulate the making of Chinese American rhetoric without incurring these problems? I think the answer to these questions may be found in the Chinese fortune cookie—not so much in the "good fortune" it regularly dispenses as in the ways in which it evokes and embodies two distinctive traditions.

I often give out Chinese fortune cookies to my writing students at my own school. Not that I necessarily believe in the ability of good fortunes inside Chinese fortune cookies to lift up the spirits of my students, but that I see these fortune cookies as a generative analogy for the kind of rhetoric I want to articulate and promote both for my students and for myself. Crispy, sugary, and dumpling-shaped, a Chinese fortune cookie serves as the finale of, and in fact represents a constitutive ingredient/ritual of, a Chinese meal in Chinese restaurants in America. We would probably feel cheated if we didn't get served with fortune cookies at the end of such a meal. While we may indulge ourselves in eating a fortune cookie, we may not be cognizant of the two traditions it faithfully represents. On the one hand, the fortune cookie represents a centuries-old Chinese tradition of using message-stuffed pastry as a means of communication—a tradition that started in fourteenth-century China as a covert means to share information and to get organized without being detected by the authorities.[7] On the other hand, serving dessert at the end of a meal is a European American tradition, because the Chinese traditionally do not eat dessert at the end of a meal. That is why we do not find fortune cookies in restaurants in mainland China, Hong Kong, Taiwan, or Europe at all—and we don't feel cheated either for not eating them at the end of such a meal over there.[8]

In a sense, the Chinese fortune cookie becomes a product of contradictions: it is born of two competing traditions and made viable in a border zone where two cultures come into contact with each other and where gastronomical narratives are punctuated by rhetorical performances. At the same time, the Chinese fortune cookie makes no effort to mediate these two very different traditions or to deny each its own history and its proper place in a Chinese meal. On the contrary, the two traditions are allowed to co-exist with each other in every single Chinese fortune cookie, which in turn has served its dual function faithfully—both to initiate a fortune-sharing communicative activity and to remind its participants that it's time to pack their bags.

While I know how quickly one can overextend the significance of any useful analogy, I cannot help but submit that the making of Chinese American rhetoric bears an unmistakable resemblance to the birth of the Chinese fortune cookie—a resemblance stemming not so much from any shared essence between them as from the associations they invoke with both Chinese and European American traditions. I draw comfort, too, from Ien Ang who, as indicated in the first epigraph for this chapter, also appeals to the Chinese fortune cookie in her efforts to highlight how Chineseness takes on new form and content in its new, diasporic environment.[9] Like the Chinese fortune cookie, the making of Chinese American rhetoric is born of two rhetorical traditions, and made both visible and viable at rhetorical borderlands as a process of becoming. It is this kind of rhetoric that I want to develop and advocate in this book, and beyond.

A word or two may be entered at this early juncture to clarify my use of "Chinese American." By characterizing this emergent hybrid rhetoric as *Chinese American*, I do not intend to suggest that only Chinese Americans use and experience this rhetoric. Rather, it can be used and experienced not only by Chinese Americans, but also by Chinese, European Americans—or any other individuals for that matter. At rhetorical borderlands, which have become increasingly more visible and geographically less confined, Chinese, Chinese Americans, and European Americans can participate in the making of Chinese American rhetoric, as long as Chinese and European American rhetorical traditions are being brought together and as long as relations of power continue to make their presence felt in the process.

Further, the realization of Chinese American rhetoric can be observed by *either* our success in achieving those "articulated moments in networks of social relations and understandings" (Massey 154) *or* our failure to engage, to overcome silence and prejudice—almost like one can observe an existing rule by either honoring or breaching it. Chinese American rhetoric can be realized not only by our own (successful or failed) practices, but also by our reflections of others' experiences—be the latter articulated, silenced, or embedded in their own historical, social, and linguistic contexts. These reflections enable us border residents to imagine what is like from the other tradition's perspective—whether it be Chinese or European American—and to interrogate its discursive practices and material conditions. In the process, our reflections and our interrogations help cultivate and nurture a subject position that negotiates between two rhetorical traditions and that challenges and contests the discourse of essentialism and duality. They in fact become, I submit, the stuff that Chinese American rhetoric is made of.

In addition, the making of Chinese American rhetoric does not necessarily embody the "growth pattern" in which it evolves from an emergent ethnic rhetoric to an established one. Nor does it necessarily follow the model in which it could be passed from generation to generation to a point where it may become indistinguishable from European American rhetoric. As a process of becoming, Chinese American rhetoric may not settle into a discourse of established or blurred identity any time soon. The reason is perhaps straightforward: not only will relations of power remain highly asymmetrical for a long time to come, but also communication at rhetorical borderlands will continue to be inflected with ambiguities, uncertainties, and even contradictions. In a word, contingency and contestation are almost immanent to the making of

Chinese American rhetoric insofar as there are border residents at rhetorical borderlands.

Let me now start with the concept of border zones or borderlands,
which Rosaldo and Anzaldúa talk about and which I have so far referred
to only briefly. In her preface to the first edition of *Borderlands,* Anzaldúa
characterizes borderlands as "physically present wherever two or more
cultures edge each other, where people of different races occupy the
same territory, where under, lower, middle and upper classes touch,
where the space between two individuals shrinks with intimacy" (19).
And Giroux describes the borderlands as a space "crisscrossed with a
variety of languages, experiences, and voices" that "intermingle with the
weight of particular histories that will not fit into the master narrative of
a monolithic culture" (209). In fact, we can go so far as to say that we all
now live at borderlands, given the fact that this world of ours has become
increasingly interconnected and interdependent. It is at these borderlands, both literal and metaphorical, that Chinese American rhetoric, or
any other ethnic rhetoric, has the potential to become visible and viable,
though the risk is equally great of it becoming "frozen for inspection"
(Rosaldo 217) or not getting listened to and heard on its own terms—a
point to which I will return shortly. Not because Chinese American rhetoric can achieve its uniqueness and thus legitimacy through coherence
at the borderlands, but because the borderlands provide a generative
space where, Ang writes, "fixed and unitary identities are hybridized,
sharp demarcations between self and other are unsettled, singular and
absolute truths are ruptured, and so on" (164). To describe the matter another way, the borderlands become, in the words of Bhabha, a
"third space" that "enables other positions to emerge" and "sets up new
structures of authority, new political initiatives" ("Third Space" 211). As
a result, Chinese American rhetoric can gestate and coalesce at these
spaces. It can begin to yield multiple acts—of signification, ambiguity, as
well as contradiction—creating identities that are implicated in the old
relationships and indicative of the new ones. As such discourse emerges
as a creative and viable form of communication, these in-between spaces
become both highly rhetorical and intensely interpersonal.

Anzaldúa further characterizes borderlands as "vague and undetermined," as places that are "in a constant state of transition" (25). For
her, too, borderlands are both metaphorical and physical: they are
places where the mestiza "operates in a pluralistic mode—nothing is
thrust out, the good the bad and the ugly, nothing rejected, nothing
abandoned" (101). And these are places where divergent thinking is

taking place, "characterized by movement away from set patterns and goals and toward a more whole perspective, one that includes rather than excludes" (101). Further, her own experience of living on the borderland between Mexico and the United States, of claiming and celebrating this mestiza status, is not a matter of desire, but one of survival and resistance (Ang 166).[10] Rhetorical borderlands are no exception: they are vague and undetermined, not only because they are in transition, in movement, but also because there is always, for each discrete communicative act, an excess of meaning yet to be processed, yet to be fully grasped. It is this excess of meaning, both in its production and in its consumption, that further aggravates this sense of ambiguity, indeterminacy, and vulnerability.

I cannot help, at this moment, but recall experiences, both my own and others', of reading fortunes inside fortune cookies in Chinese restaurants in America. More often than not, our fortunes, be they terse predictions, pithy proverbs, or Confucian sayings, tend to be "happy" or "auspicious." However, we never fail to fret over, perhaps half seriously, the unspoken, the silenced, and the yet-to-be-decoded. We know that there is always a nagging "but" ready to punctuate the good fortune popping out of every fortune cookie. Take, for example, this apparently auspicious prediction, "You shall never worry about wealth in your life"—one that pops out often from fortune cookies we eat at the end of a Chinese meal. But such fortune is no less burdened with an excess of meaning that could quickly deflate the happy moment. "Does that also imply," a good friend of mine once reminded me, with all seriousness, as I exhibited some jealousy for not getting such good fortune at regular intervals, "that the person in question is not going to be around for too long?" While I refuse to subscribe to this kind of ominous reading, I have become more cautious about, or less boastful of, the happy fortunes I have come into possession of these days because of their potential ambiguity, indeterminacy, and vulnerability. And as I move back and forth between gastronomical narratives over the import of fortunes stuffed inside fortune cookies and discursive experiences felt and realized at rhetorical borderlands, I have become all the more mindful of how unsettled or indeterminate the process of production and consumption can be—which presents, in turn, both opportunities and challenges.

Rhetorical borderlands bear an unmistakable family resemblance to what Pratt calls "contact zones." Contact zones, according to Pratt, are "social spaces where cultures meet, clash, and grapple with each other, often in contexts of highly asymmetrical relations of power" ("Contact Zone" 34). At the same time, contact zones provide, she suggests, creative energy for new forms of expression, and one such form is what she calls "autoethnographic text"—where "people undertake to describe themselves in ways that engage with representations others have made of them" (35). That is, autoethnographic texts, composed by conquered others, are "*in response to* or in dialogue with those texts" that Europeans have constructed of their conquered others (35; emphasis original). These texts are outcomes of "a selective collaboration with and appropriation of idioms of the metropolis or the conqueror," and they are "merged or infiltrated to varying degrees with indigenous idioms to create self-representations intended to intervene in metropolitan modes of understanding" (35). These autoethnographic texts, while representing "a marginalized group's point of entry into the dominant circuits of print culture" (35), have to negotiate with both metropolitan audiences and indigenous or local discourse communities. Thus, their fate can be highly indeterminate, if not perilous: they could suffer "miscomprehension, incomprehension, dead letters, unread masterpieces, absolute heterogeneity of meaning" (37).[11] In short, autoethnographic texts are "a phenomenon of the contact zone"—similar to, Pratt tells us, the process of transculturation whereby "members of subordinated or marginal groups select and invent from materials transmitted by a dominant or metropolitan culture" (36).[12] And I might add that this process of selection and invention by subordinated others is always filtered through their own particular experiences, through their own historical memories, and through their own "terministic screens" (Burke, *Language* 45).[13]

Rhetorical borderlands create and nurture new forms of expression, too. That is to say, rhetorical borderlands make it possible for Chinese American rhetoric to be created and to be experienced. Like autoethnographic texts, Chinese American rhetoric may face similar perils ranging from misunderstanding, to misrepresentation, to wholesale rejection. At the same time, Chinese American rhetoric does not just "select and invent from materials transmitted by a dominant or metropolitan culture" (Pratt 36). Rather, it selects and invents from *both* Chinese rhetorical tradition *and* European American rhetorical tradition, and it engages these two traditions in a way that may blur boundaries and that may disrupt asymmetrical relations of power. Such rhetoric may further enable its border residents to take the other's perspectives as seriously as one takes one's own (Rosaldo 207)—however antagonistic or ambiguous the other's perspectives may sometimes turn out to be.

Caution must be exercised here. As a metaphor, "borderland" or "contact zone" is likely to be heir to some of the ills that affect most, if not all, metaphors. Generally speaking, the use of metaphor allows us to represent or understand one kind of experience or concept in terms of another (G. Lakoff and Johnson 5). Further, our understanding or representation is normally focused on one particular aspect of that experience or that concept. So, by stating that "Argument is war," one is singling out the battling, winner-taking-all aspect of arguing, while neglecting or overlooking other aspects or characteristics about arguing (10). As we all know, in almost any sincere argument there is the basic need to demonstrate one's willingness to understand the other's point of view and to be cooperative in securing each other's uptake. And take "Time is money" as another example. By comparing time to money, we are highlighting the economic, monetary aspect of time so that we can put our time to good use, to generating economic capital. But in doing so, we are obscuring other aspects that are perhaps just as important to our understanding of time—such as the fact that time normally cannot lead to greediness and corruption, but money can, or the fact that time does not fluctuate in value, but money does. Therefore, the use of metaphor is never total, but always partial, incomplete, and inflected with a particular orientation or ideology. As G. Lakoff and Johnson rightly point out, "if it were total, one concept would actually *be* the other" (13; emphasis original).

In *Imperial Eyes,* Pratt tells us that she borrows the term "contact" from the phrase "contact language" used in linguistics. Contact language refers, in linguistics, to an improvised language that develops in places, such as ports, trading posts, plantations, and colonial garrison towns, where most speakers have no common language.[14] By using the term "contact," Pratt aims to "foreground the interactive, improvisational dimensions of colonial encounters so easily ignored or suppressed by diffusionist accounts of conquest and domination" (7), and she wants to treat such relations between colonizers and colonized *in terms of* "copresence, interaction, interlocking understandings and practices" (7).

However, as we embrace the promises of this metaphor, Hall and Rosner remind us, we tend to gloss over its perils or to overstate "its potential for cultural mediation" (103). Or as Ang points out, there is a clear inclination "to value, if not celebrate and romanticize notions of the borderland, the 'third space', the liminal in-between" (164). More bluntly put, borderland or contact zone tends to be imagined "as a utopian site of transgressive intermixture, hybridity and multiplicity" (Ang

164). For Hall and Rosner, this kind of characterization reflects a desire to stabilize and tame what is otherwise a dynamic concept (96)[15]—a position that I share. However, the dynamic, processual characteristic they ascribe to the definition of Pratt's "contact zone" does not stem from her own revisions of the concept in her subsequent work as they seem to be suggesting (99). Rather, what has emerged from Pratt's later work is a more focused effort on her part to address "highly asymmetrical relations of domination and subordination" (*Imperial Eyes* 4; also see 7) and to highlight "how differences and hierarchies are produced *in and through contact* across such lines [of difference]" ("Criticism" 88; emphasis original).[16] Likewise, the making of Chinese American rhetoric is necessarily dynamic amidst some highly asymmetrical relations, not because the concept of rhetorical borderlands is "in the making" (Hall and Rosner 103), but because the making of Chinese American rhetoric is always a process, an instance of comings-to-be.

For Ang, this celebratory, romanticized inclination simply fails to recognize that borderlands or contact zones are "not a power-free site for unrestrained and heteroglossic dialogue and exchange, but a contested terrain where concrete, differentially positioned subjects have to forge particular strategies to speak and to be heard" (169). Even in a most idealized speech situation, where cooperation is assumed and expected (Grice 26), there is still this matter of the transfer of meaning, which, following Grice again (31–37), is to be accomplished not by securing a one-to-one correspondence between words and meanings, but by calculating whether or not the (ideal) speaker means more than or other than what he or she says. In places like rhetorical borderlands, it should come as no surprise that efforts to communicate and to make oneself understood become exponentially more problematic and contentious.

In light of these cautionary observations, we should then resist any move to idealize rhetorical borderlands as simply liberating, empowering, or equalizing, because we can't lose sight of the partiality and incompleteness immanent to the (metaphorical) image of rhetorical borderlands or contact zones. After all, borderland heterogeneity and interlocking co-presence, while potentially transformative, may very well in the process aggravate—rather than alleviate—communication and mutual understanding.

There is another related question I must address at this point. Namely, is it then appropriate to view the making of Chinese American rhetoric at rhetorical borderlands as an example of hybrid rhetoric, given the fact that it is constituted by both Chinese and European American rhetorical traditions? It is perhaps reasonable, and even logical, to view Chinese American rhetoric as a hybrid because it indeed invokes and involves two kinds of rhetorical practices and their underlying traditions. However, just as the characterization of any ethnic rhetoric as "alternative" may have already marginalized it relative to its dominant counterpart, so the use of "hybrid" to characterize the making of Chinese American rhetoric engenders its own problems—problems that have to be confronted and properly dealt with if we want to achieve a more informed understanding of Chinese American rhetoric as a borderland rhetoric.

To be blunt, the use of "hybrid" as a borderland image may foster an illusion that the creation of hybrid rhetoric will contribute to a discursive harmony, which in turn will make our border-crossing experiences both easier and more risk-free (Bizzell, "Basic Writing" 7–8). By definition, the term "hybridity" entails the emergence of things new or different out of two or more heterogeneous or incongruous sources (*The Oxford English Dictionary*, 2nd ed.). Or, as R. Young puts it, it implies "a disruption and forcing together of any unlike living things" (26). Not only does the term suggest the "impossibility of essentialism" (R. Young 27), but also it can represent a promising response that mediates the real and potential differences between its (two or more) originating sources. Therefore, the making of Chinese American rhetoric as a hybrid can serve to fuse or synthesize differences evidenced in these two individual rhetorical traditions. The fact that Chinese *and* American rhetoric are now mixed into and contained within one single, if not unified, whole called "Chinese American rhetoric" suggests at least a blurring, if not erasure of, rhetorical hierarchies and discursive boundaries.

However, it is quite easy, Ang reminds us again, to "extol uncritically the value of hybridity without carefully understanding its complexity and its contradictions" (194). It is indeed tempting to tout an emergent hybrid like Chinese American rhetoric as a symbol of "harmonious fusion or synthesis," which Ang dubs "liberal hybridism" (195). But such optimism fails to recognize the basic fact that differences or divisions may not be completely erased, no matter what. And as my second epigraph by Shohat indicates, the hybrid as a symbol of happy fusion fails to consider or discriminate those specific power relations and historical conditions that configure our encounters and that determine the natures of our hybridity—not to mention the fact that any hybrid, like Chinese American rhetoric, once stabilized into a harmonious whole, can simply be overwhelmed by the dominant tradition, given the unequal, imbalanced power relationship that exists between them (Dobrin 46–47, 51).

Then, there is this (intractable) problem with the use of metaphor. The characterization of Chinese American rhetoric as a hybrid in this context of rhetorical borderlands is metaphorical and quite appealing. For one thing, the image of a hybrid certainly blurs the boundary between two rhetorical traditions. For another, it can lead us to recognize the inescapable impurity of all rhetorical traditions. But as I have suggested above, the use of metaphor is inevitably partial because it keeps us from focusing on those other aspects of the same concept that are often incommensurable with the metaphor in question. In this case, the image of a hybrid, when applied uncritically to the making of Chinese American rhetoric, simply abstracts different histories and experiences from situated practices. That is to say, the image of a hybrid severs the concrete link between different histories and experiences and their corresponding particularizing contexts, but it is precisely the intermingling of these two sides that produces and informs the particular manifestations and distinctive experiences of Chinese American rhetoric. Herein actually lies a paradox: the image of a hybrid purports to transcend *situated* rhetorical differences and dominance, but it is the situated, the specific, that grounds our experiences and that underpins our complex forms of participation.[17]

By opening up the problems and complexities associated with the term "hybridity" or the image of a hybrid, I am not suggesting that we reject the term or the image altogether—because that would be almost like fighting a losing battle, given the fact that we are all implicated in each other's lives or that we live in what Ang calls "complicated entanglement" (194). In other words, hybridity is here to stay.

For the last several years, I have been attending the annual party sponsored by my local Chinese American community to celebrate Chinese New Year. I enjoy the food, the company, and the festive atmosphere. The highlight, for me at least, has to be the performances that showcase Chinese culture and tradition, performances that I look forward to every year. But I am also no less eager to see how the organizers every year mix the show with performances that celebrate European American culture and tradition as well. So, in one year I watch Chinese American and European American girls perform jazz and tap dances together, to be followed by Chinese folk dance featuring a group of Chinese students wearing authentic ethnic Chinese costumes. In another year, I become almost mesmerized by a group of local high school American students performing Chinese martial arts (武术, "wushu")[18] with both grace and precision, and their performance is preceded by twelve Chinese

American couples participating in ballroom dances accompanied by Chinese traditional folk music.

I marvel at these mixed performances—examples of hybridity—but I also wonder what they mean exactly to these performers and to the spectators. Could they mean that cultural differences can be overcome and traditional boundaries crossed? Could they also mean that multiracial harmony can be attempted and indeed become quite successful—at least at these levels and on these occasions? While I am not a skeptic by nature, I cannot resist asking, in my heart of hearts, if there are tensions that cannot be reduced or if there are differences that cannot be fully absorbed. And what are some of those specific conditions or power relations that have motivated these performances and that have shaped, if not forced, other encounters and their hybrid consequences? I begin to feel ambivalent about these performances, and I begin to feel even vulnerable—because I am just as implicated in these performances as my fellow performers.

I marvel at the image of the Chinese fortune cookie, too, because it is nifty and real, and because it literally embodies a happy fusion of two traditions—one uses message-stuffed pastry as a means of communication and the other serves dessert at the end of a meal. But I also begin to spot the rupture and fission sneaking up on this fusion. For example, the Chinese fortune cookie, while it considers America its "home," is no less attached to a Chinese tradition, because it is always known as the *Chinese* fortune cookie. And although the fortune inside is regularly written in, and communicated through, American English, their consumption has never been fully disengaged from a (superstitious) Chinese frame of mind operating in the background. Such signs of tension are almost irreducible, ready to disrupt the harmony projected by the otherwise coherent fortune cookie. In spite of this newly-found awareness on my part, the Chinese fortune cookie, insofar as I can tell, continues to serve its dual function without missing a beat.

What should we do, then, with hybridity, with the making of Chinese American rhetoric being characterized as a hybrid rhetoric? In view of the complexities and challenges made real by the discourse of hybridity, Ang writes:

> What we need to question, then, is not so much hybridity as such, which would be a futile enterprise, but the depoliticization involved in the reduction of hybridity to happy fusion and synthesis. I would argue that it is the *ambivalence* which is immanent to hybridity that needs to be highlighted,

as we also need to examine the *specific contexts and conditions* in which hybridity operates. (197; emphasis original)

It is these "specific contexts and conditions" that I am most interested in uncovering in the making of Chinese American rhetoric. And it is both the ambivalence and vulnerability—which are in fact constitutive of hybridity—that I am committed to elucidating.

To begin to examine these "specific contexts and conditions in which hybridity operates," we must first recognize that there will be times when instances of incommensurability become irreducible. In fact, we should not treat discursive encounters at rhetorical borderlands as living examples of how differences from two incongruous traditions can now co-exist in a new, benign hybrid. Rather, we should seize such encounters or moments of co-presence as an opportunity to trace the complex past that has informed their respective experiences, and to recover the different paths each has traveled to arrive at this borderland destination. After all, rhetorical forms are never innocent, and they always encode particular stances, situated modalities. In so doing, we can begin to see and address those particularizing aspects and their underlying structures that a metaphorical hybrid may very well hide or elide.

Second, the making of Chinese American rhetoric as an emergent hybrid should not be seen as an occasion for celebration, because there is nothing to celebrate. To bring back Anzaldúa again, to practice Chinese American rhetoric at rhetorical borderlands is not a matter of desire, but one of survival. Because identity continues to be privileged as "the naturalized principle for social order" (Ang 200), hybridity is still seen as problematic, as anomalous, even though, paradoxically, it is almost everywhere in our world now. In this regard, we should mobilize Chinese American rhetoric as an emergent rhetoric to address and deal with this paradox. We need to highlight the fact that our rhetorical practices are forever entangled now, and that our identities are being shaped and nurtured by a multitude of interrelationships, by a web of interweaving movements. To the extent that we succeed, we can then begin to challenge "the fundamental *uneasiness* inherent in our global condition of togetherness-in-difference" (Ang 200; emphasis original).

Third, while I have no intention of diminishing the dialogic opportunity the making of Chinese American rhetoric presents, I don't want us to overlook the fact that hybridity is also "about the contestations and interrogations that go hand in hand with the heterogeneity, diversity and multiplicity we have to deal with as we live together-in-difference"

(Ang 200). To put it more matter-of-factly, at rhetorical borderlands where there is more than one language, more than one culture, and more than one rhetorical tradition, if nothing else, the basic question of communication never goes away in terms of who has the floor, who secures the uptake, and who gets listened to. Therefore, unless we are prepared to deal with these challenges and complexities inherent in the making of Chinese American rhetoric, or any other emergent ethnic rhetoric, we may end up either idealizing the making of Chinese American rhetoric or overlooking altogether how tensions between two traditions become manifested in particular, specific practices. In short, what I intend to focus on in this book is a rhetoric that seeks not uniqueness-qua-coherence from within, but complexity, heterogeneity, and ambiguity from both within and without—from a space where different rhetorical practices meet, clash, and grapple with each other, and where their encounters are always inflected with highly asymmetrical relations of power. While there may not be any recognizable logic to its formation, there is a lot of authenticity in its representation, in its expressiveness, in its articulated moments. It is, to use Ang's felicitous term, "togetherness-in-difference"—rather than harmony-in-difference—that becomes constitutive of the making of Chinese American rhetoric.

If the making of Chinese American rhetoric is now about togetherness-in-difference, one major question remains: How should we border residents actually go about practicing or realizing this togetherness-in-difference as we enter into these highly asymmetrical relations of power? Or how can we effectively negotiate this co-presence of two rhetorical traditions—deeply inflected with their own historical identities, with their own modalities—without either underestimating their inherent challenges or idealizing their combined creative potential? Critical discourse analysis, in my view, may provide some helpful perspectives over these paradoxical moments.

Critical discourse analysis views language as a type of social practice, as a socially conditioned process (Fairclough 18–19). Any communicative action—an example of discourse—involves not only a text, but also a corresponding process of production and consumption to be completed in social context. As a matter of fact, it is social context that serves to influence and to determine the process of production and consumption (20–21). Consequently, any text, be it written or spoken, is no longer seen as an innocent instrument of representation, but as the discursive performance of socially situated speakers and writers who are necessarily connected to the process of production and consumption, on the one hand, and to the structures of power and domination, on the other (Kress 85–86).

In fact, critical discourse analysis aims to put into crisis, or denaturalize, these kinds of connections. More precisely put, it seeks to problematize those underlying "common sense" assumptions that "rationalize" these connections (Fairclough 76–77, 88–89).[19] To the extent that these "common sense" assumptions act to disadvantage, to control, particular groups or subject positions at a given moment in society, critical discourse analysis seeks to effect change "not only to the discursive practices, but also to the socio-political practices and structures supporting the discursive practices" (Kress 85). In this sense, it is unabashedly partial, and it becomes, in my own words, "discourse analysis with an attitude."[20]

At rhetorical borderlands, we border residents are deeply situated and our rhetorical practices are intensely social. We therefore face enormous constraints, for example, on what we say, on what relations we enter into, and on what subject positions we occupy. In turn, such constraints exert structural effects on how we form our knowledge and beliefs, on how we establish our social relationships, and on how we cultivate our social identities (Fairclough 38–39, 61–62). However, Fairclough reminds us, constraints are enabling, too. That is to say, socially situated participants are "only through being so constrained that they are made able to act as social agents" (32), and in fact being constrained, for Fairclough, is "a precondition for being enabled" (32). In this regard, we still have to *act* as subjects in order to draw upon discourse types and patterns to perform our own speech acts, to enter into or deal with particular relations, and to engage with representations that others have made of us (Pratt, "Contact Zone" 35). Through these instances of interaction and interrogation made possible by borderland heterogeneity and multiplicity, we can begin to challenge and to put pressure on these constraints and on these asymmetrical relations of power—though we should have no illusion that differences will disappear because of co-presence. More importantly, we can begin to represent and name our borderland experiences with our own voices, with our own hybrid rhetoric—a necessary first step toward creating new cultural, discursive realities.

There is another paradox that we may experience in practicing togetherness-in-difference. As I have suggested above, the making of Chinese American rhetoric involves the process of selecting and inventing from both Chinese and European American rhetorical traditions. On the other hand, we may not be free all the time in (performing the act of) selecting and inventing from these two traditions or from their specific practices—whether our purpose is to facilitate everyday communication or to initiate social transformation. To put it bluntly, borderland choices can be quite limited, and borderland access can be very restricted—herein lies the paradox.

Critical discourse analysis recognizes this kind of paradox, too. As Kress points out, the available linguistic—and rhetorical I must add—forms have been formed by past interactions, which are imbued with power differentials and which are filled with preferred, canonical structures or patterns. As a result, no linguistic, rhetorical forms are neutral or immune from their own histories and precedents (90; also see Gee, *Discourse Analysis* 54). There also exists this urge, regularly embraced and actively promoted by the dominant culture in society, to standardize or to foreclose on meaning potential in order to forestall the potential of meaning heterogeneity.[21] In addition, the value of a word very much depends on the relationship of that word to all other related words in the same cluster or in the same discursive field (Fairclough 78–79).[22] For example, the value of the word "individualism" depends on and is indeed made complete by other related terms, such as "rights," "independence," "personal property," and "democracy." Together, they form their own cluster, and together they convey a set of meanings particular to the discursive field they inhabit.[23]

However, texts or communicative behaviors don't just instantiate prior meanings embedded in a single word, in a cluster of words, or in a stretch of utterances. Rather, texts or communicative behaviors enact their own meanings and engender their own associations between participants and in particularizing contexts. Similarly, what makes Chinese American rhetoric enabling and generative is not so much the birth of a hybrid as what I call "the occasion of use," which makes the birth of a hybrid both possible and potentially promising. That is to say, the occasion of use necessarily ascribes agency—however constrained—to us border residents, and it yields new meanings—however limited—to each and every communicative process. In fact, it is through these recurring occasions of use that we cultivate new ways to think of ourselves, of others, and of our world.

I often grow restive, if not defensive, whenever the subject of conversation turns to Chinese fortune cookies. My past experience tells me that in spite of its present-day ubiquitousness, the Chinese fortune cookie continues to inspire a sense of exoticism, and it continues to generate a discourse that shows both an appreciation of the other and a desire to frame the other in a context that often is not its own. For some individuals, it seems, a Chinese fortune cookie can only become "palatable" if it is "peppered" with this kind of discourse.

I invariably want to challenge this kind of discourse because it simply fails to represent the Chinese fortune cookie. I want to tell this "migration story" about these two traditions inside or behind the Chinese fortune cookie, and I want the Chinese fortune cookie to be represented not as some detached, exotic artifact, but as an example of cultural hybrid that is both unified and contradictory. But I am also nervous, because I don't want my narrative to be misconstrued as *just* critiquing this discourse of vacillation.[24] While it is a critique, the narrative is also my sincere attempt to narrate, as directly as possible, a history for the Chinese fortune cookie and to trace the path that it has traveled. Not infrequently, I feel unsure of its uptake by my interlocutors.

I worry about the fate of Chinese American rhetoric, too. As an emergent ethnic rhetoric, Chinese American rhetoric, like other emergent minority voices, challenges a society "that espouses universalistic, univocal, and monologic humanism" (JanMohamed and Lloyd 1). To the extent that it does, and to the extent that it serves to empower its users and to enhance their agonistic effectiveness, its (oppositional) significance should be valued and celebrated. What becomes problematic is when we treat Chinese American rhetoric *simply* as an oppositional discourse,[25] as a mode of resistance to the dominant rhetoric. As I have argued above, the making of Chinese American rhetoric is promising because it represents a hybrid that serves to blur the boundary and to destabilize the binary between the dominant and the subordinated. To come back, then, to set up Chinese American rhetoric *only* as an oppositional discourse may detract from, however inadvertently, the very attempt to challenge the discourse of duality and to articulate the positive values of Chinese American rhetoric or its togetherness-in-difference.

Here it is useful to reflect on JanMohamed and Lloyd's efforts to ward off attempts to view minority discourse as simply oppositional or antagonistic. For them, that is to say, "an emergent theory of minority discourse must not be merely *negative* in its implications" (8; emphasis added). Rather, such theory should articulate the positive practices and values embedded in the works of minorities, and it should further reaffirm that "even the very differences that have always been read as symptoms of inadequacy can be reread transformatively" (8). So should, I suggest, the making of Chinese American rhetoric. As a matter of fact, Chinese American rhetoric as an emergent rhetoric cannot be treated only as an oppositional discourse, because it is always in the state of constant negotiation and adjustment and because it is always attended by this fluid, dynamic process. It is best, therefore, to characterize Chinese American rhetoric as a rhetoric of becoming.

Almost opposite of this treatment is a liberal desire to endorse and embrace Chinese American rhetoric or any other emergent ethnic rhetoric as part of an on-going drive to promote multicultural rhetorics. While I am not necessarily opposed to multicultural rhetorics, I do want to address a few problems that this kind of embrace and inclusion seems to have ignored or pushed into the background.

The emergence of multicultural rhetorics represents a serious attempt to challenge rhetorical homogeneity and to recognize and validate the need for different rhetorics and their communities to co-exist with each other. But it does not address the complexities as well as uncertainties that necessarily arise when these different rhetorics come to interact with each other as they have to. Drawing upon Ang's critique of multiculturalism, the promotion of multicultural rhetorics is almost based on a rhetorical fantasy that "the social challenge of togetherness-in-difference can be addressed by reducing it to an image of living-apart-together" (14; also see 138–49).

Further, the inclusion and celebration of rhetorical diversity by multicultural rhetorics does not solve the asymmetrical relations that remain between the dominant rhetoric and other emergent ethnic rhetorics, such as Chinese American rhetoric. To be sure, multicultural rhetorics are predicated upon an understanding that differences should be encouraged, included, and embraced—an understanding that should be applauded and encouraged on its own. The question, though, becomes this: Who is giving and who is receiving this encouragement, this inclusion, and this embrace? And is this process unidirectional or bidirectional? It seems clear that it is still the dominant rhetoric that does the giving, whereas emergent ethnic rhetorics serve as passive recipients. In other words, the embrace and inclusion promoted by multicultural rhetorics are not without conditions and constraints—not to mention the fact that "new" rhetorics can quickly be framed or contained within the old paradigm, multicultural rhetoric or not. Absent any immediate solutions to such problems, I feel increasingly ambivalent about these "additive" moments in our desire to celebrate pluralism in general, and about any specific efforts to add Chinese American rhetoric to multicultural rhetorics in particular.

I think Pratt is right when she warns us of the complexities and perils in connection with the reception of autoethnographic texts at contact zones. As I have been arguing so far, such complexities and perils attend, in more ways than one, Chinese American rhetoric at rhetorical borderlands. As an example of "complicated entanglement" (Ang 194), the making of Chinese American rhetoric is intensely performative as two different rhetorical traditions come to grapple with each other amidst some highly complex relations of power. And Ang is equally right when she reminds us that rhetorical borderlands are filled with contestations and interrogations because of their immanent heterogeneity, diversity, and multiplicity (200). At the same time, I want to emphasize the importance of being reflective, being able to imagine what it is like from the other tradition's perspective, as we participate in these contestations and interrogations. Indeed, reflection is a must at rhetorical borderlands, and it must go hand in hand with our complicated entanglement. Otherwise stated, our practices of togetherness-in-difference have to be coupled with the ability to interrogate ourselves, to imagine what our practices may look like from the other side, from the other's perspective.

To be reflective in these kinds of moments is more than just professing our own position or ideology—a familiar move regularly adopted in personal narratives these days. That is to say, it must be acknowledged that we always start from somewhere in the making of Chinese American rhetoric. More bluntly put, we usually start from where we *are,* and with terms, concepts, and lived experiences that are close to our (ancestral) home and tradition, to which we often claim a real or imagined allegiance. Wittingly or unwittingly, we take part in this (constrained) creative process at rhetorical borderlands by relying on our own tradition, on our own primary Discourse.[26]

There is more. To be reflective also means taking ourselves beyond admitting where we initially are and examining where we have been. To put it more directly, we must reflect on how we use our own lived experiences to engage the unfamiliar, to grapple with the other's representation of us, and to direct our critical gaze at discursive experiences and material conditions that constitute the other rhetorical tradition (read as European American). By using our own "terministic screens," so to speak, we can better assess and engage its history, its underlying ideology, and its entangled relationship with our own (Chinese) rhetorical tradition. Self-reflection, as a result, helps yield an awareness of differences between these two traditions without any "exaggerated notions of uniqueness and incommensurability" (Ang 175) and without any assumed or imposed notions of hierarchy and superiority.

In a word, to be reflective is to refuse linear progression and closure as the only mode of representation. Indeed, each reflective moment begets another, and each process raises the level of understanding, and further enriches and perhaps complicates subsequent reflection. To draw upon

Bakhtin, just as each situated utterance is "a link in the chain of speech communication" ("Speech Genres" 93), so each on-going reflection is related not only to preceding, but also to future reflection. Together they become a form of meta-discourse as well: they serve as a running commentary that unpacks the history and ideology of each embodied tradition and that critically reflects upon the tensions, ambivalences, incommensurabilities, as well as the creative potentials, at the point of contact when one tradition meets with the other and when, to appropriate Geertz, "experience-near" and "experience-distant" concepts are brought together into simultaneous and interconnected view (57, 68–69).[27]

Allow me to return to the analogy of the Chinese fortune cookie to conclude this chapter. If my reading so far offered of Chinese fortune cookies is persuasive enough, it is fair to say that no shared attributes have existed or have been developed between the tradition of using message-stuffed pastry as a means of communication and that of eating dessert at the end of a meal. At the same time, the lack of commonality between the two has not prevented both traditions from sharing a joint membership that emerges out of, and further solidifies itself through, each and every Chinese fortune cookie—in spite of those tensions and contradictions inherent in almost any hybrid product.

Likewise, the making of Chinese American rhetoric as an emergent hybrid involves and embodies two very different traditions. However, these two traditions have also established an emergent joint membership in a space that is inhabited by asymmetrical power relations, crisscrossing movements, and co-existing but divergent voices. Further, Chinese American rhetoric is made possible through contestation, interrogation, *and* reflection. In fact, this kind of interactive process can be characterized as an example of "heterogeneous resonance." By "heterogeneous resonance," I mean that while there is no shared essence between these two traditions, there is a great deal of proximity-induced interaction and realignment. Further, these instances of interaction and realignment are tied to each particular speech event or to specific acts of communication,[28] and they are realized through competing voices and through ambivalent yearnings. In the process, they contribute, in ways big and small, to the making of Chinese American rhetoric. In short, it is these borderland moments of togetherness-in-difference that I want to focus on and articulate in the rest of the book. It is these processual instances of heterogeneous resonance that are in fact scaffolding much of my discussion in this chapter and that will soon pervade my discussions and representations in the next five chapters.

2

FACE TO FACE
Chinese and European American

*It should be added that the principles which regulate "face" and its
attainment are often wholly beyond the intellectual apprehension of
the Occidental, who is constantly forgetting the theatrical element, and
wandering off into the irrelevant regions of fact. To him it often seems
that Chinese "face" is not unlike the South Sea Island taboo, a force of
undeniable potency, but capricious, and not reducible to rule, deserving
only to be abolished and replaced by common sense.*

(Smith 17)

*A person may be said to have, or be in, or maintain face when the
line he effectively takes presents an image of him that is internally consistent . . . . At such times the person's face clearly is something that
is not lodged in or on his body, but rather something that is diffusely
located in the flow of events in the encounter and becomes manifest only
when these events are read and interpreted for the appraisals expressed
in them.*

(Goffman, "On Face-work" 6–7; emphasis original)

I have chosen to begin this chapter with Arthur Smith, an American mis-
sionary who went to China in 1872 and lived there for over twenty years.
His first-hand experiences in China led him to write *Chinese Characteristics*,
which was published well over a century ago. I find his description of
the Occidental with respect to Chinese face practices eerily relevant.
The Occidental, portrayed by Smith, saw Chinese face practices as
irregular, irreducible, and fundamentally irrational, and such practices,
therefore, should be replaced by European American "common sense."
While Smith's Occidental may largely have been discredited, the binary
disposition evidenced in these descriptions continues to color people's
perspectives and to cloud their vision. Commenting almost four decades
ago on the longevity of this kind of dichotomizing discourse, Raymond
Dawson concluded as follows: "This polarity between Europe and Asia
and between West and East is one of the important categories by means
of which we think of the world and arrange our knowledge of it, so there

can be no doubt that it colours the thoughts even of those who have a special interest in Oriental studies" ("Western Conceptions" 22). What follows, then, is my attempt to challenge this kind of polarity, to repudiate those efforts to replace Chinese face with European American face, and to cultivate the rhetoric of togetherness-in-difference through a face-to-face dialogue between Chinese and European American face.

Nothing at rhetorical borderlands is probably more exposed and more vulnerable than our face. As border residents, we look different and we may choose to act differently, too—so that we can better claim allegiance to our face and to what our face represents (that is, to our ancestral home and culture). Our face becomes both a liability—we get "recognized" because of it—and an asset—we are a "model minority" in spite of it. As we meet with European Americans face to face, both sides may first appeal to each other's face as a way to discern meaning from what is inscribed on the face and from what is lurking behind the face. In a word, we are both empowered and trapped by our own face.

As a Chinese American at my own school, I am no doubt quite visible to my students and to my European American colleagues. My face in part gives away my identity, and I get recognized instantly. But my rhetoric, my way of communication, does not have to be as visible—especially if and when I choose to play it safe, to avoid tensions, or simply to blend in. Ironically, it is this acute awareness of my own face, both physical and metaphorical, that serves as a source of conflict and as a catalyst for the making of Chinese American rhetoric. To get these reflective encounters under way, it is perhaps appropriate for me to begin by enacting the European American directness paradigm—namely, by trying to get to the bottom of things as directly as I can. After all, I am just as implicated (and trained, too) by this paradigm as I am by the Chinese indirection paradigm.

Face is a regularly invoked discursive construct in Chinese rhetorical repertoire.[1] Its visibility and longevity have recently caught the attention of Western linguists, communication scholars, and rhetoricians—thanks in part to Arthur Smith's initial characterization of Chinese face as "a key to the combination lock of many of the most important characteristics of the Chinese" (17). Ironically, their attention, if not infatuation, has only made it become less visible. This is how. Sociolinguists Brown and Levinson have characterized face as a public-self image that people, across discourse and culture, want to claim for themselves in face-to-face communication. Further, their characterization of face consists of two related aspects: negative face and positive face. They define negative face as the basic desire for freedom of action and freedom from imposition, and any given individual in society is entitled to such a desire. They characterize positive face as the desire to be appreciated and approved (61–62). To put it more mundanely, negative face refers to an individual's desire to be left alone, and positive face refers to an individual's desire to be stroked on his or her back.

While recognizing that face content is culture-specific and subject to much cultural elaboration, Brown and Levinson maintain that the notion of face constituted by these two basic desires is universal (13). Such a claim, however appropriate or relevant to the communicative dynamics of white, middle-class European Americans, is highly problematic to Chinese face, because central to Chinese face is an emphasis on the public, on the community. While such popular expressions as "saving face" or "losing face" continue to circulate in North American public discourse, their popularity in fact rides on the myth of the individual, of the individual's need either to be free or to be liked. On the other hand, the significance of this public, communal orientation, which underpins the original concept of Chinese face, becomes increasingly diminished as face becomes more of a personal, rather than a public, property. Herein lies, for me, a most revealing contradiction: the very reason that Chinese face fascinated western scholars in the first place may have something to do with its visible emphasis on the public, on the interdependence between self and other. But as their fascination turned into concrete efforts to develop European American face and beyond,[2] the central feature of Chinese face fast recedes into the background, if not into oblivion. While Chinese face has become better known on this side of the Pacific thanks to these efforts, it has also become less visible, and thus less Chinese, because it is now just like European American face, or it is being adjudicated on the strength of, if not already replaced by, European American face. Therefore, any move to revive or to reenact (the public characteristic of) Chinese face risks either being co-opted or being dubbed "not individual enough."

How can I address this contradiction? How can I practice togetherness-in-difference with Chinese and European American face? To answer such questions, let me first turn to cultural anthropologist Hsien Chin Hu. In an influential essay titled "The Chinese Concepts of 'Face,'" Hu characterizes Chinese face as consisting of two specific constituents: "lian" (脸) and "mianzi" (面子).[3] According to her, 脸 refers to "the respect of the group for a man with a good moral reputation," and it embodies "the confidence of society in the integrity of ego's moral character," constituting "both a social sanction for enforcing moral standards and an internalized sanction" (45). Echoing Hu's characterization, Cheng sees 脸 as signifying "the basic dignity and respectability that one has" and identifies it with "the sense of honor, integrity, and shame of a person" ("The Concept of Face" 334–35).

On the other hand, Hu defines 面子 as connoting prestige or reputation, which is either achieved through getting on in life or ascribed (or even imagined, I might add) by members of one's own community (45). 面子 in this sense becomes a property obtained and owned by the individual in a public arena and in relation to one's own community. Similarly, Cheng associates 面子 with what one has achieved in one's life and with the position one officially occupies or is in charge of ("The Concept of Face" 332–34).[4]

While it is important to recognize their different emphasis, the distinction between 脸 and 面子 is not absolute, and the two characters can on occasion be used interchangeably. The context can also lead one to determine which of the two meanings is being conveyed by either character (Ho 868).[5] But one thing seems to have remained constant: the moral connotation or social judgment of character that informs 脸 is, at most, secondary in 面子.[6]

Drawing upon these characterizations of Chinese face, I want to define Chinese face, consisting of 脸 and 面子, as a public image that self likes to claim or enhance for him- or herself from others in any communicative event. This is an image that signifies a reciprocal balance, at any given point in time, between self and those others as they engage in a face-to-face interaction. In this sense, Chinese face in general is not a private or an internalized property "lodged in or on his body," but an image that is supported by the judgment of others in the situation and that is "diffusely located in the flow of events" (Goffman, "On Face-Work" 6–7). More specifically, Chinese 脸 encodes a moral and normative connotation as it places self in the judgment of others, and as it establishes and/or reinforces a link between the integrity of self and his or her community. According to Cheng, 脸 cannot be lost or broken "without suffering a disgrace in the eyes of others or oneself" ("The Concept of Face" 334–35). On the other hand, Chinese 面子 places its primary emphasis on securing public acknowledgement of one's reputation or prestige through social performance or by the social position one occupies in the community (Ho 883). Therefore, to lose 面子 is not as damaging as is to lose 脸—though to suffer the loss of 面子 certainly can result in shamefulness, resentment, and even hatred (Cheng, "The Concept of Face" 334).

As a dynamic concept whose significations are tied to each and every interactive moment, Chinese face (脸 and 面子) cannot be held constant in value, nor can it be held up for inspection divorced from particularizing contexts. In other words, Chinese face must be negotiated and constructed in the flow of events, because it is always embedded in and enacted through individual practices. While the dangers are obviously real of pursuing Chinese face to an extreme at the expense of ethics or even justice, it can potentially serve as an empowering site where old relationships can be solidified, new relationships cultivated, and the circle of interdependence further expanded.

There is a lot of 脸 at stake the moment I step into my classroom. In order for me to earn my 脸, I must comply with all the necessary conventions and requirements associated with good, effective teaching, and I must meet and exceed the expectations of my students. And for my colleagues and peers in the profession, I must demonstrate my ability to channel my research to classroom practices. I can further enhance my 脸 by proving to my students that I am an intelligent, dedicated, and caring teacher in the classroom. Consequently, my failure to do all of the above would cost me a great deal of 脸, because being thought of as an ineffective, unintelligent teacher exerts a smearing effect on my 脸, on my professional integrity in the eyes of my academic peers. Seen in this light, my 脸 is no longer so much about *my need* to be liked or appreciated by the students and my colleagues as about the kind of image I can claim *from* them in my role as their teacher and as their peer. Because of this strong normative and communal connotation associated with 脸, any loss of my 脸 necessarily erodes, if not completely damages, my 面子—that is, my reputation, my prestige.

On the other hand, my 面子 will accrue if, for example, I never miss my office hours in any given semester or if I grade and return my students' assignments in a timely manner. My 面子 will suffer accordingly if I deviate from these performances. Because they are not directly tied to my (otherwise exemplary) classroom performance, these deviations may not exert any immediate smearing effect upon my 脸, upon my effectiveness as a teacher in the classroom. On the other hand, if such lapses persist, the damage to my 面子 may bleed into, and eventually impair, my hard-earned 脸 inside the classroom. In other words, the longer I let my 面子 deteriorate, the more likely my 脸 will be adversely impacted, and the more likely my relationship to my students, to those I am most intimately associated with, will be strained, if not damaged beyond repair. While Chinese 面子 does involve an individual's need to secure public acknowledgement of his or her prestige or reputation, there always is a fine line between maintaining an appropriate level of 面子 and pursuing it at any cost, to the point of being seen as vain or excessive.[7] Differently stated, too much of 面子 has to be carefully avoided—because to gain 面子 at the expense of 脸 will in the end cost both. Managing this kind of interlocking relationship between 脸 and 面子 can be characterized as performing face-work (Goffman, "On Face-work") or face-talk (Cheng, "The Concept of Face").

What about, then, Chinese discourse patterns? Do they manifest and realize the same kind of face-work or tug of war between 脸 and 面子? If Chinese face (脸 and 面子) is a quintessential public image to be constructed and negotiated between self and other in a communicative process, why have we not mobilized it, on this side of the Pacific, to account for Chinese rhetorical practices and to inform our understanding of their discursive patterns? Why have we regularly characterized Chinese and Chinese American writers—or their East Asian counterparts for that matter—as being prone to use their writings to promote *not* individualism *but* harmony and social relationships (Yum 375–76)?[8] Why is it still so common to resort to this binary discourse that pits individualism against harmony and collectivism and that contributes to terms of contact marked not by reflection but by opposition? Why have we not already appealed to some "experience-near" concepts—concepts that the natives might naturally and effortlessly use to define what they or their fellows see, feel, think, or imagine (Geertz 57),[9] and concepts that recognize the Other, to quote Zhang Longxi's apt description, "as truly Other, that is, the Other in its own Otherness" (127)?

In light of my preceding discussion on Chinese face, it seems appropriate to characterize the desire to promote and preserve social harmony, on the part of Chinese and Chinese American writers writing in English or in Chinese, as a rhetorical move to appeal to Chinese 脸 and to connect themselves to their community and to its history and culture. That is to say, if our discursive practices, past and present, are intricately linked to each other, and if they together constitute an integral part of our social-cultural environment, any writerly efforts to reinforce this connection and to cultivate a harmonious whole amount to demonstrating one's membership and conviction in this larger social-cultural environment. To the extent one succeeds in doing so, one has actualized and enhanced one's own 脸 (one's own credibility and authority) or, to use Bourdieu's term, one's social capital or "membership in a group" ("Forms" 51).

While it is important to recognize and to restore this connection between Chinese 脸 and the writer's discursive preference for harmony and cultural order, we should resist the temptation to see this connection necessarily as an example of Chinese and Chinese American writers consciously rejecting Western individualism. Instead, this discursive preference and this appeal to 脸 should be treated more as an outcome resulting from the writers' earlier literacy training or from their earlier exposures to a discursive construct that favors harmony and cultural continuity. It could also be an indication of border residents connecting to their formative culture of birth for inspiration, for means of representation.

One may ask, "Does this discursive preference also have anything to do with Chinese 面子?" The answer to this question is affirmative. If this connection between Chinese 脸 and the writers' general desire to promote harmony and to secure a sense of credibility is plausible, it should come as no surprise for the same individuals to show a corresponding preference for proverbial expressions, literary citations, or canonical precedents in their writings.[10] The deployment of such strategies can be viewed as their way of securing and enhancing their 面子—their ability to showcase their knowledge of a long, venerable tradition and to comply with the convention to incorporate these discursive moves. To the extent that they have the ability to pull this off, they will have solidified the approval of their audience. In fact, the securing of 面子 in this context almost becomes a prerequisite for enlarging their 脸, for establishing a link to their larger social-cultural environment. As is the case with oral communication, any tendency to show an over-dependence on proverbs, precedents, or citations—thus an example of showing-off—amounts to an excessive concern over one's 面子. Such a tendency necessarily will erode and damage the writers' credibility and authority, that is, their 脸.

By bringing back, as it were, Chinese face (脸 and 面子) to the foreground so that it can be "seen" again, I am heeding Geertz's call to pay more attention to experience-near concepts, to how such concepts can help us overcome this discursive binary. More importantly, I want to make Chinese face visible on its own terms, not on terms that are deeply inflected with European American face or with its individualistic paradigm—so that its characteristics will be clearly recognized and so that its "otherness" will be neither exoticized nor exorcized. In so doing, I do not want to set up, however inadvertently, another opposition between Chinese face, on the one hand, and relations of power, on the other, or to have the former somehow trump or overshadow the latter. In fact, for one to claim a public image *from* others in any communicative event— and vice versa—involves just as much consideration of power dynamics as does any other communicative act.

One point is perhaps worth emphasizing here, though. That is, the restored visibility to Chinese face must not be automatically translated into an argument in favor of rhetorical uniqueness. As I have argued in Chapter One, our discursive practices readily find echoes and resonances in other individuals' practices and in other individuals' voices. And as Rosaldo has rightly pointed out, "our everyday lives are crisscrossed by border zones, pockets, and eruptions of all kinds" (207). Therefore, the emphasis encoded in Chinese face on an individual's connection to, and indeed his or her dependence upon, the public may very well be found in other "faces" belonging to other cultures or to other communities. After all, we are all implicated in each other's face—both because we determine and appraise (the value of) our own face through another's face and because face, if Levinas is correct, "renders possible and begins all discourse" (87). Otherwise stated, Chinese face may find its own mirror image in other faces, in other discourses that share the same kind of communicative dynamics and transformative potentials.[11]

What happens, then, when Chinese face (脸 and 面子) meets with European American face (positive and negative face)? What actually transpires when I interact, face to face, with my students in my own classroom where different cultures intersect and where different languages clash? There surely will be conflicts and confrontations when we face each other or when these two concepts of face are brought together through our respective face practices. As I have suggested above, European American face focuses on the needs or wants of the self, and on discovering and expressing one's distinct attributes. Even when others' wants or expectations are being considered, these wants or expectations are "incorporated into the individual's own subjective frame of reference, that is, into his own definition of their significance for his own action" (Ho 882). In contrast, Chinese face puts an emphasis on the interconnectedness between self and public, and it symbolizes this ever-expanding circle of face-giving and -receiving in one's own community and beyond.[12]

Just as conflicts and confrontations are bound to arise, so are creative responses and re-alignments or "articulated moments in networks of social relations and understandings" (Massey 154). More specifically, such moments recognize and embrace these face-to-face differences and conflicts, and they represent individual face-experiences and face-acts on their own terms. In fact they become part of togetherness-in-difference, because the emphasis now is no longer on adjudication, assimilation, or dissolution, but on co-existence, on processes of hybridization characterized by discursive tensions, semantic vagueness, and asymmetrical relationships of power. Out of these moments emerges a new sense of identity that is both relational and expansive, whose energy, according to Anzaldúa, "comes from continual creative motion that keeps breaking down the unitary aspect of each new paradigm" (102). And it is this energy—"a source of intense pain"— that nurtures a third element, a new consciousness (Anzaldúa 101–2). These articulated moments, as they actively construct rhetorical experiences brought on by borderland face-to-face encounters, become examples of Chinese American rhetoric.

My conceptualization here of Chinese American rhetoric, to some extent, bears some important resemblance to Scott Lyons' efforts to develop a mixedblood pedagogy of conflict and contact and to "revise the narratives of captivity that govern the discourses, material conditions, and lived experiences of people all across the educational system—and beyond" (Lyons 88). For Lyons, such revision in part lies in the recognition that his Indian students produce their own mixedblood narratives "against, within, and in tandem with the grand narratives of contemporary American life and culture: race and racism, intelligence and learning, literacy and orality, success and failure, them and us" (88–89). Reinscribing the history of conflict and contact, these narratives constitute examples of what Lyons calls "contact heteroglossia" (89): "truly ironic, playful, infuriating, and hopeful, substituting for the prison neither the asylum nor the battlefield, but rather *a different language*" (91; emphasis added).

So, I share my 脸 and 面子 with my writing students—most of whom are from white, middle- or upper-middle-class family backgrounds—to try to establish this web of interdependence where my public image needs their blessings as much as do theirs. In this context, I tell them that it is no longer my need either to be liked (as their teacher) or not to be bothered (when I am not in the classroom or when I am not having my office hours) that should be respected and satisfied. Rather, it is about whether they can grant me the kind of public, teacherly image that comports with their overall expectations, and with what they believe to be appropriate teacherly activities and behaviors both inside and outside the classroom. At the same time, I ask my students to tell their stories of how their own face wants have been left unfulfilled because of my concern over what I imagine to be their need for 脸 and 面子. They tell me—somewhat nervously because of the nature of their "oppositional" discourse and because of the asymmetrical relation of power—that my compliments or good grades are not as forthcoming as they have expected in spite of their solid work, and that they are often puzzled and frustrated by my tendency not to spell out what I want from them, but to emphasize what should be expected of them by their peers and by the (imagined) community with which they are affiliated. They think I am too "non-committal," "hard to read," and even "tricky." Through these kinds of exchanges, fragmented and tentative, we begin to see beyond the limits of our own face and of our own boundaries, and we begin to experience, perhaps still indirectly, the dynamics of the other face in its own otherness. We do that, I insist, not to dissolve or disown our own face because we can't, but to nurture, to negotiate togetherness-in-difference in a space that yields a narrative fraught with internal tensions but incongruent with "the master narrative of a monolithic culture" (Giroux 164).

I use discursive examples by Chinese speakers and writers in my writing classroom, too. In so doing, I seek to share further with my students the dynamics of Chinese face and to mobilize them to put themselves in the perspective of the other. Using these Chinese examples helps generate the kinds of reflections that will engage both Chinese and European American face and that will promote an in-between subject position at rhetorical borderlands—just as much as do Chinese American and European American examples. In other words, the making of Chinese American rhetoric can emanate from *both* our own borderland experiences involving Chinese and European American face-work *and* our borderland reflections of Chinese face-work or any other Chinese rhetorical practices. That is to say, I want my students and myself to experience the ways in which Chinese face-work can be received at rhetorical borderlands; to interrogate the knowledge such reception induces or implies; and to talk about our own biases and about our own points of origination. These reflective, thick descriptions, so to speak, help bring together Chinese and European American face without denying each its own history and its own cultural imperatives. They in turn contribute, in no small way, to the making of Chinese American rhetoric.

For example, I discuss with my writing students personal narratives written in English by some Chinese students, and I point out to them a tendency in these narratives to provide a detailed chronological past as a way to address the future, or to link the future back to the past and the present. Such a strategy, I want to suggest to my students, is intricately tied to the dynamics of Chinese 脸 and 面子. For example, the following is the first paragraph of a four-paragraph statement of purpose submitted to one of our graduate programs by a female Chinese applicant:

> Born in a doctor and teacher's family, I had my childhood dream of becoming a doctor or teacher. I learned to be diligent and independent at an early age. At the age of 15, I attended a provincial key high school. As the school was about 15 miles away from home, I had to leave my parents and lived at school during weekdays. It was certainly not easy for a girl of that age. In China, kids, especially girls, are usually not educated to be very independent before they grow up. Besides, being the class monitor and a member of the school's Field and Track team, I had to do more than just taking care of myself. However, despite all the difficulties, I managed to do things well.

A statement of purpose should be expected to provide personal information about the applicant's past in order to respond to the question of her present and her future. Yet, it is quite striking that the applicant focuses on her past right from the get-go, and in such a detailed manner. Rather than telling her audience why she is applying for graduate work, the applicant chooses to focus on how she was born into a doctor and teacher's family, and how she became very independent and hardworking at a very early age. In fact, except for the last paragraph, the rest of her statement amounts to a detailed chronological account of her past accomplishments, which, not by accident, are wrapped around a nurturing family and a supportive community. By making so much of her past into her statement, she has in effect "laminated" her private self, to borrow a term from Goffman (*Framing Analysis* 82), onto a public that she expects would endorse and embrace such a self. In this sense, this process of lamination becomes a process of earning her 脸. In other words, her success in securing her 脸 almost depends on her ability to project her past onto the present and to tie her foreseeable future to her worthy past.

Since any statement of purpose is expected to answer the question of "now and future," the applicant saves her answer in the last paragraph of her statement. But even there she still clings on to her very past, to her established 脸:

> I understand that the interesting curriculum and training provided in the program will help to enrich my knowledge in science and to improve

my writing and interpersonal skills. I believe that, with my previous background and help from the faculty members and fellow students from the program, I will become a better communicator in scientific, technical, and other fields. I'd like to use the skills I learned to help make technical and scientific information more understandable and useful to people in China and in North America.

This paragraph consists of three ordinary sentences. What is somewhat extraordinary, though, is the fact that each sentence serves as a comparison with her established past that precedes this last paragraph. First, she compares what should be her future knowledge of science and interpersonal skills with the knowledge she has so far acquired—knowledge that needs to be enriched and expanded. Second, she believes she "will become a better communicator" than she has been. Third, she will develop the necessary skills to help others, skills that she does not have right now. These three sentences, in a word, take her future right back into her already established past and present. Out of this web of interdependence emerges a secure, confident 脸, one that in turn lends credit and respectability to her 面子, that is, to a sense of well-deserved recognition that she has arrived.

How do North American applicants compose their statements of purpose? How do they convey their positive and negative face wants, and how do they go about projecting themselves to their intended audience? The following is the first paragraph of a statement of purpose submitted to one of our graduate programs by a North American applicant:

In applying to the doctorate program in Rhetoric and Composition, I'm endeavoring to combine my interests in language and its multitude of systems and pedagogies, with a dual focus on sociolinguistics; attempting to gain relatable knowledge of the interrelatedness of all aspects of communication processes with social and cultural ideologies. In other words, I intend to pursue insights into how we, as individuals and as a culture and a society, perpetuate and maintain behavior and thought through language and communication strategies.

Unlike our Chinese applicant, this applicant does not address her past or her own success stories right away. Rather, she focuses on why she is applying to our graduate program, and on the future: what she intends to pursue after joining us. Her need to be liked, and thus to be accepted, does not depend so much upon initially sharing her past accomplishments as upon what she can become in the near future—

because positive face is not about the past, but about the present and the future. In other words, to relive your glorious past alone probably will not get you into the graduate school, but to imagine a real, challenging future, of which you will be a part, will.

These reflections, limited and selective, enable my students to become gradually aware of their own discursive preferences, of their own positive and negative face wants. They help enact a discourse that engages both Chinese and European American face and that reflects on the limit each face presents to the understanding of the other. Such discourse, at once heterogeneous in its own utterances and potentially resonating with other ethnic discourses, allows us to be better prepared to respond to frustration, incomprehension, or rejection that has often been the fate of many emergent ethnic discourses. It also provides us a means to resist the temptation "either to silence or to celebrate the voices that seek to oppose, critique and/or parody the work of constructing knowledge in the classroom" (R. Miller 407).

As must be emphasized, there is always a limit to this kind of reflection, to the practice of togetherness-in-difference. As Ang points out, "there is only so much (or so little) that we can share," and "any process of 'translocal connecting' not only needs hard work, but, more importantly, can only be partial also" (176). The making of Chinese American rhetoric as a hybrid rhetoric does not necessarily dissolve all the differences and conflicts. What it represents is a contested encounter either of one's own choosing or brought about by forces beyond one's control.

To be a bit more specific, the process of revealing and articulating our respective "face experiences" can be quite discomforting, because feeling tensions and conflicts face to face, coupled with the existing teacher-student hierarchy in the classroom, can be at least unsettling, if not threatening. On the one hand, my students, in spite of my disclaimers to the contrary, will probably never stop asking, perhaps in the back of their minds, Is this what the professor wants? Or, How can I get him to like my writing or my argument? On the other hand, I cannot help but ask how this web of interdependence called for by my own yearnings for 脸 and 面子 will ever get past my students' discourse of "wants" and "likes," and whether they will ever become an integral part of this web of interdependence upon which my own face depends. These unsettling, interrogating voices entangle our articulations, and they further complicate our own face needs and our own nagging ambivalences about them. However, as they inform and construct my students and myself in the classroom, they become no less of the form and content of Chinese American rhetoric.

Not surprisingly, these kii.ds of unsettling voices also resonate in Min-Zhan Lu's *Shanghai Quartet: The Crossings of Four Women of China*—a memoir, addressed to Lu's own daughter, of her Haopo (grandma), her Mmma, her nanny, and herself. A naturalized Chinese American who first moved to America in 1981, Lu tells us, in story after story, how these four women overcame adversities not of their own making, and learned to live with differences and with other-imposed circumstances that often challenged their very existence. Through these stories, both real and imagined, and drawing upon "yi" (移)—the Chinese word for "immigrate" or "move," to which I might add "transform," Lu points out that we are in fact all immigrants, because we move from one place to another as best exemplified by her own crossing from China to America; from one circumstance to another, like her Haopo, who had to rely on her "cunning obedience" (*Shanghai Quartet* 8) to deal with her alienation after she was married to Lu's grandpa, a traditional, less-educated man; and from sorrow to triumph and back to sorrow again when her Mmma switched from hot water to coffee and tea after China survived the Three Years of Natural Calamities in the mid-1960s, and back to hot water again during the Cultural Revolution to "keep pace with the deprivation her husband suffered behind prison bars" (*Shanghai Quartet* 235). As Lu tells her daughter in the Prologue, "we can't keep ourselves from wanting to *yi*—fuse, confuse, and diffuse—set ways of doing things" (*Shanghai Quartet* xi). In my terms, it is these "transplanting" and "transforming" movements that give rise to such ambivalent and entangled encounters—both of which are to be further enriched and complicated at rhetorical borderlands by both sides and on some most basic communicative levels.

For example, in as trivial or mundane an activity as setting up the dinner table and eating dinner with her "foreigner husband," Lu confronts and experiences one of her "yi" moments. In this case she needs to decide whether the dinnerware should be plate and silverware or bowl, chopsticks, and Chinese porcelain spoon, or whether *both* sets should be made available on their mission oak table. What is at stake is whether Lu can choose to slurp soup and shovel rice with chopsticks, or whether her husband can work through the vegetables, meat, and rice—"one at a time, always in that same order" (*Shanghai Quartet* 196). This moment of "togetherness-in-difference," while it has taken them a long time to arrive at it (*Shanghai Quartet* 196), continues to be filled with ambivalence and contradiction. For slurping and shoveling on Lu's part never fail to evoke visceral reactions in her husband, whereas her husband's eating habits remain "foreign" to Lu—because cutting everything into pieces just wastes the juice, the best part, on the plate, and smearing rice onto the fork simply ruins its very texture and flavor (*Shanghai Quartet* 196–97).

It is these moments that make them aware of both their culinary needs and their cultural prejudices. Their voices emerging from them can be quite unsettling, discomforting, and no less transformative. While not so easily generalizable, these moments share a family resemblance to other "yi" moments, to other border zone encounters like mine. Through encounters like this one, Lu and her "foreigner husband" can ask, "are we making love when we sit over bowl, chopsticks, porcelain spoon, and steamy tea across from plate, silverware, and French wine?" (*Shanghai Quartet* 197). They can then "stay and move forward together" (*Shanghai Quartet* 197) with differences, with ambivalences.[13]

Similarly, because of our own yearnings for our own face wants both inside and outside the classroom, I can ask of my students and myself: Are we ready to accept each other's face dynamics and to weave this web of tension-filled interdependence collectively? I can further challenge us by asking: How can we mobilize and put to practice a hybrid rhetoric that creatively engages both "experience-near" and "experience-distant" terms and that openly cultivates not a harmonious fusion, but a togetherness-in-difference rife with tensions and potentials? These voices, perhaps halting and perhaps enabling, nonetheless signify the making of Chinese American rhetoric.

To continue these face encounters and to bring about more of these "yi" moments, I have also used the Chinese film, "The Story of Qiu Ju," in my classroom. This is, once again, my effort to bring Chinese face-work to our rhetorical borderlands in order to help generate reflections that will creatively engage both Chinese and European American face. In so doing, I want to cultivate further this discourse that enriches both faces without denying each its characteristics, or without turning one into merely an obverse of the other. Directed by Zhang Yimou and released in 1992, the film—which is widely available with English subtitles on this side of the Pacific—portrays how Qiu Ju, a village woman, goes on a personal odyssey to seek justice and to restore her damaged face. The film begins with Qiu Ju and her sister-in-law taking Qiu Ju's injured husband, Wan Shanqing, on a rickshaw to the doctor's office. Her husband's injury—he was hit by their Village Chief in the crotch— results from an argument between him and the Chief over the Chief's refusal to allow his family to build a new drying shed on their own land for the chili peppers they raise. Her husband, resentful of the Chief's unjust use of authority both in his refusal and in his having four girls when everyone else is only allowed one child, insults him this way: "You would have no heirs. You only raise hens." In response, the chief kicks him between the legs.

Initially the Chief shows no remorse. Confronted by Qiu Ju for an explanation, he flatly refuses. "Do whatever you want" is his response. To issue an apology amounts to an admission of wrongdoing, thus constituting a serious threat to his 面子—his prestige in the eyes of his fellow villagers—and eventually to his 脸, as such an admission would significantly contribute to their poor judgment of him.[14] The same is almost true of Qiu Ju: not to receive an apology from the Chief is a threat to her 面子 (her standing in the eyes of her fellow villagers), and subsequently to her 脸 (their normative judgment of her). Given her lower social status, however, the damage probably would not be as severe because the "size" of her face, so to speak, is small in comparison with that of the Chief's. Regardless, the dynamics of Chinese 面子 and 脸 shape their respective behaviors, which, in turn, enhance or diminish their own 面子 and 脸.

Determined to redress the wrong inflicted upon her 面子 and 脸 by the Chief's refusal to issue an apology, Qiu Ju, who is pregnant, begins her long quest for justice—first with the Village Public Security Bureau, then with the County Public Security Bureau, and finally with the Municipal Public Security Bureau. After the initial mediation by Officer Li from the Village Public Security Bureau, the Chief agrees to offer Qiu Ju 200 yuan—a significant amount—for the medical cost and lost wages, but no apology. In fact, as he puts it, his payment is not an indication of his regret over his assault, but a gesture to "give 面子" to Officer Li, who is being inconvenienced by their dispute. And Qiu Ju is also advised by Officer Li not to take away all of the Chief's 面子, which her insistence on an apology might just do. To assert further that his face (面子 and 脸) is not diminished at all with his agreement to the mediation, the Chief tosses the money—twenty 10-yuan bills—at Qiu Ju's feet so that she will have to pick them up by bowing her head in front of him. As he tauntingly puts it, "You'll bow your head to me twenty times. Then we'll be even." Qiu Ju refuses to oblige, and walks away with this response: "I'll decide when we'll be even!" And this entire confrontation plays out in front of a group of their neighbors watching in the distance, and most likely weighing if the Chief still "deserves" all the face that has been accorded him so far and if Qiu Ju can face up to someone, the size of whose face is presumably bigger than hers.

Qiu Ju now decides to take her case to the county, and later to the city after she learns that the county has agreed with Officer Li's mediation and that the Chief shows no sign of compromise, unwilling, for example, to say any "面子話" ("mianzi hua," "words that anoint one's 面子"). And the Municipal Public Security Bureau returns with the same decision, except to increase the monetary compensation by 50 yuan. This time, the Chief invites her husband to his house and leaves the money on the table for him to take home. In spite of this conciliatory gesture, the Chief still manages to keep his face intact. He not only makes no apology, but also avoids facing up to Qiu Ju. After all, it is the Chief's wife who actually hands the money to her husband, who in turn takes the money home.

Qiu Ju's 面子 and 臉 would definitely suffer if she agreed to resolve the matter on these terms and under these conditions. Instead, she confronts the Chief face to face and tosses his money back at his feet, thus challenging in particular the Chief's 臉—that is, his moral, communal superiority. She travels back to the city and, with the help of a lawyer, takes her case to court—only to be told later that the court stands by the city's decision. Undeterred, she appeals to the Intermediate People's Court, and eventually wins her case only because the x-ray shows that the Chief has also broken her husband's rib, which constitutes the crime of assault, punishable by fifteen days in detention.

However, when Officer Li arrives at her house to deliver the verdict and to inform her that the Chief is being taken away to serve out the punishment, Qiu Ju is stunned. Not only because earlier the Chief came to her rescue when her labor went badly, but also because the verdict comes in the middle of her family's party, where the whole village has been invited to celebrate her boy being one full month old. As the news breaks, and as the people at the party slowly start to comprehend what has transpired in front of their very eyes, Qiu Ju runs out to chase after the police car, apparently to stop the police from taking the Chief away. As the siren gradually fades away with the film coming to the end, Qiu Ju looks utterly lost and deeply distressed. Although she has finally won her case, she has also lost a good deal of her 面子 and 臉. Her 面子 suffers because she has failed to secure an apology. More damagingly, by helping put away someone who has just saved her and her child's life, Qiu Ju now appears to be completely "ungrateful" and "unreasonable." In the eyes of her community, she has lost her 臉, and she may also have "lost her personhood" ("diu ren," 丢人), which exacts by far the most serious consequences.

How would they react if they were in Qiu Ju's situation? I ask my students. Would they take the money the second time around—instead of tossing it back at the Chief's feet—and move on? Who is to blame here for her not getting an apology and for her losing her 面子 and 脸, and, most likely, her personhood in the end? And how would they characterize the Chief: a local bully who abuses his power and who deserves to be detained for fifteen days, or a tragic figure that lost his 面子 and 脸 because, ironically,[15] he is incapable of sacrificing some of it for the sake of someone else's 面子 and 脸? Can we transform Chinese face without erasing its otherness (read as its emphasis on the public, on the communal)—so that the Chief can apologize without severely damaging his 面子 and 脸 and so that Qiu Ju can move on with her life without an apology, but with her 面子 and 脸 relatively intact?

As perhaps expected, my students and I do not agree on our answers to these questions—in part because of our own irresistible face yearnings. Paradoxically, though, because of these different yearnings, our encounters with the film and with each other have also fostered a new awareness, and they have yielded, however tentatively or haltingly, a new discourse—one that brings our two faces together not to form a harmonious whole, but to create a reflective dialogue where one face does not impose itself upon the other and where re-alignments and new imaginings become possible and indeed necessary.

For example, my students begin to use Chinese 面子 and 脸, or what each stands for, to analyze the face-work of Qiu Ju and the Chief. They begin to see Chinese face in its own otherness, rather than through the lens of negative and positive face wants. As a result, they move from "Both Qiu Ju and the Chief have to be responsible for their own actions though both seem to be dealt an unkind hand" or "One has to pay a price for what one believes in" to "They just don't have a lot of choices to begin with because their hands are tied by (the dictates of) their face" or "Chinese face is simply being messed up by the Chinese justice system—especially when the latter finally delivers 'justice.'" Through these movements or "yi," they have come to see the complexities of Chinese face, to realize more concretely how Chinese face is inextricably linked to social relationships, to normative expectations.

For me, I have come to see, more clearly, both the limits of Chinese face and the importance of negotiating a proper balance between self and public. On the one hand, the Chief is so determined not to lose his own face that he loses sight of his own agency—his will power to provide some 面子-soothing remarks and to issue an apology when it counts the most. On the other hand, Qiu Ju is convinced that her damaged face can only be restored by the Chief's apology, so that she fails to move beyond apologies to redress the face imbalance between herself and the Chief and to regain her standing in the eyes of her peers. Because of their respective failures, they both have lost their face: the Chief is deprived of his freedom for fifteen days and Qiu Ju is seen as "ungrateful," as not possessing "renqing" (人情, "human feelings").

These kinds of reflective encounters, once again, enable us to see each other's face without assumed or imposed biases. For European American face, my students and I can now contemplate discursive possibilities where the need to be liked or to be left alone does not have to be centered upon the individual as the point of origination, and where the same need can be imagined as being discursively distributed at every point of contact and as being shared and experienced by both sides. For Chinese face, we can now return to this pervasive preference for the public not to erase it, but to nurture it in a way that will enable us to critique 面子 and 脸 with self-reflection and self-renewal, and to see through the false sense of security promised by or associated with the performance of an apology. To do so is to eliminate those communicative occasions where one either becomes so obsessed with one's face that one loses one's necessary agency or risks having one's face reduced to such an extent that one could lose one's personhood altogether.

Face encounters and the discursive opportunities they present for the making of Chinese American rhetoric are certainly not confined to classroom interactions or to academic writings. The consequences of not seeing each other's face in their own otherness, of not practicing togetherness-in-difference, can be far more serious outside or beyond the classroom. No example is probably more telling than the accident that exploded over the South China Sea several years ago.

On 1 April 2001, there was a mid-air collision over the South China Sea between an American E-P3 spy plane and a Chinese F-8 jet fighter. The collision crippled the E-P3 and forced it to land on China's Hainan Island without prior clearance. Meanwhile, the Chinese F-8 crashed into the sea immediately after the impact and the pilot was presumed dead. After the collision, China demanded that the United States make an apology to the Chinese government and its people, but the United Stated initially refused because the United States had nothing to apologize for, according to Secretary of State Colin Powell (Sanger). After eleven days of intense negotiation, which has since been dubbed "apology diplomacy" (Gries and Peng 173), a compromise was worked out:

a letter of "regret" by Ambassador Joseph Prueher was sent to Chinese Foreign Minister Tang Jiaxuan in exchange for the safe return of the entire E-P3 crew. While the word "apology" was never used, Ambassador Prueher did state in the letter that President Bush and Secretary of State Powell had expressed "their sincere regret" to the Chinese people and to the family of the pilot, and they were "very sorry for their loss."

Different explanations have since surfaced in the United States to account for China's insistence on an apology. Many seem to have singled out the Chinese concept of face, or its face-saving culture, as the root cause of this "intransigent behavior"—though none of these explanations distinguishes between 面子 and 脸. What seems most ironic is that as these explanations appeal to Chinese face for its explanatory power, they stop seeing it in its own otherness, or they simply characterize it as the obverse of European American face. Such interpretive efforts not only perpetuate the stereotypes about Chinese face-saving culture as mysterious, as irrational, reminiscent of Smith's description of the Occidental, but also reinforce this perceived dichotomy between Chinese and European American face and between (the Chinese preference for) emotion and (the European American disposition for) reason. Not to mention, of course, the diplomatic impasse and international instability such a discursive move contributed to.

Kagan and Kristol's editorial in the *Weekly Standard* is an example of this misguided, stereotyping effort. As the title of their editorial—"A National Humiliation"—indicates, they view the Bush administration's decision to express "their sincere regret" as a "profound national humiliation" (11). On the other hand, they attribute, in large measure, the Chinese leaders' insistence on an apology to a culture that "places an unusually high premium on honor and 'face,'" and that makes it impossible for them to "admit error and to accept responsibility" (12). Further, Kagan and Kristol characterize face encounters as a game of one-upmanship where one saves face at the expense of the other losing face, and where the locus of attention is focused on how face can either be saved or lost through antagonistic encounters, not on how it can be saved, enhanced, or lost through collectively managing each other's relationship to a series of events on a public continuum. Therefore, according to them, by insisting on a public apology from the United States, the Chinese government not only is saving its own face, but also is forcing the United States to lose face and to admit its weakness (12). Such behavior becomes, in their eyes and minds, an example of "irrational emotionalism" (Gries and Peng 174), and it should naturally be rejected out of hand.

Therefore, unless Kagan and Kristol stop seeing Chinese face through the mirror of their own (European American) face, they cannot help but characterize Chinese face in such a way that it becomes either "a petty issue of 'face'" (14) or utterly unrecognizable in the eyes and minds of the Chinese on the other side of the Pacific or of us border residents on this side of the Pacific.

From the point of view of the Chinese leadership, the justification for apology (read as Chinese face) cannot be based solely on isolated incidents, on individual face wants, or on individual responsibility and culpability. Rather, it has to be based on a cluster of interlocking events, both present and past. It is these events that should frame the expectations and that should determine corresponding face-work. For the Chinese leadership, the "present" events include the fact that the accident occurred just off the Chinese coast, and at a time when the United States was increasing the frequency of its surveillance flights. The "past" events have to do with the 1999 American (accidental) bombing of the Chinese Embassy in Belgrade, with the Bush administration's repudiation of Clinton's China policy of "engagement," and with its decision to brand China as a "strategic competitor" (Gries and Peng 175). Consequently, it sees the United States' refusal to "apologize" as its selective blindness to these "incriminating" events, as another sign of the sole superpower's arrogance and hegemony.

On the other hand, by being so steadfast on its demand, the Chinese leadership makes the issuing of an apology the only remedy to force the other side to acknowledge the larger context. But in so doing, it only pushes the other side further away—away from seeing its face dynamics (面子 and 脸), away from understanding its yearnings for interconnectedness, for appealing to the past as a way to face up to the present and the future.

Because each side chose to cling to its own face, the letter of "regret" and the safe return of the entire EP-3 crew did not help at all to dissolve the fundamental biases that led to the diplomatic impasse between the two countries in the first place. In other words, each side seemed to be handicapped, if not crippled, by its own frame, by its own face—so much so that the other face becomes either too exotic (thus threatening and deserving to be replaced) or too invisible (because the other side simply couldn't imagine another world in which some different face could possibly exist and operate). Consequently, the call for retaliation against China for its "irrational behavior" had already been made, even when the plane carrying the entire crew of the E-P3 was still on its way to the

United States (Kagan and Kristol 14). Similarly, on 11 April 2001, the same day when the resolution of this impasse was announced to the public, the *People's Daily* wrote an editorial praising the Chinese leadership for standing up to America's hegemony and for forcing it to "apologize" to the Chinese people ("Let Patriotism"). In a word, both sides were back where they started or worse: in spite of eleven days of face-to-face negotiation, China was seen to be obsessed with its face and the United States with its superpower (self) status.[16]

As I have argued in Chapter One, rhetorical borderlands constitute a potentially transformative space where new voices and new consciousnesses emerge and take shape. On the other hand, rhetorical borderlands are no guarantee that this creative process should materialize or that some hybrid rhetoric should be born out of this contact or out of this co-presence of two different cultures. In addition, the making of any hybrid rhetoric is inevitably attended by the possibility that it may suffer the fate of miscomprehension or incomprehension.

The Chinese leadership, by insisting that its Chinese face be anointed only with an outright apology, is obviously not contributing to the making of "interlocking understanding" (Pratt, *Imperial Eyes* 7). By extracting a letter of "regret" from the United States, it may have succeeded, however temporarily, in asserting some form of moral and symbolic power. However, by not engaging the other face in its own otherness, the Chinese leadership unfortunately compounds the face divide. In so doing, it withdraws into its own discursive enclave, into its own cultural arena. In the end, the Chinese leadership may have failed to challenge substantively the existing power imbalance on the international stage.

Kagan and Kristol, by insisting that all China is concerned about is saving face (and making the other lose face), are not contributing to the making of interlocking understanding, either. By equating Chinese face-work with "irrational emotionalism," they have certainly succeeded in using this polarizing discourse to account for Chinese face dynamics to their own satisfaction. In so doing, they may have accounted for nothing. In the end, they have only managed to perpetuate the stereotype and to reinforce the existing power imbalance.

What does all this mean? Why doesn't any interlocking understanding or hybrid rhetoric take shape when two cultures or two faces come into contact with each other? Let me develop three answers to these questions as a way to bring this chapter to a close.

First, when two cultures or two faces are brought together "in contexts of highly asymmetrical relations of power" (Pratt, "Contact Zone"

34), such a face-up or co-presence does not necessarily translate into the making of a third face or a hybrid rhetoric. As this "apology diplomacy" has forcefully demonstrated, if either side chooses to apply its own face logic to the other, no reflective encounters are ever possible, and no togetherness-in-difference is ever going to come to fruition. However, the inability to nurture the rhetoric of togetherness-in-difference has far-reaching consequences.

Without the rhetoric of togetherness-in-difference, prejudices and stereotypes may continue to be touted as "truths," as "common sense." Further, the binary disposition that pits "us" against "them" will remain as the dominant mode of discourse in thinking of ourselves and the world, and in creating knowledge and meaning—with the dominant culture invariably deciding who can speak, what should be spoken of, and whose face should serve as the norm of both production and consumption. By not engaging each other in a truly dialogic fashion, both sides squander the opportunity for self-discovery and self-renewal; they together fail to cultivate a third discourse—one that has the potential to transcend hierarchical binaries, and one that helps nurture and promote an interlocking understanding of different cultures, different faces.

Second, I agree with Pratt that autoethnographic texts are a phenomenon of contact zones ("Contact Zone" 37). But what needs to be emphasized here is that rhetorical borderlands are also a double-edged sword: there are just as many articulated moments of Chinese American rhetoric as there are failed or silenced ones. That is to say, for any culture that has suffered the slings and arrows of colonialism and other forms of humiliation, self- or other-imposed silence is likely to accompany moments of communication and articulation, and temptations to withdraw into one's own discursive space for self-protection are never far behind the need to challenge "common sense" and to practice togetherness-in-difference. And for the dominant culture, it is not uncommon to vacillate between exoticizing and excoriating the other and to deploy the discourse of appropriation that decides which features of the other should now be "on loan" or "on display" for their "newly-found usefulness." In a word, neither the existence of rhetorical borderlands nor the clashing of two faces is a sure ticket to a celebration of hybrid rhetoric. What both do provide is a set of conditions conducive to or generative of practices and interlocking understandings that can destabilize the hierarchical boundary and promote a sense of interconnectedness.

Finally, from these failed moments or missed opportunities we border residents can, in fact, draw some additional lessons. That is, contacts or face-to-face encounters at rhetorical borderlands are one thing, but to be able to face each other without prejudice and without the "othering" impulse—by, say, not "disfiguring" the other face or disowning one's own, but seeing both faces in relation to their own contexts and imagining them together in a new environment—is entirely another. Therefore, we should guard against confusing sight with vision, and we should not forget that vision is seeing through both faces, by means of cultivating an in-between subjectivity that engages both faces and that re-aligns them in relation to each and every instance of contact, of "yi." If we want to move beyond the discourse of dualism and beyond what it entails, we must take the initiative to cultivate such a vision and to develop a different way of naming and communicating. While I am fully aware that vision of this kind is to be achieved through practice, and that the rhetoric of togetherness-in-difference is to be had through joint efforts, I am anxious to move ahead to do my part and to spur my interlocutors to be part of this borderland, interlocking dialogue. In a word, I want to continue these reflective encounters, to take full advantage of the transformative potential such encounters embody, and to contribute further to the making of Chinese American rhetoric.

3

INDIRECTION VERSUS DIRECTNESS
A Relation of Complementarity

Thus for something to be noble it must take the humble as its root;
For something to be high it must take the low as its foundation.
(Daodejing 138)

A human act is a potential text and can be understood (as a human
act and not a physical action) only in the dialogic context of its
time *(as a rejoinder, as a semantic position, as a system of motives).*
(Bakhtin, "Problem of the Text" 107; emphasis added)

As a style of communication, Chinese indirection is quite visible. Not
only have China observers, from missionaries to sinologists,[1] studied
it, linking it to the Chinese preference for harmony and stability, if
not to the image of inscrutability, but it has also been consistently con-
trasted, as a quintessential feature of Chinese communication, with the
direct style of communication in European American culture. While
Chinese indirection has been attributed to the long-held tradition in
China "to nurture the subtle, fragile bonds and links in human relations" (L. Young 58–59), this style of communication is not that unique.
Indirection has been frequently characterized in terms that are reminiscent of Hall's "high-context" communication in which "very little is
in the coded, explicit, transmitted part of the message" (79), or of
Bernstein's characterization of "restricted code" as verbal signaling with
condensed meanings and reduced clues (126–28). Further, as Fox has
demonstrated, this tendency to communicate through subtle, indirect
strategies, through innuendoes and allusions, are shared by many other
cultures in the world (18–22). Many of her world majority students, she
tells us, are puzzled and frustrated by "the western need for clarity, even
transparency, in written communication" and by "the spare, relentless
logic of the western tradition" (21). These kinds of frustrations or confu-
sions only add, perhaps not in the most positive light, to the visibility of
indirection at rhetorical borderlands, be it Chinese or otherwise.

And more directly put, Chinese indirection has often been singled out as a weakness, as a lack. For example, many Chinese are said to be reluctant to make their requests at the outset, even though there is no perceived power hierarchy between their interlocutor(s) and themselves.[2] They are also said to be reluctant to develop bold, transparent statements up front in their written discourse—whether or not these statements are to be substantiated later in the same text. Instead, they prefer to establish first a shared, sometimes elaborate, context where their requests or statements can be better judged and appreciated. Further, such a context may not be tied *directly* to the requests or statements that they will later make or develop—a connection that the interlocutors/readers may have to make on their own. In this manner, the requests can then be seen as expressions of cooperation, and the delayed statements as gestures of deference (L. Young 37–39). Unfortunately, such discursive moves have not been appreciated as such at rhetorical borderlands—except, at times, to associate them with an Asian preference for inductive reasoning (Scollon and Scollon, "Topic Confusion"). Nor has any serious effort been made to reconfigure Chinese indirection, to characterize it not as a direct opposite, but as a complementing equal, of European American directness—a point I will come back to in greater detail shortly.

In the widely anthologized "The Language of Discretion," Amy Tan tackles similar misconceptions. For example, it is said that the Chinese language lacks direct linguistic means to perform assertions or denials, and that Chinese people are incredibly discreet and modest, only capable of performing phatic (or indirect) speech acts (64, 67). But as Tan tells us, these are no more than misconceptions and stereotypes—though they are not only annoying, but also insidious in perpetuating stereotypes and in compounding misunderstandings. Her own experiences growing up in a bicultural, bilingual family tell her that Chinese people in fact know how to answer "yes" or "no" directly relative to each specific speech event, and that their language may seem indirect or cryptic only to those uninitiated or on the outside looking in (66–67). Further, as she explains elsewhere, it is the richness of her linguistic experiences negotiating between her mother's "broken" English and her own "watered down" translation of her mother's Chinese ("Mother Tongue" 201–2), not any personal preferences for "wishy-washiness," that helps Tan speak "of two minds" ("Language" 63), and that makes such a style of communication an ill candidate for the characterization of "indirection."[3]

But there is more. Chinese indirection has also been feminized. For example, according to L. Young, the need to be indirect and to nurture this sense of commonality or bonds "bears a striking similarity to some of the goals pursued by American women when conversing with American men" (59). Following Gilligan and Tannen, L. Young tells us that when European American women ask questions in a conversation with European American men, they are often doing so not to get answers to their questions, but to keep the conversation going (59). Like the Chinese, European American women want to "nurture and affirm the other's existence and presence" (60) because they are more interested "in seeing themselves functioning within a network of relationships" (61). But as Garrett warns us, such a comparison can become part of this recurring effort to associate Chinese culture—Chinese indirection being an important part of it—with "a valorized feminine" that "hardly squares with the overtly patriarchal nature of the Chinese family, state, and culture" ("Methodological Reflections" 58). Put differently, this kind of comparison, however good-intentioned, inevitably runs the risk of over-generalizing each communicative style and of decontextualizing its internal complexities. Not surprisingly, feminizing Chinese indirectness may in the end help turn the visible—Chinese indirection—into the less visible, because, for now at least, the Chinese talk *just* like European American women.

This "valorized feminine," incidentally, almost becomes the mirror image of the "demonized feminine" associated with colonial discourse. That is to say, the category of "woman," one of the important markers in colonial discourse, regularly signifies irrationality, hysteria, and backwardness, and these negative attributes then feed into and further justify masculine supremacy and colonial domination (Pennycook 61–64). Images of the feminine—be they "valorized" or "demonized"—serve to construct and subsequently control the "other," which always seems so alien or so threatening to the established order.

Chinese written discourse is regularly cited (or sighted) as a typical example of Chinese indirection—though no adequate consideration has been developed to account for its underlying cultural context. How can we, then, evaluate Chinese indirection seen from this side of the Pacific without applying an orientalist logic—a logic that relies on invoking the Western public address paradigm as its norm, as its adjudicating authority in studying Chinese indirection? And how should we, as teachers/writers at rhetorical borderlands, respond when we encounter well-known quotations, literary allusions, and celebrated sayings in our

Chinese or Chinese American students' prose? What should we say when we discover that some of these references might not include their specific sources, or that some of them might not be directly linked to the main ideas they want to get across? As expected, we've seen a wide array of responses over time to these examples of Chinese indirection, ranging from romantic adulation or idealization, to utter condescension, to total frustration.

Amid these responses, I often feel so out of place simply because I share none of them. I fear that I would probably be deemed out of order should I decide to speak out directly. I wonder why, and I want to know how the context that underpins Chinese indirectness has been so conveniently left out.

The discourses so far produced on Chinese indirection have also created their own discursive reality—however removed that reality is from the real dynamics of Chinese indirection or from its underlying context. Such discursive—rather than ontological—reality in turn helps construct cultural stereotypes and shape individual experiences, even though these experiences may not have anything to do with indirectness, Chinese or otherwise. In other words, Chinese and Chinese American students may end up invoking these kinds of discourses in order for their own communicative practices to "make sense" both for themselves and for their European American audience. Or they simply rely on these discourses to "self-critique" their writings and to showcase their meta-knowledge. These maneuvers may not be predicated at all upon their ability to speak and/or write in Chinese, because what they are negotiating is not necessarily between two languages, but between two discursive, cultural realities (of indirection and directness) that are constructed, shaped, and disseminated by such discourses.

For example, according to Jarratt, Losh, and Puente, one of their Chinese American students, Chao, when asked to analyze his own writing, described it as "indirect," as containing too many passive sentence structures (14). They were very surprised by his characterization because there was such a wide discrepancy between his writing and his own characterization of it. For one thing, he used only eight passive constructions in a nine and a half page paper, and several of these constructions were "of a conventional type that would have sounded awkward in an active voice" (14). For another, the arguments he presented in the paper were generally free from qualification or hedging, and his treatment of sources was quite summary (15). In short, there was nothing "indirect" about Chao's writing, in spite of his own meta-discursive efforts to the contrary.

What we are seeing here is a disconnect between referencing or naming, on the one hand, and the referent or what is being named, on the other. Such a disconnect only speaks to the discursive power of these discourses on Chinese indirection: they create knowledge, and they condition our ways of thinking because they now operate as a social and discursive reality. Such discourses perform, in the words of Ang, "the continuing and continuous operation of 'fixing'" (25) on the formation of our rhetorical practices and/or on the formation of our meta-knowledge about these practices. They inevitably produce a "truth" effect, a belief that there is a "fit" between the proposition and the world—even though, most ironically, such discourses hardly reflect truth, and they hardly "word" the world.[4]

So, what, then, is the underlying context that informs Chinese indirection? What is the real referent that has been so obscured, if not erased altogether, by these kinds of discourses? Simply put, Chinese indirection becomes much more complex when viewed in its larger cultural context, and in fact it should not be viewed as just the (inferior) opposite of directness—be it European American or that of any other speech community.

Before I proceed to uncover this context, this much has to be noted right away. First, my effort to re-evaluate Chinese indirection should not be rationalized, directly or indirectly, as an example, on my part, of cultivating harmony over discordance between Chinese indirection and European American directness. Nor should such an effort be construed in any shape or form as an attempt to accommodate Chinese indirection to the terms of the directness paradigm. Either interpretive move is, at best, to cancel important, productive opportunities for reflective encounters at rhetorical borderlands. Such encounters interrogate and contest hierarchical stereotypes and structures that have, in my view, so crippled our understanding of Chinese indirection and European American directness. As I have argued in Chapter One, encounters of this kind—through heterogeneous resonance—help reconnect to the complex past that has informed their respective manifestations at present. They generate dynamic, complex relationships, yielding a new awareness that is intricately implicated in, though not causally derived from, points of contact between Chinese indirection and European American directness.

Second, my re-evaluation of Chinese indirection in relation to European American directness should not entail that the latter is monolithic or unchanging—though it is quite tempting to describe European

American directness, or European American rhetorical tradition for that matter, as such—so that we can use it as our own easy target, as our own rhetorical foil. Not only does European American directness, like any other mode of communication, manifest itself in each and every particular context of situation, which necessarily is cause enough for variation, improvisation, and transformation, but also European American directness can quickly find itself overlapping with other modes of communication associated with other rhetorical traditions. What remains constant, therefore, has to be people in positions of power, who hold European American directness in place and who further reify[5] it as their own preferred, celebrated norm.[6] Incidentally, the disconnect between referencing and the referent that I discussed above concerning Chinese indirection applies, just as fittingly, to European American directness—though with differing consequences. That is to say, for Chinese and Chinese American students, to describe their communicative practices as "indirect" reproduces and reinforces cultural stereotypes, and it squarely places them at the bottom of this hierarchy that pits indirection against directness. For European American students, to dub their communicative practices "direct" provides a positive cover for them, if not cultural capital. Such an outcome serves them well: it matches with and further enhances the discursive desire for clarity and transparency.

There are, admittedly, a multitude of components shaping Chinese cultural context—if we consider China's long history, and its changing social and political conditions. In this chapter I want to focus on two of them—correlative thinking and the topic-prominent characteristic of the Chinese language—because these two are quite central, in my view, to the subject matter *at hand*, and to my overriding concern to reconnect (the act of) referencing to the referent, the past to the present. Naturally, my selected focus here does not imply that other components are not important; rather, it means that they are *presently* not as important.

Correlative thinking has been characterized as a fundamental Chinese characteristic,[7] one that is "grounded in informal and hence ad hoc analogical procedures presupposing both association and differentiation" (Hall and Ames, *Anticipating China* 125). By putting items or events in groups as interrelated sets within a scheme explainable in terms of analogical relations, correlative thinking uses the association of image- or concept-clusters to yield similarities or contrasts and to produce richly vague significances. This mode of thinking parts with other modes of thinking that rely upon "natural kinds, part-whole relations, an implicit or explicit theory of types, or upon causal implications or entailments or anything like the sort one finds in Aristotelian or modern Western logics" (124; also see 125–41). To use Hall and Ames' example of totemic classifications for illustration, when a clan, or a family, or a group is associated with a particular animal or natural object, a meaningful correlation gets established—though no shared essence or causal connection, as would be expected by Western logic, underpins such association. The selected animal or natural object has characteristics that help create feelings and behaviors in the human beings associated with it. In turn, these feelings and behaviors help to establish their character and identity as individuals, as well as their patterns of communal association (125).

Let me use another example—the twelve animals of Chinese astrology. According to the Chinese zodiacal system, which consists of a twelve-year cycle, each year of the cycle is named after one of the twelve animals: the Rat, Ox, Tiger, Rabbit, Dragon, Snake, Horse, Ram, Monkey, Rooster, Dog, and Boar.[8] Each animal accords a set of distinct characteristics to its year, and a person who is born in that year then takes on these characteristics, and in fact his or her future or fortune is determined by the year of his or her birth, by this association, by this assigned relationship. For example, if you are born in the year of the Dog, you are then trustworthy and faithful, and you are adept at assessing information and will always fight for truth (Kwok 14). Further, your association with the Dog also entitles you to certain kinds of relationships with other individuals. As a Dog, you are suited to the Horse (that is, the individual born in the year of the Horse), but not the Dragon, Ram, or Rooster (Kwok 16–17). Once again, no efforts are being expended to connect you to the characteristics of a given animal from a causal perspective, nor are any gestures being made toward establishing some shared essence or identity between you and the animal. Rather, by clustering together the images and characteristics of the twelve animals within the twelve-year zodiac cycle,[9] Chinese astrology creates, for individuals associated with each of these twelve animals, meanings and significances that are informed by a correlative logic—by an exclusive focus on "the correlational implications between different signs" (T. Chang 312) and on their mutually-dependent characteristics.

To suggest that correlative thinking is a central characteristic of Chinese culture should not lead us to conclude that it is necessarily unique to the Chinese mind. Such a conclusion would be too extravagant because "it ignores or undermines the well-developed Greek interests in correlations" as is seen in the Pythagorean Table of

Opposites reported by Aristotle (Lloyd 114–15). Similarly, according to Graham, correlative thinking was the dominant mode of thought in the West until Galileo, and the correlative cosmos was then the only game in town, so to speak, until the development of modern science, beginning with the Scientific Revolution around 1600 (*Disputers* 315–19). In the words of Graham, "Until the Scientific Revolution, the choice was between a correlative cosmos and no cosmos at all" (*Disputers* 318). Such (scientific) development then began the shift away from correlative to causal thinking, and it began to assume "an objective ground that can underwrite standards of evidence, allowing claims to certitude or plausibility" (Hall and Ames, *Anticipating China* 126). As a result, even modern Western astrology—the most recognizable artifact evidently shaped by correlative thinking, is being rationalized, and much of its language is not correlative, but causal (131).

Almost by the same token, the dominance of correlative thinking in Chinese culture does not mean that causal thinking is non-existent—the technological achievements throughout Chinese history provide sufficient evidence for its existence and for its influence. As Hall and Ames point out, all cultures possess both correlative and causal modes of thinking, and what makes one mode run roughshod over the other is that the dominant mode tends to "inform and recast the recessive mode" (131). Ironically, because of its importance in Chinese cultural tradition, correlative thinking has been singled out as one major "culprit" contributing to the lack of scientific and technological advances in Chinese history. Namely, since correlative thinking does not follow the kind of rational, deductive reasoning associated with Western tradition, with the Enlightenment, China missed out on the opportunity to join the ranks of the West in the area of science and technology. And correlative thinking has also been recast in causal, logical terms, and it has been invested in a context that is altogether not its own. The reason appears simple: since correlative thinking is so important in Chinese culture, it must have embodied some logical deep structure, or it must have somehow followed the same kind of rules and rationale as in Western culture. Consequently, the Chinese zodiac system should now be understood less in terms of its immanent associations and corresponding significances, but more in terms of metaphor (similarity) and metonymy (contiguity) (Bodde 98–99).[10]

What must be underscored in any discussion of Chinese correlative thinking is that interrelated sets or correlatives within a given scheme of twos, threes, fives, or nines are not logically or causally related. Nor are they necessarily or always hierarchically ordered or distinguished, with one being superior to, and more valuable than, the other. Correlatives like "day" and "night," "heaven" and "earth," and "action" and "inaction" in a classificatory scheme of twos should not be characterized, as often been the case, as opposites that conflict, but as opposites that complement (Graham, *Disputers* 331–40). Otherwise stated, the contrast between these correlative pairings does not mean that one excludes the other, or that one logically entails the other. Nor does it mean that they together yield completeness or totality. Rather, they become what Raphals calls "complementary polarity"—a polarity that emphasizes the need for balance and interdependence between the two items (*Sharing the Light* 151).[11]

Let me use "yin" and "yang" to illustrate further this characteristic. "Yin" and "yang" initially appeared as two of six "qi" (氣, "energy")[12] in fourth-century (BCE) works such as the *Zuo Zhuan* (左傳, *Zuo Annal*), which chronicled the reigns of twelve rulers of the State of Lu (722–481 BCE). "Yin" and "Yang" began to assume the role of the quintessential polarity in China in the third and second centuries (BCE), first as a cyclic model that "emphasized the alternation of day and night or darkness and light (晦明) and the four seasons" before it became part of the language in an explanation of social, political, and cosmological processes (Raphals, *Sharing the Light* 143; also see Graham, *Yin-Yang* 91–92;). Therefore, "yin" and "yang" are always interdependent, and they are always in the process of *becoming* in relation to one or more other pairings of polarities. So, the chest is "yin" (receptive, soft, submissive) in relation to the back, which is "yang" (creative, hard, aggressive). However, in relation to the abdomen, the chest becomes "yang." And these relations can be further transformed with any other changes in the human body, such as a broken leg or a pinched nerve (Ames and Rosemont, "Introduction" 25). On the other hand, the "yin-yang" complementary relationship is not immune to social and political forces, which have in fact led to a skewed, though self-serving, emphasis on maintaining a hierarchical distinction between subordinate and superordinate in each and every paring (Raphals, *Sharing the Light* 151). As a result, the "yin-yang" polarity, the basis for ordering all binary correlatives in Chinese cosmology,[13] has been frequently interpreted as representing only hierarchical, irreversible contrasts in social realms to justify, for example, the separation of the sexes— women as "yin" suited only for the "inside" and men as "yang" belonging to the "outside"—or to maintain the status quo—those who dare to challenge the existing social system are described as upsetting the "yin-yang" balance and thus ruled out of order.

On the strength of this binary, distorted understanding of the "yin-yang" contrast, Chinese indirection has often been characterized as a direct and subordinate opposition to the European American directness paradigm. Any attempts to complicate or to reject this binary characterization will then be naturally faulted for not observing the "yin-yang" balance, and thus dismissed as having no value at all. While the use of this binary discourse to define Chinese indirection can certainly be attributed to a lack of contextual knowledge, it reveals, to my mind, a far more serious, deep-rooted disposition to construct, in this case, Chinese indirection according to the "exnominated" (read as invisible) norm.[14] Once this kind of disposition is set in motion or put to work, the rest about Chinese indirection is, as we say in English, history.

Not too surprisingly, the Chinese language seems to have suffered an almost identical fate. According to Tong, Chinese has been characterized as "lacking principle and incapable of self-generation" because it does not have a system of inflection (46). Such a characterization or "fixing" becomes possible only because of the adjudication administered by the "exnominated" norm, by the model of Western European inflected languages. This kind of characterization, to quote Tong, is based upon "a frame of reference that belongs to the Western tradition" (46). Or, in my own words, it is made possible and discursively real by the discourse of hierarchical polarity that opposes a (subordinate) noninflectional Chinese language to (superordinate) inflectional Western European languages.

Analogical, correlative associations are not always binding, though. Their discursive forces are predicated upon the extent to which these associations have been fully institutionalized or firmly entrenched within structures of power. For instance, there is a notable difference between Hall and Ames' example of totemic classifications and my example of the twelve animals of Chinese astrology. When a clan or a family becomes associated with a particular animal or natural object, they may not have much choice except to embrace or to adjust to those feelings and behaviors that emanate from such associations, and that help establish their identity and their future alliances. The reason is perhaps easy to comprehend: such totemic associations have been assigned an institutional value that is both expressive and deterministic. To reject them is to reject their own community, to upset this "yin- yang" order of communal significance.

On the other hand, individuals that are born in the year of one of the twelve animals under the Chinese zodiacal system can indeed subscribe to or consult with corresponding associations—whether they are trustworthy or whether they should associate themselves with individuals born in the year of a different animal. Or they don't have to take these associations seriously, and they can even reject them altogether without necessarily incurring any serious consequences or penalties from the community. While Chinese twelve-animal astrology does create meanings and identities for individuals associated with each of these twelve animals, these meanings and identities are yet to be institutionalized or incorporated into the larger constitutive order of discourse in Chinese society. Until and when they are, individuals can either remain free of their associative influences or use them to their advantage.

Let me now turn to the second component—the topic-prominent characteristic of the Chinese language. In a quite influential essay on language typology, Li and Thompson demonstrate in some detail that Chinese is a topic-prominent language because topic-comment structure is its significant typological feature ("Subject and Topic" 460)—though they admit that they are not the first to make this proposal (477). Unlike English, a subject-prominent language which prominently features subject-verb structure, Chinese has, as its basic sentence type, topic-comment structure, with the topic always being definite, in the initial position, and the center of attention (464–66).[15] For example,

> Z[h]eijian shiqing ni bu neng guang mafan yige ren.
> (这件事情你不能光麻烦一个人.)
> this (classifier) matter you not can only bother one person
> The matter (topic), you can't just bother one person. ("Subject and Topic" 479)

Here the relationship of "z[h]eijian shiqing" ("this matter") and "ni bu neng guang mafan yige ren" ("you can't just bother one person") is not subject to object, nor is it subject to predicate. Rather, "ni bu neng guang mafan yige ren" serves as a comment on the topic "z[h]eijian shiqing." Differently stated, "z[h]eijian shiqing" provides a framework or establishes a theme for the discourse—hence the topic-comment structure.[16] The same sentence also contains both the subject ("you") as actor and the topic ("this matter") as patient.

Li and Thompson further suggest that the topic in Chinese topic-comment structure essentially belongs to discourse. For example, by relating the sentence, of which it is a part, to some preceding sentence, the topic functions in "the context in which a given sentence occurs, whether it is a conversation, a paragraph, a story, or some other kind of language situation" (*Mandarin Chinese* 100). The function of the topic as a discourse element to establish a framework for the rest of the discourse is further reinforced by other connective pairs in Chinese, like "yinwei ...... suoyi......" (因为......所以......) ("because...so...").[17] Like the topic in topic-comment structure, "yinwei" ("because") establishes a "causal" framework, one that is not necessarily confined to one dominant factor or agency; nor does it have to be realized by just one or two sentences. And such a framework is essential for the comment-like "suoyi" ("so") part to emerge.

Drawing upon *Shuowenjiezi*, the first comprehensive Chinese lexicon compiled by Xushen in the second-century Han Dynasty, L. Young takes into account the classical meanings for each constituent in this modern connective pair. In this context, "yinwei" is better defined as "'accommodating' or taking into account those contingent conditions," and "suoyi" means "'thereby' a particular 'place' or 'position' is configured as a center of these *yin* [accommodation] conditions" (40). In other words, what "yinwei" connotes is a cluster of contingent conditions or relationships upon which the "suoyi" part of the discourse depends. The "yinwei ......suoyi......" construction, as L. Young points out, "suggests a peculiarly Chinese sense of causality in which a full range of conditions must be elaborated and considered as causes for a particular event" (40), and it represents "a holistic disposition in the movement of foci from big to small" and "a kind of bidirectional responsiveness in which each party 'moves toward' the other" (43). In short, both topic-comment structure and connective pairs like "yinwei ...... suoyi......" in Chinese foster a discursive tendency where "topics" or clusters of conditions precede "comments" or definitive statements, and where information is being packaged as "one gigantic unit" (L. Young 83), analyzable only in terms of topic-comment structure or regularly signified by connectives like "yinwei ...... suoyi......."

Discussing the ways in which syntactic units in Chinese are sequenced, Tai proposes that Chinese word order "corresponds to thought flow in a genuinely natural way" (64). That is, Chinese word order, in Tai's terms, is "natural" or iconic rather than "salient" (64–65). For example, "Because John went walking in the freezing rain he caught cold" is in natural order, and "John caught cold because he went walking in the freezing rain" is in salient order (65). While one may argue over the semantics of the word "natural" in describing the syntactic order of a given language, Tai's characterization of Chinese word order further reinforces this discursive tendency evidenced in the topic-comment structure and in the use of connective pairs like "yinwei ...... suoyi......"—a tendency to cluster initially a range of conditions as causes for a particular event that follows, or to provide a frame of reference that precedes the presentation of facts or events.

Along a similar line—though with more of a philosophical focus, Ames and Rosemont describe classical Chinese as "an eventful language," whereas they characterize English as a "substantive and essentialistic" language ("Introduction" 20–21). More specifically, classical Chinese displays what they call "a more relational focus"—a concern to describe how events stand in relation to other events at a given moment in time, rather than how they are in themselves despite differing appearances ("Introduction" 23).[18] Because of this relational focus, the meaning of a given word in classical Chinese becomes dependent upon its relationship with other words that it becomes associated with or that it comes in contact with. For example, "jun" (君) ("exemplary person") is defined by its cognate and phonetically similar "qun" (群) ("gathering"); similarly, "gui" (鬼) ("ghost") is defined as "gui" (歸) ("return") because presumably the ghost "has found its way back to some more primordial state" ("Introduction" 28–29). This kind of discursive interdependence thus underscores "the primacy of process over form as a grounding presupposition in this tradition" ("Introduction" 29). To put it another way, the "meaningfulness," not the "essence," of these terms lies not in the unchanging Form that transcends the human realm, but in a long-held recognition that the only constant is change itself.

The eventful properties of classical Chinese, coupled with the fact that classical Chinese does not have definite articles, copulas, plurals, or tenses, have often been viewed as evidence that Chinese remains highly ambiguous, because these "eventful" properties lead to a "cryptic and ambiguous style (Becker 80).[19] This view is patently mistaken. As I have been suggesting, the contextual interdependence is in fact "a decided communicative asset" or an example of "productive vagueness," because it "requires the reader to participate in establishing an interpretation and to internalize the given passage in the process of doing so" (Ames and Rosemont, "Introduction" 42). In addition, such a view assumes, without adequate explanation, that this lack of "precision" in classical written Chinese necessarily shades into speech and that classical written Chinese was more or less a transcription of speech.[20]

My discussion so far of the eventful characteristics of classical Chinese is perhaps far too brief, but it seems evident that this focus on discursive interdependence, on how events stand in relation to other events, is shared by both classical written Chinese and modern Chinese. The fact that this affinity has been maintained for all these years is significant if one just considers how much has changed in the language since the use of oracle bone inscriptions ("jiaguwen," 甲骨文) in the late Shang Dynasty (circa 1200 BCE)—from Archaic Chinese, to Medieval Chinese, to Pre-Modern Chinese, to Modern Chinese (P. Chen 2). On the other hand, one may also argue, as I am doing right now, that nothing substantive has changed after all, because this relational focus has remained a central underpinning that informs and reinforces how Chinese operates as a language, how its users use the language to interact with the world. In fact, without making any explicit connection to the topic-comment structure in modern Chinese, Ames and Rosemont propose a heuristic for how to read classical written Chinese: read pictograms, which are stylized direct representations of objects, as nouns or *topics*, and read ideograms, which are created by joining two ideas or pictures, as *comments*—as long as there is no contextual evidence to the contrary (*The Analects of Confucius* 304; emphasis added). Therefore, not to articulate the eventful properties of classical written Chinese, and not to associate them with the topic-comment structure in modern Chinese, are tantamount to denying Chinese one major defining characteristic. Similarly, to characterize this relational focus as a discursive liability rather than an example of productive vagueness once again reminds us of the orientalist logic that relies on some Western model to evaluate non-Western phenomena and that treats those "recalcitrant exceptions" as instances of liability or deficiency.

So, how, then, is our understanding of Chinese indirection going to be different in this new context informed both by correlative thinking in cosmology and by this relational, topic-comment focus in the language? To begin with, Chinese indirection should not be seen, without discrimination, simply as an example of a nontransparent style of communication or, worse still, of indecision and incoherence. Chinese indirection, be it realized or articulated by repeated appeals to tradition/authority or by recurrent parallel statements with or without a transparent progression of ideas, takes on new meanings or associations within its (newly-developed) context. To put the matter another way, the contextualized nature of the Chinese language and the dominance of correlative thinking in Chinese culture both constitute a central context to understand the rhetoric of Chinese indirection more completely and provide a meta-discursive language to talk about and reflect upon it more felicitously.

For one thing, they can now be viewed as part of an ever-present effort to establish a field of conditions or contingencies. It is quite possible that these discursive moves may contribute to the impression that there are too many piles of facts, quotations, and anecdotes that seem unconnected to the original argument. But it is precisely these facts, quotations, and anecdotes that help create this relational focus.[21] Namely, they help explore how one set of facts and anecdotes stands in relation to, and becomes, another set of facts and anecdotes, and how the latter creates new meanings and associations from the former.

For another, as examples of productive vagueness, they serve as "contextualization cues," as linguistic features that signal contextual presuppositions and that suggest how the entire discourse should be understood (Gumperz 131–32). In other words, they initiate and invite the audience to make necessary associations, to recognize the interdependence of texts, and to participate in the overall meaning-making process. Naturally, audience participation in meaning-making can be fraught with uncertainty and incompleteness. And there will always be a surplus of meaning in communication—in the sense that meaning is both always deferred and always yielding new meanings to those who resonate with this mode of thinking (Hall and Ames, *Anticipating China* 228–29). And Chinese indirection makes no effort to control that surplus; in fact, it thrives on this kind of meaning surplus to create "richly vague significance" (*Anticipating China* 124). Therefore, to characterize Chinese indirection simply as an example of a "lack" or of "Chinese inscrutability" is to miss the point altogether. And no less off the mark is the effort to feminize Chinese indirection, to compare it, however charitably, with European American women's style of communication.

Here then is the question: How will this new understanding of Chinese indirection influence our encounters at rhetorical borderlands, at places where different cultures engage each other and where the disadvantaged, the disempowered negotiate with the dominant? It surely creates tensions if I choose to compose prose in English with clusters of initial "topics" or with repeated efforts to embed my argument within allusions and analogies—both are being attempted, perhaps indirectly, in this chapter and throughout this book. Such a move most definitely conflicts with the "directness norm" in analytical writing, and it challenges the expectation that precise definitions and explicit statements of cause and effect be provided and that paragraphs begin with general statements to be followed by appropriate examples (Fox xviii).

However, a conflict of this kind helps foster a more open, rigorous recognition of the values and assumptions associated with each style of communication, with its concomitant view of the world. And such recognition becomes crucial in any dialogic knowledge-making process. To be more specific, by creating this tension, I can begin to highlight, for Chinese indirection, a sense of co-existence or interdependence, and I can explore this focus on how some "events" can become other "events" in a world that depends not on univocal meanings, but on clusters of images and inferences. For European American directness, I can be more understanding of the need, if not the compulsion, to go directly to the marrow of a subject in order to be credible and to be authoritative. I can become equally attentive to the history behind the "directness norm," to the emergence of essayist literacy in Europe in the eighteenth century when language came to be viewed "as a transparent representation of the natural order of the universe" (Scollon and Scollon, *Narrative, Literacy and Face* 44), and when "an explicit, decontextualized presentation" was valued over an unclear, contextual, and symbolic presentation (52). As I reflect on European American directness from this point of view, however, I continue to feel the pull from my own yearnings for events, contexts, and indirectness.

Associated with this emergent recognition is a corresponding sense of indeterminacy and ambiguity. Whenever there is more than one language involved, and whenever there is more than one style of communication invoked, any hope of an immediate, seamless correspondence between words and the world dissipates quickly. And the fact that norms of production and consumption are yet to be laid out fully and explicitly further aggravates this sense of indeterminacy and ambiguity, both of which, in competition with well-definedness and clarity, are being realized through symbolic and strategic articulations. It is indeed in these rhetorical spaces that we border residents can begin to take advantage of this opportunity to develop and try out new ways of speaking, and to reconstitute rules of relationships and patters of communication—without, of course, underestimating the constraints and uncertainties that necessarily will intrude upon these efforts, these experiences.

Any such attempts on my part to upset the discursive or "exnominated" norm in English analytical writing entail consequences, both material and rhetorical. While the reflective encounters and enabling practices that I am describing here do emerge from rhetorical borderlands both in and outside the classroom, their reception, or the securing of their uptake, is never assured and is filled with tensions and ambiguities. As I have argued in some detail in Chapter One, to gloss over these problems overstates borderland potentials and romanticizes the power of cultural mediation over heterogeneity of meaning—not to mention those moments when co-presence only leads to miscomprehension, to hiding behind one's own discursive space, as discussed in Chapter Two.

At the same time, my decision to enact a particular rhetoric—Chinese American rhetoric in this case—is not just my own personal choice so that I can break out of this cacophony over Chinese indirection and move beyond this discourse of "othering."[22] Rather, my decision is very much grounded in my own desire to align myself with my own (Chinese and Chinese American) community, to secure its approval and its blessings. Further, I know my discursive alignment or rhetorical "footings"—to borrow a term from Goffman (*Frame Analysis*)—can never be totally divorced from European American directness, from its culture, and from its overwhelming co-opting power. Once again, I find myself to be cultivating something of an in-between subjectivity that negotiates between the subject position of the exile and that of the immigrant. Those conflicting ideologies are forever implicated in, and continuously impress themselves upon, my rhetorical inventions, upon my yearnings to bring on board both Chinese indirection and European American directness at rhetorical borderlands.

Again, to bring out these contextual underpinnings informing each style of communication is not, as one might expect, to engineer some sort of harmony between them, because there is really none to be had. Nor am I advocating, in doing so, a relativity of values, because each style constitutes a distinct method of investigation and signifies a distinct aspect of cultural reality. While no assimilation should be attempted in this kind of encounter, the kinds of reflections I am articulating here are mobilized through heterogeneous resonance, through togetherness-in-difference. That is to say, they embody how we may be able to participate in "events" while still being cognizant of the context of "things," and they reveal how we can get to the bottom of "things" with the realization that other conditions and other events may eventually turn the bottom into the top again. Seen in this light, Chinese indirection does not have to be viewed as the undesirable opposite of European American directness. On the contrary, it should be seen as a necessary equal to the latter—since, after all, indirection and directness, like "yin" and "yang," like the noble and the humble or high and low, as aptly illustrated in the first of the two epigraphs for this chapter, are never not fluid and fluctuating, and the value of one is always parasitic upon that of the other, and vice versa. Or to paraphrase Bakhtin, quoted in the second epigraph, European American directness can only be understood in the dialogic context of indirection or it can only exist in conjunction with it.

What now? I will, for the remainder of this chapter, further illuminate this interlocking tension as Chinese indirection engages European American directness. I first discuss Min-Zhan Lu's work again, followed by a reading of Kingston's *The Woman Warrior*, through the lenses of both indirection and directness. In so doing, I want to highlight how such tension can yield a new way of communicating, of referencing the world, and how Chinese indirection and European American directness can "join hands" to realize togetherness-in-difference. I close this chapter with a personal story of mine, which shows, once again, both the promise and peril of practicing Chinese American rhetoric.

So, let me begin with Min-Zhan Lu's work, turning my attention to *Shanghai Quartet.* Once again, it provides some telling examples of how Chinese indirection and European American directness are entangled in complex ways, and how their entanglements help illustrate the making of Chinese American rhetoric.

One of the stories she tells us in the memoir is centered upon her coffee-drinking experience. People regularly ask Lu, when she either accepts or declines coffee when green tea is also being offered, "Do the Chinese drink coffee?" (231). Confronted with such a straightforward question, Lu feels the need to be direct: to give a "yes" or "no" answer to this question, and to present "a single, all-encompassing story" (230). But she can't, because "taste and distaste for coffee are often as much matters of economics and politics as of palate or habit" (231), and because no single story can get to the bottom of things. For her, therefore, any direct answer to such question has to start from "the seemingly insignificant incidents of every day life" and from "variations and collages of little stories" (230). For her American audience, however, this kind of answer may become a bit too "indirect," if not too inscrutable.

Growing up in an upperclass household where coffee was served on all occasions involving her surgeon father, Lu coveted the taste of coffee early on, though she had to wait until age ten before she was granted a few drops. By 1961, she was old enough to drink coffee, and she quickly formed the habit of mixing it with milk and three lumps of sugar, though both milk and sugar were rationed in those years in China. She only began to realize her privileged position when her nanny's two-year-old adopted grandson asked for "a bowl of life-saving sugar water" to fight off his dizziness (237). Now she takes her coffee straight because she discovered, soon after coming to America, that the dishwater variety served at most places could not have been taken any other way. Yet, to reject sugar and milk when offered with coffee remains emotionally challenging, because they conjure up so many past memories about her growing up in Shanghai, about her trips, with her "foreigner husband," to a local Vietnamese restaurant "where coffee was still served *our way*" (238; emphasis original).

These memories or these felt experiences make it only fitting for Lu to provide a full range of conditions, and to set up a necessary frame of reference, in order to answer or to talk about whether or not the Chinese drink coffee. On the other hand, an otherwise all-encompassing response would necessarily become quite incomplete or too abstract—no matter how "direct" it might be. Her own acute awareness of the inadequacy evidenced in this "direct" approach makes the telling of her story all the more appropriate (and quite direct to her) —no matter how "indirect" it might appear to her American interlocutors. The use of such a story and her reflective efforts to talk about "Do the Chinese drink coffee?" are therefore imbued with both Chinese indirection and European American directness, and they constitute a situated example of Chinese American rhetoric.

Min-Zhang Lu's decision to select a particular episode from the past to address and to inform the present resonates with, or conjures up an affinity to, Kenneth Burke's concept of "representative anecdote" (*A Grammar* 59–61),[23] and to his overall insight that language both reflects and deflects reality (*Language* 45). For Burke, a "representative anecdote" is a dramatistic conception that is "supple and complex enough to be representative of the subject-matter" it is chosen to represent or inform (*A Grammar* 60). Because it contains the terminological structure, a "representative anecdote" develops "a systematic terminology," out of which "another kind of summation looms up" (60–61). Burke calls this summation the "paradigm" or "prototype" (61). Of course, be it a "representative anecdote" or the "paradigm," any discursive effort to reflect reality also necessarily functions as a deflection of reality, as a "terministic screen" that directs our attention to a particular slice of reality that the anecdote or the paradigm is designed to reflect and to symbolize in the first place—in the same way that different color filters can give us some very different photographs of the same objects (*Language* 45).

Lu's story about her own childhood coffee-drinking experience in the midst of social, political upheaval may indeed be viewed as an example of "representative anecdote" because it is chosen to answer most directly "Do the Chinese drink coffee?", thus reflecting the kind of reality that she wants her European American interlocutors to see and to believe. But there is a significant difference: this story becomes rhetorically appropriate and effective because it grows out of a critical and inventive engagement, as Chinese indirection grapples with European American directness. Not only does the danger exist of having such a story misheard or not having it heard at all, but also its meaning is always in flux, contingent upon specific encounters, upon specific contextual variations. And there is simply no "paradigm" or "prototype" to be had at rhetorical borderlands. In a word, stories of this kind remain stubbornly local, because their meanings need to be renegotiated and rearticulated every time these stories get told and get heard. They are, in a word, part of our reflective encounters, part of the making of Chinese American rhetoric at rhetorical borderlands.

In my writing classes, I regularly teach Kingston's *The Woman Warrior* to illustrate, for my mainstream American students, how Chinese Americans, like Kingston, are negotiating between two powerful cultural traditions, and how memories, dreams, and "talk-stories" shape and influence their experiences and their sense of who they are. More importantly, I want to use these teaching moments to demonstrate how Chinese indirection acquires its new form and content at rhetorical borderlands as it grapples with the logic of European American directness. In short, I want to articulate, both for my students and for myself, the making of Chinese American rhetoric. While they are real and direct most of the time, I know, in the back of my mind, some of these teaching moments can be just as imagined, just as informed by my own private longings for Chinese indirectness, and for a discourse that is not about "othering" on either side of the Pacific, but about productive engagement at rhetorical borderlands. Once again, I feel the tug of both the exile and the immigrant.

The "general" American readers, according to V. Chen, view *The Woman Warrior* as both interesting and confusing, and they think that "Kingston does not write clearly" because "it is difficult to tell where her fantasies end and reality begins" (4). Reflecting the mood of the "general" American readers, critics have measured the book "against the stereotype of the exotic, inscrutable, mysterious oriental (Kingston, "Cultural Misreadings" 55).[24] A good number of my students share a similar reading experience: while they all enjoyed reading the book, they were puzzled by its recurrent use of Chinese myths and fairy tales in the construction of Kingston's personal journey. To use my terms, this inability to appreciate the blurring, the border-crossing, reflects, to a large extent, the tendency to read the Chinese "events" through the framework of European American "things"—that is, they were expecting a transparent, causal progression from a text that thrives upon meaning interdependence and upon productive vagueness. The failure of their expectation conveniently matches, and perhaps reinforces, their culturally-conditioned image of the Chinese as the exotic, as the inscrutable. For me, then, it becomes crucial to move beyond discourses that simply dub *The Woman Warrior* an example of "fictional autobiography" and that quickly condemn "the ghostly otherness" in Kingston's Chinese American experience to the exotic Orient (Kingston, "Cultural Mis-readings" 57). Instead, I must develop discourses that can, as Kim suggests, stake our claim on America without relinquishing "our marginality" (147), and that can, to draw on my preceding discussions, claim "the ghostly otherness" as part of this togetherness-in-difference at rhetorical borderlands.

The Woman Warrior should be read, I tell my students in no uncertain terms, as a story of Chinese indirectness in contexts that cut across different times, spaces, and cultures. Throughout the book, Kingston weaves the personal with "talk-stories" to yield a complex tale of her experience growing up as a Chinese American. The book begins with a story of "No Name Woman," Kingston's aunt, who drowned herself in the family well with her just-born infant because she became pregnant while her husband was on the other side of the Pacific. Because of this disgraceful act and the shame it created, the family didn't want to even acknowledge that she had ever existed, and her mother warned Kingston not to tell the story to anyone else (3, 18). But for Kingston, this story has to be told first (19), because doing so not only rebels against her mother's injunction not to tell, but also transforms an absence of fifty years (19) into a haunting presence—both of which are necessary for her own account to come out later. Her No Name Aunt had to commit suicide so as to repair "the break she had made in the 'roundness'" (14) of the patriarchal tradition, to make the family whole again by removing herself and her illegitimate child—both of whom proved to be "malignant growth" that had to be fixed. Kingston has to tell, and tell on, her aunt's story as a necessary introduction to her own story—where ghosts have to be "talked-story" and experiences of growing up in America have to be recounted in the spirit of a Chinese woman warrior (24). To the extent that No Name Woman serves as a haunting analogy to Kingston's own struggle to break free from old traditions, the first chapter becomes a good example of Chinese indirection, and of creating part of an ambiguous, cyclical world—a world that Kingston inherits and tries to mold in her own way.

In the second chapter, "White Tigers," Kingston mixes history with myth to tell a story of a Chinese woman warrior, who, against all odds, led an uprising and eventually overthrew a dynasty—only to come home to be a filial daughter and daughter-in-law (53–54), to complete the cycle that was broken temporarily when she left home following the call of a bird into the mountains at the age of seven to become "a female avenger" (24, 51). Like the story of No Name Woman, the creation of this woman warrior becomes Kingston's way of anticipating her own struggle, while growing up, with Chinese values and traditions—such as lying to be polite (25), feeling loved on New Year's morning by receiving red money in her pockets (36), rejecting the constant drumming that "girls are maggots in the rice" (51), and dealing with the fact that "even now China wraps double binds around my feet" (57). Again, the woman warrior serves as a compelling "topic"—one that is about a mythical past and one that fully prepares for, to use Kingston's word, "the climax" ("Cultural Mis-readings" 57) or, to use mine, the comment in the final chapter, "A Song for a Barbarian Reed Pipe."

My students, so far, are not quite convinced. While they remain interested in the plot of the story and in the Chinese myths and traditions, they keep asking, "Why doesn't Kingston start telling us more about her own growing-up experiences?" "How can we tell for sure which is real, and which is myth?" It is clear that they are getting impatient when confronted with the flow of "events," because they have yet to recast the frame of their own directness norm with the discursive tendency to lay out the "topics" first.

Things are not going to get any more direct for my students for now—though in my world of indirectness, they are just events holding out for more events, more relations. Therefore, the next two chapters— "Shaman" and "At the Western Palace"—are still not directly focused on Kingston herself. They are more about her mother ("Shaman") and about her aunt Moon Orchid ("At the Western Palace"). Like Kingston, we may not be able to tell, in these two chapters, "where the stories left off and the dreams began" (24). But with these two chapters, Kinston has unfolded two more sets of conditions or topics that are necessary for her own memory and for her own self-realization. Since they reveal how her mother and her aunt meet and grapple with the other (American) culture, these topics have to be spelled out first, so to speak, before her own climax can be reached or the final comment offered.

It is not until the last chapter that Kingston begins to deal with her own memory *directly* of growing up as a Chinese American, who struggles, for example, between her parents' injunction to hide secrets from all kinds of ghosts in America (212–13) and her own need to talk, to explain things so that she can remain sane (216). In the process, Kingston begins to connect all the "preceding topics" to reach for the climax. For example, unlike her No Name Aunt, who could only repair the "roundness" she had broken by committing suicide, Kingston can now repair the "roundness" by trying to sort out what is real and what is imaginary (239) without having to yell out to her mother "the hardest ten or twelve things on my list all in one outburst" (235). But like the woman warrior, Kingston has to leave home, too, "in order to see the world logically" (237)—only to come back to tell her mom that she now also "talks-story" (240). And finally, she completes, though with a telling twist, the story that her mother began (240)—thus signifying that the family tradition is now being passed down. The story is based on the cycle of poems known as "Eighteen Songs of a Nomad Flute," credited to Cai Yan (Ts'ai Yen,[25] 蔡琰), the daughter of the eminent poet and statesman Cai Yong (133–92). These eighteen poetic compositions, in some most direct, most passionate expressions, portray how Cai Yan was captured by a Southern Xiongnu (Hsiung-nu 匈奴) chieftain, of how she spent the next twelve years among the barbarians with a grieving heart, and of how she had to break her heart again when she had to abandon her two Nomad sons to return to her ancestral home.[26]

As Kingston is about to conclude the climax, the boundary between the real and the imagined continues to be blurred and to be crisscrossed. While Cai Yan did return to her homeland to be remarried so that her deceased father could have Han descendants, her return was not without hardships, not without ultimate sacrifices on her part: she had to leave forever behind her Xiongnu husband and her two sons. This pain of losing home twice permeates the entire eighteen songs. Yet Kingston chooses to focus on Cai Yan's pain of losing her ancestral home when she was abducted by the Xiongnu tribe, and on her longing for return after she became a mother of two sons in the harsh and alien land. On the other hand, she chooses to edit out Cai Yan's anguish and grief at giving up her second (barbarian) home—a key condition for her ransomed release from the tribe.

Kinston's omission here in the creation of Cai Yan is deliberate and revealing, I tell my students. Namely, Kingston may need Cai Yan's safe and uncomplicated return to her ancestral home to shore up her own reunion with her family, to help her search for new possibilities from this world with blurred boundaries and shifting paradoxes (V. Chen 10) —a search that is fraught with ambivalences and ambiguities. While her mother's story may have begun with a tragic development (the loss of a daughter to a barbarian tribe), Kingston creates for it a happier, more settled ending—where Cai Yan was rescued and reunited with her ancestral family and where no mention was made of her gut-wrenching loss of her loved ones. Such an ending perhaps helps Kingston better prepare for her own on-going crossings—crossings that have taken her through a culture that is mythical and ambiguous to a culture that commands a different logic or, as she put it, "the new way of seeing" (237). For Kingston, both cultures will continue to vex, if not antagonize, each other because they are forever entangled in America where they "meet, clash, and grapple with each other" (Pratt, "Contact Zone" 34). While no harmony is in sight, their entanglement makes it possible for them to co-exist with their differences, and it is this co-existence that leads Kingston to allow both cultures to wrap double binds around her feet (57). Such narrative, in turn, gives me hope that Kingston may eventually be able to draw positive energy, for example, from her childhood agony and trauma of speaking English; from the haunting presence of her No Name aunt; and from her struggles in navigating these cultural cross-currents. At the same time, I cannot help wondering: Is she going to "talk-story" to her own children in the same way that her mother did to her? What would she do if they should accuse her of "lying" as she did to her mother? And will this crisscrossing between the real and the imagined continue to dominate her life?

My students, I can tell, may not be particularly thrilled by these kinds of open-ended questions or by the way I have been reading Kingston. But I want to use their discomfort to help them realize that their classroom is part of rhetorical borderlands where they must learn to recognize their own rhetorical tendencies and where they must prepare to negotiate with other perspectives, with other ways of reading and writing. For me, on the other hand, to read *The Woman Warrior* as an example of Chinese indirection is in large part to claim, as directly as I can, "the ghostly otherness" (read as "Chinese tradition") that American reviewers have tried so hard to exorcise (Kingston, "Cultural Mis-readings"). No less real is my desire to enter a dialogue that will also allow me to start where my students are, to imagine how a directness approach can be recast so that we can read *The Woman Warrior* without measuring it against the stereotype of the Chinese as mythical or exotic. After all, indirection and directness should not be viewed necessarily as an example of opposing polarity. As I have argued above, they are a pair of complementary opposites, whose values or meaningfulness could change at any time in relation to changes in the context of other complementary opposites. It is this kind of discourse that can engage both styles of communication without either feminizing one or idealizing the other. And by practicing togetherness-in-difference, this kind of discourse becomes part and parcel of Chinese American rhetoric—a rhetoric that, I imagine, both Kingston's mother and her children may very well appreciate and come to embrace.

Since I came to America in the mid-1980s, people from all walks of life have asked me, countless times, the question "Where are you from?" I am certainly not alone in encountering this question, as many of my fellow border residents would be able to testify.[27] I often feel torn by the question, in spite of its apparent directness and simplicity. The fact that I am now a naturalized Chinese American does not make the job of answering this question any easier. In fact, my answer may very well have been complicated by my (legal) status and by my (discursive) in-between subject position. Not because I don't know the answer to the question, but because I don't know which of the two answers I should give, and at what cost. I really don't question in general the sincerity of my interlocutors' interest in the origin of my identity—perhaps due to the fact that my face and my demeanor have either piqued their general curiosity about otherness or reminded them of a similar migration story. However, I have also discerned, on rare occasions, a sense of superiority on the part of a very few interlocutors, as if to tell me, however indirectly, that "We are native and you are not." Regardless, I fumble with my answers and I think often of the reasons for my fumbling, and for my discursive indecision. Here is why.

On the one hand, I know what my interlocutors would like to hear. They would like to hear an answer to where I am *really* or *originally* from—rather than an answer that encompasses all the stops I've made in between. But like my fellow border residents, I often feel incapable of providing such an answer because I don't want to admit, to myself and to my interlocutors, that I have yet to be completely assimilated into the "melting pot" in spite of my genuine efforts to assimilate myself for twenty years now. I can't bear the thought that "I am still being 'recognized.'" Nor do I want to surrender to the notion that "where you are *originally* from" will necessarily mark you off as different, if not deviant, from the normal, from the "native."

On the other hand, I know what kind of answer I *want* to give: I want to tell my interlocutors all the places I have been associated with, from where I was born to where I am at. I want to tell them that each of these stops that I have made along the way informs where I am at, and indeed may predict where I will be. For me, this is a more appropriate, more direct answer to the question "Where are you from?" And in fact this is the only answer I feel comfortable giving. So far, I haven't quite succeeded in doing that on a consistent basis. Not infrequently, as I am about to begin with the last place I was at (Minneapolis, that is), then gradually tracing all the way back to my birthplace, Shanghai, I get interrupted by something like "But no, where are you *really* from?" For my interlocutors, my answer appears too *indirect*—hence those friendly interruptions—because they want to "get to the bottom of things" and "to call a spade a spade." For me, what they want is not *direct* enough in the sense that the "preferred" answer—"I am from Shanghai"—does not *directly* address how the cultural context of where I am at has been constituted by, and in turn helps rearticulate, the meanings of where I have been (Ang 35). To give in to the "preferred" answer almost becomes tantamount to admitting that the origin of where I am from may continuously overshadow the reality of where I am at. Which I loathe to admit, and which I so very much want to reject.

I am far from giving up trying my direct answer. On the contrary, I have lately been more insistent on giving *my* answer to the question "Where are you from?" in spite of repeated interruptions, and at the risk of vexing, perhaps even alienating, some of my interlocutors. Not only do I want to direct the attention of my interlocutors to a new reality, to a new awareness of what each of us wants from the other, but also I want to practice Chinese American rhetoric—a way of communicating that critically engages both traditions and that calls forth both Chinese indirection and European American directness to talk about our own "origin" story, to reject cultural stereotypes, and to cultivate a much needed sense of togetherness-in-difference.

As I am about to close this chapter and to end this narrative, I must confess that my direct answer here is not quite complete or direct enough, because it has left behind another, no less important, subtext that has never failed to lurk behind this communicative event. Namely, as I press on with this direct answer of mine these days, I often ask myself, in the back of my mind, "What would I think if this question—'Where are you from?'—has never been asked of me at all?" In other words, how would I react if my interlocutors decided to say nothing at all about (their curiosity concerning) my origin? Could I then take their silence or their lack of curiosity to mean that I am no longer "recognized?" Or, to be more realistic, is it more of an indication that they are just not interested in my difference? And worse still, would I consider their silence as a "direct affront" to my Chinese face, to my Chinese American identity? I begin to grope for answers. And there is more. What would I do if I were in my interlocutors' position? Would I ask the same question or would I choose to say nothing? What does either discursive move really mean to me, acting now as my interlocutors? I begin to feel ambivalent again. Once again I see the complexities and challenges that both sides to this interaction in fact face and share. And I realize, too, that the promise and peril that the making of Chinese American rhetoric presents affect us border residents and our European American interlocutors alike—another example of complicated and productive entanglement when both practices are brought into simultaneous and interconnected view.

4

TERMS OF CONTACT RECONFIGURED
恕 ("Shu" or "Reciprocity") Encountering Individualism

To be most fully and perfectly a human being, to be a person, is inherently to live certain human relationships with other persons . . . ."
(Fingarette, "The Music of Humanity" 339)

Trust thyself: every heart vibrates to that iron string.
(Emerson 121)

I have long noticed—with a certain degree of ambivalence—that the English word "individualism" has become a necessary part of my communicative repertoire: I use it often in my classroom and in my own writings to characterize certain discursive behaviors. Not that I have come to embrace its underlying ideology,[1] but that I often feel compelled to invoke it either to help describe, both for my students and for myself, European American rhetorical practices, or to help draw distinctions from Chinese rhetorical practices. However, every time I perform these acts, I feel a sense of inadequacy, because individualism entails its own ideology and its own conceptual cluster, both of which may not necessarily exist in a Chinese context, and both of which are being enacted in complex ways at rhetorical borderlands. As I employ individualism to navigate through these different situations, I cannot help but think of the Chinese word "恕" ("shu"), which can be translated as "reciprocity" or as "putting oneself in the others' place." I cannot help but think of how 恕 can contribute to a discourse of togetherness-in-difference, to the making of Chinese American rhetoric. The more I reflect upon what individualism and 恕 each stand for in their own historical and cultural milieu, the more engaged I feel as I bring these two words into a direct dialogue within the borderland context. In the process, I have not only grown to be more acutely aware of my own place and my own identity, but I have also become eager to embrace the processual characteristics of these reflections. These reflections and their ensuing practices are, I argue again, products of rhetorical borderlands and living examples of Chinese American rhetoric. I start with a few preliminary remarks.

Chinese rhetorical practices have often been characterized, in various ways, as discouraging or impeding individual expression or development, as restricting or disapproving originality and inventiveness. So in ancient China, to quote Robert Oliver, author of *Communication and Culture in Ancient India and China,* "individuality was suppressed rather than encouraged" and the ancient Chinese guided their daily lives "less by personal preference than by an intricate system of prescribed ritual" (91; also see 143, 145, 261). For Oliver, one of the defining characteristics about ancient Chinese rhetoric, or about Asian rhetoric for that matter, is that its primary function "is not to enhance the welfare of the individual speaker or listener but to promote harmony" (261). What is lurking behind these descriptions, to my mind, is the concept of individualism, or more precisely, its absence in ancient China.

In modern China, according to Matalene who taught English writing there in the 1980s, the primary function of Chinese rhetoric is not so much in emphasizing originality and individualism, as in preserving and promoting communal harmony and cohesion ("Contrastive Rhetoric" 795). While trying to tease out the characteristics of contemporary Chinese expository writing style, J. Gregg predicates her analysis upon an assumption that the individual's expressive needs within the Chinese value system are subordinated in order to promote the welfare of the community (355–56). Similarly, when attempting to analyze social, cultural, or what he calls "ethnologic" influences on Chinese rhetorical practices (267–72), Jolliffe notes that "the ideal Chinese writer is a cooperative member of a collective, not a novel, independent, individual" (268). He further suggests that "this subordination of the individual to the group, moreover, leads the ideal Chinese writer to employ a characteristic, recognizable mode of reasoning" that is characterized by the repeated use of maxims, analogies, and authoritative statements (269). More bluntly put, it is the lack of Western individualism that has contributed to their composing behavior. Or it is selflessness and submission to central authority that are emphasized for "achieving unity and harmony between man and nature as the principal goal of communication" (Cushman and Kincaid 9).

By citing these studies, I do not intend to reject their work or ignore their places and significances in their own time. Oliver's study of Indian and Chinese rhetorical tradition was certainly ground-breaking at a time when there was hardly any study concentrating on non-Western rhetorical traditions on their own terms (Oliver 3, 261; also see Mao, "Reflective Encounters"). And as Matelene has pointed out, her work ("Contrastive Rhetoric"), in spite of the criticisms it has received (Y. Liu, "To Capture the Essence"), reflects her genuine motive to "understand and elucidate and dignify the rhetorical practices of Chinese culture, a culture of extraordinary textual complexity and richness as well as of unequaled continuity" ("East and West" 162). Such a motive is definitely something to be applauded. My job here, though, is to identify an underlying methodological bias that relies on Western concepts (like "individualism") to help understand Chinese rhetorical practices. This bias, if truth be told, ought not to surprise anybody: to study another rhetorical tradition for comparison or for understanding, we must start somewhere. More often than not, we begin with principles or concepts that are most familiar to our own sensibilities and to our own common sense. However, what is surprising, and what becomes highly problematic, is how we lose sight of this bias, and of the likelihood to impose, perhaps unknowingly, our own principles or concepts on the other tradition, creating, in its wake, a discourse of deficiency or a discourse of forced fit. Not to mention, of course, the fact that such an imposition has often been unidirectional from West to East in modern times, fostering a rhetorical and cultural hierarchy with far-reaching consequences.

How can we, then, move beyond such bias? How can we initiate a different kind of discourse, where other voices can be heard and listened to, and where terms like "deficiency," "absence," or "lack" can be replaced by an insistence to search for "experience-near" categories or ways of speaking? How can we, finally, practice togetherness-in-difference in our classroom and beyond, with a rhetoric that reconfigures terms of contact with a careful examination of their respective histories and precedents, and that engages this co-presence (Pratt, *Imperial Eyes* 7) without minimizing the sense of ambivalence and vulnerability?

To respond to these questions, I first unpack the ideology that underpins "individualism"—an ideology that has become naturalized and thus invisible. I suggest that it is this underlying ideology that makes the term "individualism" ill-suited for describing Chinese rhetorical practices. Should one insist on such an alliance, dissonance and disconnect are bound to materialize. Second, to illustrate how we can understand Chinese rhetorical practices on their own terms and in their own context, I use the Chinese term 恕, and I propose that what 恕 represents and entails should offer a more appropriate, more compelling framework for this undertaking. Third, I articulate the comings-to-be when 恕, on the one hand, and individualism and "ethos," on the other, are in dialogue with each other, and when their dialogue is enabled both by the proximity of togetherness and by a sense of tension and asymmetry.

Before I go on, a disclaimer of sorts is warranted. Namely, my focus here is to identify those key ingredients that have come to constitute the ideology of individualism. In doing so, I am not prepared to suggest that those ingredients are fixed or unchanging—because values, beliefs, or assumptions do change over time, and they do adjust and even morph relative to the changing times or to the evolving interests of the ruling class in society. This much, however, is what I want to suggest. To the extent that the ideology of Western individualism has become a dominant force over the last two centuries or so, those underlying ingredients have been stabilized or abstracted to serve the interests of the ruling class, and to create their own social and discursive reality. Not that the ingredients identified below are by nature adverse to change, but they have been held constant in order to serve the interests of the people in power. In short, I am most interested in uncovering their underlying points of commonality—with the full realization that generalizations of this kind might potentially end up obscuring the diversity within Western tradition, because the ideology of individualism, like any other ideology, is always being realized and experienced, across time and space, in different situations and through specific discursive practices.

So, what is the ideology informing Western individualism? First, individualism invokes a relatively modern belief in Western culture, thanks in large part to the Romantics and the Enlightenment.[2] This belief emphasizes that there is an inherent separateness of distinct persons and that its normative imperative is to become independent from others and to discover and express one's distinct attributes (Markus and Kitayama 226). It conceives of an individual as a bounded, distinctive, and independent whole, which is set both against other such wholes and against its own social and cultural background (Geertz 59). My own classroom practices embody this belief in ways big and small, and at times I have to serve as its loyal spokesperson, as its effective conduit.

For example, I emphasize the importance of originality, of creative expression, and I underscore the need for my students to acknowledge, in their writing, other people's ideas. And I never fail to excoriate those who fail to comply with this need by waving, in front of their very own eyes, the "dangling sword" of a plagiarism charge. These practices of mine, and my students' subsequent responses, manifest a collective effort to establish an independent, unique self. Similarly, in class discussions, I make sure that my students listen to each other without unnecessary interruption, and that their verbal contributions proceed in an orderly fashion. To regulate their turn-taking is once again an attempt to honor the individual as a bounded self that is entitled to autonomy and to the right to speak uninterrupted.[3]

Of course, other Western beliefs or concepts have surfaced in modern times to compete with this discreet, bounded self. For example, individuals have also been conceived of as socially constructed beings or as an integral part of a larger whole. The social psychologist George Herbert Mead represents this social turn in the conceptualization of the individual. For him, it is the social process, or "the generalized other," that enters into "the experience of any one of the individual members of it [a social group]" (154). Mead defines "the generalized other" as "the organized community or social group which gives to the individual his unity of self" (154). As he explains, "the individual possesses a self only in relation to the selves of the other members of his social group" and "the process out of which the self arises is a social process which implies interaction of individuals in the group" (164). Such a conception in fact continues to vie for attention and representation in our on-going dialogue about the relationship between individuals and their communities.

Mead's "social turn" is further powered by his distinction between "I" and "me." For Mead, self is not just the individual combined with the social attitudes of others; it is constituted by both an "I" and a "me." "The 'I' reacts to the self which arises through the taking of the attitudes of others. Through taking those attitudes we have introduced the 'me' and we react to it as an 'I'" (Mead 174). Otherwise stated, the "I" is within the experience of the individual, whereas the "me" "represents a definite organization of the community there in our attitudes calling for a response" (178). Taken together, they constitute a self as it presents itself in some organized form in social experience (178).[4]

In spite of this social turn, the binary bias evidenced in Mead's "self-as-subject" ("I") and "self-as-object" ("me") is unmistakable. Further, this "self-as-subject" in fact becomes another version of the inner self, which remains "as the epicenter of consciousness" and which "relates outward across the boundary of *interpersonal self* into the arena of relationships with other selves, and the physical environment" (Johnson 109–10; emphasis original). It seems, therefore, that this "self-as-subject" ("I") comports well with individualism's persistent emphasis on a self-defining, self-initiating individual. Such an emphasis differs sharply from the discourse of 恕 that constructs self as irreducibly social, as forever intertwined with other selves and with an ever-expanding circle of relations, without at all committing to this binary bias. I will return to this point in greater detail shortly.

Second, individualism embraces a corresponding means of realizing this very belief. That is to say, associated with this brand of individualism is an exclusive, much revered dependence upon an individual's own internal repertoire of thoughts, feelings, and actions. This self-dependence is characterized by its persistent appeal to reason and rationality rather than to sentiment and emotion. So, for John Locke, the individual—not society or tradition—assumes total control over meaning, over his or her own thoughts. By insisting on sensation as the sole source of all knowledge, Locke sees language as mere tools subordinate to individual ideas, as "promissory notes that have no value unless they are backed by ideas on deposit in people's minds (Peters 390). In doing so, Locke "places individuals in the center of the universe and marginalizes commitment, language and culture as the shaper and substance of human knowledge" (Peters 390). Emerson, by declaring that "nothing can bring you peace but yourself" in "Self-Reliance" (137), also looks inward to the self for truth, freedom, and authenticity. While endowing individualism with a moral and religious significance, Emerson appeals to the individual's soul as "the fountain of action and of thought," as "the lungs of that inspiration which giveth man wisdom, and which cannot be denied without impiety and atheism" (128).

One caveat is probably in order here. This kind of inward-looking characteristic does not automatically exclude the possibility of the individual being responsive to the external, to "the generalized other" (Mead 154). Indeed, as Roskelly and Ronald have suggested, it is inaccurate to characterize Emerson as advocating self in exclusive opposition to society. For, as they tell us, Emerson not only looks inward, but also outward to the world surrounded by the signs of the New England community (59–60). For Emerson, "the knowledge of self attained in the process of self-examination becomes a lesson on how to be a self in a world populated by other selves" (Roskelly and Ronald 60).

Such a reading of Emerson, however more dialectic, is perhaps still indebted to this binary bias, one that continues to presuppose a division, though not necessarily an opposition, between self and other selves. In other words, a world populated by a (higher) self and other selves is predicated upon a dualistic ontology that situates the individual outside of or independent of the society. Moreover, whatever social responsiveness or knowledge such self-examination may induce "often, if not always, derives from the need to strategically determine the best way to express or assert the internal attributes of the self" (Markus and Kitayama 226). Differently stated, any outward search in order to connect to other selves becomes only necessary and useful insofar as it benefits the self, and insofar as it secures and reinforces the self as the point of origination.

Third, individualism, being a product of the Romantics and the Enlightenment, endorses a sense of progression and celebrates a continuum of self-actualization with a definable objective in the end. By performing specific acts of self-actualization, an individual shapes a unitary, distinctive speaking self, a self that is being made possible both by his or her own past experiences and by formulating responses in anticipation of the future. In doing so, the individual advances toward a predetermined perfection or toward a higher self. Such an advance instantiates a moment of actuality and anticipates a full realization of potentiality. In the words of Johnson, it "implicates dynamic change as well as continuity" and "transcends the ebb and flow of transitory encounters and reflections" (95). Consequently, individualism appeals to a teleological model where individual initiatives are calculated to achieve a given objective, and where individuals are primed to carve out their own paths toward a final cause, "toward the end for which an item exists or was made" (Hall and Ames, *Anticipating China* 77; also see Lloyd 96–97).

This developmental orientation in individualism does reject an automatic closure: while there is a telos or a higher self that can potentially be realized, such realization depends on each and every instance of actuality regulated by rational mechanisms and aimed at an eventuality. This kind of characteristic thus tends to celebrate those specific instances where an individual succeeds, through his or her own actions, in moving a step closer to this predetermined perfection. This kind of celebration could also engender "an invitation to a defensive, narcissistic self-infatuation" (Johnson 120), and to a discourse more about self, more about how self distinguishes oneself from all other selves. By contrast, there seems to be no such overt recognition or celebration of self-actualization in Chinese tradition, not only because the ideal of perfection is always in the making, but also because the discourse of 恕 does not allow for such points of recognition or celebration. Instead, it encodes and celebrates a network of interdependence and interrelatedness.

One point is worth repeating at this juncture. As I have stated above, in articulating this ideology of individualism, I am not suggesting or implying at all that these three ingredients represent the full gamut of significations attributable to individualism. In addition, post-modern re-conceptualizations of individualism abound, which attempt to foreground, for example, multiple subject positions or multiple interpersonal voices (see, e.g., Ogulnick). These re-conceptualizations or other competing representations not only further help illustrate the dynamic nature of individualism, but also point to the inadequacy of relying on one essential category like "individualism" to conceptualize the complex, multi-layered process of self-actualization. By almost the same token, to state, as I am doing now, that the ideology of individualism is local, and should not be applied to Chinese rhetorical practices, does not mean that individualistic traits have never existed in China, then and now. As de Bary has argued, the Neo-Confucians in the Sung Dynasty celebrated certain individualistic qualities such as "self-consciousness, critical awareness, creative thought, independent initiative and judgment" (334). Such celebrations were nevertheless predicated upon the view that individuals fulfill themselves "through the social process and a moral and spiritual communion with others" (332). In contemporary mainland China, demands for individual expressions and personal freedom can now be heard more frequently and more persistently, especially among the younger generation (Pye; also see X. Li 73–81).

What I am suggesting, then, is that these three ingredients of individualism so far identified have been reified to be symptomatic of a particular set of values and beliefs and subsequently constitutive of a recurring point of reference and origination. They create a cultural and discursive reality at rhetorical borderlands—where contacts with and critiques of Chinese rhetorical practices are being made and where knowledge about that tradition is being both created and disseminated.

What happens, one is bound to ask, when individualism with this concomitant ideology gets invoked to describe and to make sense of Chinese rhetorical practices? What are the gains and losses when it moves out of its own cultural domain and enters into an entirely different space?

Plainly put, the use of individualism in characterizing Chinese rhetorical practices has led to a discourse of deficiency or difference. Namely, either Chinese rhetorical practices lack individualism (hence deficiency), or their concept of self or personhood is very different from Western individualism (hence difference). Commenting upon the dangers of relying on Western categories like self, person, and individual to access knowledge about the "authentic" identity of another culture, L. Liu points out that the knowledge so acquired "cannot but be tautological: either non-Western cultures are deficient in concepts of the self, person, and individual; or their concepts essentially differ from their

Western counterparts" (9). Whether Chinese rhetorical practices simply lack Western individualism, or whether they embody an entirely different brand of individualism, deficiency is not much different from difference, and both discourses contribute nothing positive to our knowledge about Chinese rhetorical practices.

To be fair, the discourse of deficiency or difference in and of itself should not necessarily be viewed as wanting: when we are engaged in any efforts to understand the other tradition or ways of speaking at rhetorical borderlands, it is not out of the ordinary to characterize that tradition or those ways of speaking as lacking some particular concept or as simply being different. However, the discourse of deficiency or difference does not operate in a vacuum, in an acontextual space. Rather, it always is laden with value judgment, and it is always imbued with an adjudicating and othering impulse. Its very enactment at rhetorical borderlands foregrounds questions of power, and issues of using one tradition as the norm, as the de facto standard. We border residents must ask: On whose behalf is this discourse being performed, and for what end? On whose terms and in whose frames are deficiencies or differences being described or inscribed? Why is the burden always on non-Western rhetorical traditions to explain or to justify those apparent deficiencies or differences? Why hasn't Western rhetorical tradition developed, say, the arts of communication that are manifested in and represented by non-Western rhetorical traditions? And why can't we utilize the discourse of 恕 to reflect on and possibly to reconfigure Western individualism?

The use of individualism in this context is further complicated, and becomes all the more problematic, because of its own linguistic and rhetorical path. The word "individualism" ("geren zhuyi," 个人主义), to begin with, is a neologism in modern China: it came into the Chinese language via the Japanese *kanji* translation "kojin shugi" of the English "individualism" at the turn of the twentieth century. It was part of the massive influx of neologisms into Chinese in the late nineteenth century and the first quarter of the twentieth century (L. Liu 18–19).[5] Since its introduction into Chinese, the word "individualism" has undergone some drastic transformations. According to L. Liu, "geren zhuyi" didn't quite become radicalized initially. Not until around the New Culture Movement in 1917 did "geren zhuyi" first become the polar opposite of Confucianism. The idea of "geren zhuyi" then began to be used as a powerful weapon to attack Chinese tradition, to cure China's illness, and to transform the status quo. Then, there was an about-face on individualism during the Communist revolution in the 1920s, when it acquired the negative status of bourgeois ideology, and when it was viewed as the opposite of socialism (L. Liu 87–91). This negative, bourgeois ideology status of individualism became solidified after the establishment of the People's Republic of China in 1949. Individualism began to be seen as nothing more than self-centeredness; as illicit, selfish behavior driven by the doctrine of spontaneous license ("ziyou zhuyi," 自由主义); and as "*un-Chinese,* with the consequences that the idea becomes a synecdoche for a negative West" (L. Liu 41; emphasis original). The economic and political reform in the last twenty-five years in China has gradually "rehabilitated" individualism, to the extent that Chinese individuals are increasingly shaping their own identities in terms of the broad strata of society, such as entrepreneurs, intellectuals, workers, migrants, students, and the like (Pye 38). At the same time, the basic conflict between conforming and self-assertion persists (Pye 39–40), and it continues to cast a shadow on the rise of individualism in contemporary China.[6]

Therefore, any characterization of Chinese rhetorical practices as lacking individualism, without attending to the latter's linguistic and rhetorical history in modern China, neglects an important part of the context that has shaped the development of individualism in China. Further, such characterization risks jeopardizing the cause that the use of individualism may have been intended to promote. Namely, if the central objective of this kind of cross-talk is to understand Chinese rhetorical practices on their own terms and to accord them authentic and authoritative voices, then this discourse of deficiency or difference practically places these practices in a context entirely not their own, depriving them of the opportunity to speak their own history, to develop their own metadiscourse. In the end, we border residents are confronted with two impossible choices: one is to allow such characterization to continue with the consequence of misrepresentation, and the other is to reject such characterization at the risk of having no representation at all.

There is yet another related problem. In "Against Relativism," comparative philosopher Rosemont develops an argument to challenge moral relativism. According to him, much of the anthropological evidence that validates moral relativism seems to be saying that a particular human action has been loathed by one culture but tolerated, if not applauded, by the other, and that such divergences in attitude and action then constitute examples of moral relativism. However, Rosemont suggests that if speakers from one culture have no term corresponding to the term "moral" in the other culture, then they cannot logically be said to have any *moral* principles. It is worth quoting him in extenso here:

[W]e might disapprove of an action that members of another culture approve. But if our disapproval rests on criteria that involve concepts (terms) absent from their culture (language), and if their approval rests on criteria that involve concepts (terms) absent from our culture (language), then it would simply be a question-begging, logical mistake to say the members of the two cultures were in basic *moral* disagreement; the term is ours, not theirs. ("Against Relativism" 60–61; emphasis original)

Put another way, if two given cultures do not share certain concepts both denotatively and connotatively, and if we end up using concepts from one culture to describe and evaluate the same phenomenon from the other culture, whatever descriptions and evaluations that emerge cannot help but being instances of non-application at best, and impositions smacking of an orientalist logic at worst.

Chinese had no words that convey the kind of ideology espoused by or associated with individualism until the latter's introduction into its lexicon at the turn of the twentieth century. Even after it became part of modern Chinese, individualism or its use has had a checkered history, as described above, and its underlying (Western) ideology has never taken hold in Chinese. What has taken hold, in its "host" country, is a set of negative connotations such as self-centeredness, undisciplined liberalism, and total disregard for collective interests. And these negative connotations have further contributed to this growing tension between the need to conform to the state or group needs, and the desire for independence and for one's actions to be unimpeded by others. Consequently, if there is no word or concept that corresponds to individualism and to its attending ideology, and if it is yet to be shown that Chinese speakers evaluate the relationship between individual and society by subscribing to the same kind of ideology embodied in individualism in English, then it becomes at best a non sequitur to say that Chinese and European American rhetorical practices differ over how to conceptualize and evaluate the relationship between individual and society, and/or that one rhetorical practice lacks and devalues individualism, and the other embodies and champions individualism.

Chinese did not have other related lexical terms—such as "rights," "independence," "personal property," or "democracy"—either, until the turn of the twentieth century when they, together with "individualism," became part of this massive linguistic influx into modern Chinese.[7] These terms are closely associated with, and in fact help constitute, the entire discursive field of which (English) individualism is an integral part. In light of Rosemont's argument against moral relativism, it is important for us to recognize that it is not adequate to seek only one term in Chinese—if there were such a term—that corresponds to (English) individualism if we are to speak comparatively about how Chinese and European American rhetorical practices represent the relationship between individual and society. Rather, a cluster of such terms should exist in both traditions, and these terms should enjoy an equivalence of meaning, featuring, as it were, individualism as a core constituent, and a host of other related terms as its lexical constellations. Now, without the presence of these terms, and without further establishing an equivalence of meaning between these terms,[8] any talk about Chinese rhetorical practices lacking or discouraging or suppressing individualism becomes vacuous. Worse still, it reinforces a stereotypical binary that unfortunately pits one against the other—a kind of discourse that this project aims to discredit and dispose of.

It would be inconceivable, however, to conclude that Chinese, a language with a history of over three thousand years, simply lacks terms or concepts that describe and codify the relationship between individual and society. It would be equally difficult to imagine that Chinese thinkers, since the appearance of oracle bone script over three thousand years ago, have not come to terms with such a relationship—especially if we take into account the overwhelming power imbalance in feudal China between emperors/empresses/princes and their subjects, as well as the catastrophic consequences when any discursive efforts were perceived to upset such a power imbalance. So, the question becomes this: What were the terms and concepts used by Chinese thinkers prior to the introduction of individualism? What kind of knowledge has been produced and passed over through the use of these terms? Is there a discursive field, too, inhabited by some core term, as well as its "cognates" or close associates? In short, why are no serious efforts being made to move beyond the lens of individualism at our rhetorical borderlands?

My efforts to call on my fellow rhetoricians to challenge the discourse of deficiency or difference share some family resemblance to some recent projects that look for and develop Chinese terms and concepts—in order not to rely on such Western terms as "rhetoric" and "persuasion" in discussions of Chinese communicative practices. For example, X. Lu argues that "ming bian" (名辯)—literally "naming" and "dispute" as two separate characters—comes closest, as a compound, to approximating "rhetoric" in ancient China (500–200 BCE), because the compound formulates "a philosophy of language, theories of logic, argumentation, persuasive speech behavior, and artistic use of language" (93). Similarly, to respond to the charge or myth that Chinese classical texts lack argumentation, Garrett focuses on "bian" (辯, "dispute"), "shuo" (說, "argue," "explain"), and "shui" (說,[9] "discuss," "persuade") as representing three discrete speech activities ("Classical Chinese Conceptions"). Her careful analysis of each of these activities, of their relation to each other, and of their concomitant philosophical and cultural contexts, ably demonstrates that there was no lack of argumentation in classical China. Together they serve to convey the kinds of meanings evidenced in "persuasion" in ancient Greece. These projects are worthwhile because of their insistence on using Chinese terms to describe Chinese communicative practices, and because they refuse to use Western rhetorical terms as both their initial and terminal points of reference.

What has motivated these projects is this desire to prove that ancient China did develop "rhetoric" (名辯) and it did practice "persuasion" (辯, 說, and 說), and that these Chinese "rhetorical" and "persuasive" practices are discursively similar to those in ancient Greece and in the West. Such a desire seems appropriate and even necessary in light of the staying power of the discourse of deficiency or difference. Since it may not be possible to find exact equivalence of meaning between rhetorical concepts from these two traditions or from any given two traditions for that matter, such projects could be seen as trying to discover what X. Lu calls "a language of ambiguous similarity" that aims to "bring together similar or shared meanings in the conceptualization of rhetoric, illuminating ambiguity and subtle differences embedded in such similarity" (92). However, this kind of language, because of its predisposition to similarity, may prove to be a bit premature. After all, we have just begun to understand how Chinese concepts or terms—such as "ming bian"—create and disseminate discursive knowledge in their own contexts, and how such knowledge is received and consumed in the shaping of social and cultural meanings. Absent an informed understanding of this knowledge-making and -receiving process, any discussions of similarity may become inadequate, either yielding superficial, reductive comparisons or producing vacuous generalizations. In light of these reservations, my attempt below is not to develop a language that seeks to "bring together similar or shared meanings," but to focus on a cluster of Chinese terms that are central to our understanding of the relationship between individual and society in Chinese context. In fact, it is these terms that create, by resonance and complementarity, knowledge pivotal to overcoming the discourse of deficiency or difference, and to nurturing a discourse of togetherness-in-difference in the making of Chinese American rhetoric.

To accomplish this task, I chiefly focus on the *Analects of Confucius*, not only because "Chineseness"—whatever we might mean by it—has often been traced back all the way to the *Analects* (Ames and Rosemont, "Introduction" 1), but also because it is in the *Analects* that we experience Confucius' teachings on and visions about how to establish and extend the relationship between individual and society. And his teachings have since been established as the dominant ideology representative of Chinese cultural values—in spite of shifting social contexts and differing, if not novel, interpretations of this ideology.[10]

The *Analects* or *Sayings of Confucius* (the *Lun Yü*, 論语) is a collection of twenty books put together by Confucius' disciples over the span of three hundred years after the Master passed away (551–479 BCE).[11] Each book contains twenty (more or less) short chapters or paragraphs. As one of the *Four Books*,[12] the *Analects* contains the main body of Confucius' philosophical teachings, and these teachings provide "a system of basic beliefs and inceptive orientations" for the study of communication (Cheng, "Chinese Philosophy" 24). As a matter of fact, the *Analects* should be seen as part of a larger body of texts that were instrumental to the development of Chinese rhetoric in ancient or pre-imperial China (1045–221 BCE) and that, in the words of Y. Liu, "had reached an impressive level of sophistication in what is readily recognizable as *rhetorical* thinking" ("'Nothing Can be Accomplished'" 147; emphasis original; also see 150). To the extent that Confucius' philosophical teachings deal with the use of discursive practices both in response to and in the shaping of social and cultural goings-on in ancient China, they become irreducibly rhetorical, and their symbolic and transformative significances become more accentuated when they are viewed through a rhetorical, performative lens.

Comparative philosophers David Hall and Roger Ames have consistently analyzed the *Analects* with a philosophical point of view. Among the insights that appeal to me the most is their recognition that (Western) dualism—a radical separation between the transcendent and the dependent—did not exist in pre-imperial China. Instead, they propose that it was polarity—"a relationship of two events each of which requires the other as a necessary condition for being what it is" (*Thinking Through Confucius* 18)—that underpinned much of ancient Chinese discursive practices, including the *Analects*.[13] Ironically, it is dualism, rather than polarity, that seems to have guided their occasional discussions of rhetoric in pre-imperial China, resulting, as a matter of fact, in their flawed understanding of rhetoric (Y. Liu, "'Nothing Can Be Accomplished'" 150–51).

More specifically, they distinguish rhetoric from logic, because rhetoric appeals to "*ethos-* and *pathos*-based arguments" and it overrides "the discipline of logical forms" to which logic appeals (*Thinking from the Han* 135). While they acknowledge that rhetoric was "the privileged mode of communication" in classical China (135), their curious association of rhetoric only with ethical and pathetic appeals has handicapped their understanding of how rhetoric actually functioned in pre-imperial China and beyond. Moreover, if the ancient Chinese only used (their version of) rhetoric, aren't they looking at Chinese rhetorical practices through the lens of dualism? Aren't they, in other words, denying the mutually-entailing characteristic they have rightly accorded Chinese tradition? By extracting logic from rhetoric, and then by pinning this version of rhetoric onto the ancient Chinese, they have divided something—rhetoric—which should not have been divided, because rhetoric and logic are mutually entailing of each other in Chinese context. In so doing, they have, perhaps inadvertently, come back to the discourse of dualism from which they have shown every intention to move away.

My analysis below of the discourse of 恕 is intended to be rhetorical, and it is deeply informed by where I am at and where I have been, and by how I position myself from the others' perspective (read as my understanding of individualism). Not only do I not want to separate rhetoric from logic or philosophy, but also I want to zero in on how a group of related terms cluster around to find resonance in each other and define and disseminate the discourse of 恕, and on how personalized and situated actions enable, and accord symbolic power to, such discourse. Further, I want to suggest, too, that the discourse of 恕 in fact indexes part of a larger social-cultural practice that responds to social exigencies and yields new discursive alignments and configurations.

So, if it is inconceivable for the Chinese language not to possess terms or concepts describing and codifying the relationships between individuals, and between individuals and society, what terms or concepts does Confucius use and develop in the *Analects*? They are, I suggest, 恕 and its conceptual "siblings" or "cognates," and they together constitute what I call "the discourse of 恕."

In paragraph 24 of book 15, his student, Zigong, asks Confucius if there is one expression that can serve as a guide to one's conduct throughout one's life. Confucius replies as follows:

"It is perhaps the word 'shu' (恕). Do not impose on others what you yourself do not want" (34).[14]

Often translated as "reciprocity" or as "putting oneself in the others' place," 恕 is interpersonal in nature. The character 恕 consists of two parts: the top 如 ("ru") and the bottom 心 ("xin"). 如 means "compare" (譬, "bi") or "be like" (像, "xiang"), and 心 stands for "heart-and-mind." In view of its semantic makeup, the practice of 恕 can be literally glossed as comparing with others by using one's own heart-and-mind. This interpretation—which should clear Confucius of any "complicity" in denying the existence of self—may call for some explanation.

The use of one's own heart-and-mind for comparison with others could lead one astray if one's heart-and-mind is either too self-centered or not in the right place. Such a scenario is easily averted, however, because 恕 requires that one, in the process of performing 譬 (comparing), should not impose one's own needs or desires on others. Rather, it is through the other persons' points of view that one begins this process of 譬 (comparing) by engaging one's own heart-and-mind. 恕, to quote Fingarette, is "to grasp analogy with the other person, and in that light to treat him as you would be treated" ("Following the 'One Thread'" 383), and it amounts to "analogiz[ing] *myself* to you" and "being your *I*" (384; emphasis original). Therefore, the analogy initiated by 恕 is the use of one's own heart-and-mind situated within, and filtered through, the other persons' perspectives or through the other I's. In the words of Hall and Ames, 恕 evokes an analogy "between oneself and other people" or "within the field of the relationship constituted by self and other" (*Thinking Through Confucius* 286).[15]

The importance of 恕 in Confucius' thinking is evident, because the concept is repeated on several other occasions in the *Analects*. For example, when Zhonggong, one of Confucius' favorite students, asks about humaneness ("ren," 仁),[16] the Master says, "Do not impose upon others what you yourself do not want, and you will not be subject to ill will at the state or family level" (28, bk. 12, par. 2). And since the conduct of 恕 is highly demanding, not everybody can practice it. When another student, Zigong, indicates that he wants to follow 恕, the Master replies, "Zigong, this is quite beyond your capability" (19, bk. 5, par. 12).

恕 has also found its way into other Confucian texts. In the *Zhongyong*, one of the *Four Books*, there is one particular passage that makes a direct reference to 恕. After explaining that the way (道, "dao") should not be far from people, Confucius has this to say:

Thus, the exemplary person ["junzi," 君子] relies on people to guide other people, and he or she does no more after succeeding in doing that. Doing one's utmost and putting oneself in the others' place do not stray from the way [忠恕违道不远]. Do not treat others you yourself do not want. (*Four Books 9*)

Confucius' comment on 恕 in the *Zhongyong* is almost identical to what he says about 恕 in the *Analects* (bk. 12, par. 2; bk. 15, par. 24), and the practice of 恕 is explicitly associated, in both texts, with the process of becoming humane.

In the *Mencius*, we again find the link between the practice of 恕 and the attainment of humaneness:

> Mencius said, "All the ten thousand things reside in me. There is no great-er joy than to learn, upon self-examination, that I am true to myself. Try your utmost to put yourself in the others' place (强恕而行) and you will find that humaneness cannot be too far away from you. (*Four Books* 76)

Suffice it to say, then, that this level of attention given to 恕 in these texts provides a good indication of its importance and currency in the larger social-cultural discourse in pre-imperial China.

Here now is the question: How does one actually put 恕 into practice? And where does one develop and acquire this ability, since not every-one, according to Confucius, is capable of doing that (cf. *Four Books* 19, bk. 5, par. 12)? To answer this question, we have to move beyond the semantic boundary of 恕; and we have to examine how 恕 is aligned with other related terms and how its meaning is joined with, and indeed made actionable by, these other related meanings or values. In a word, the rhetorical significance of 恕 cannot be fully mapped out if we don't step outside the semantic confines of 恕—both because its implementa-tion has to be taken up by *individuals*, and because its uptake has to be experienced and acted upon in *situated* practices. After all, for 恕 to be appropriately realized, one's heart-and-mind has to be in the right place and at the right time in the presence of others.[17]

In Book Four of the *Analects*, Confucius once again addresses 恕 and its central importance to his pursuit of "dao" (道, "way").[18] He states that his "dao" is bound together with one single or continuous strand, which his disciple Zengzi explains as "zhong shu" (忠恕) (18, par. 15). Here 恕 is being joined with 忠—a significant addition. According to Zhu Xi, 忠 (zhong) is defined as "doing one's utmost for the others' interests,"[19] and 恕 as "using oneself to infer the others' needs" (34). With 忠 literally at its side, 恕 is now supported by an individual's maximum effort, thus acquiring a more well-defined agency. What is also revealing is that both 忠 and 恕 share the same radical 心 ("heart-and-mind"), suggesting a discursive kinship that underscores the self's disposition to call on his or her own "heart-and-mind" to practice 恕, to exert his or her utmost to infer and serve the others' interests.

Coupled with 忠, the practice of 恕 becomes more interpersonal and more other-oriented. However, the content of this interpersonal relationship is yet to be fully defined. And the social, cultural context in which the practice of 恕 gets enacted remains too general. This apparent gap can be closed if we turn our attention to Confucius' discussions in the *Analects* of "ren" (仁, "humaneness") and "li" (禮, "ritual action" or "ritualized living").

The close, almost mutually-entailing relation between 恕 and 仁 can be easily identified in the *Analects*, because 恕 is often defined in terms of 仁. For example, when asked about the criteria one can rely upon to characterize a humane person, Confucius responds this way:

> Humane persons establish others by seeking to establish themselves and enlighten others by seeking to enlighten themselves. The ability to take as analogy what is near at hand [self] can be called the method of becoming a humane person. (21, bk. 6, par. 30)

Here the practice of 恕 no longer just regulates how self should conduct oneself in the company of others. Insofar as it is the method with which one can transform oneself into a humane person, 恕 becomes constitutive—in the sense that the practice of 恕 is the process of becoming. As one practices 恕, one is on one's way to becoming a humane person, and to becoming connected to others in this life-long project of person-making and relationship-building. Commenting on this paragraph, Zhu Xi characterizes this method of attaining humaneness as the ability to draw upon one's own needs or desires to infer and connect to those of others (60). To state the matter another way, as (the practice of) 恕 yields 仁, its interpersonal content is now more focused, more clearly articulated. According to the *Shuowenjiezi*, the word 仁 consists of two parts: "ren" (人, "person") and "er" (二, "two"). So, to become 仁 by way of 恕, one has to be related to and constituted by some other individual or individuals. Describing Confucius' view of what constitutes a person, Fingarette puts it this way: "To be most fully and perfectly a human being, to be a person, is inherently to live certain human relationships with other persons . . ." ("The Music of Humanity" 339). And when another disciple asks about humane conduct, Confucius simply replies: "Love others" (29, bk. 12, par. 22). Or in the words of another student, "rely on friends in support of humaneness" (29, bk. 12, par. 24). Once again, it is by way of aligning oneself with others (恕), either through love or through friendship, that one realizes humaneness.

Since the practice of 恕 cannot proceed in a context-free environment, what about the social, cultural context that influences, and is in turn being enriched by, this practice? For Confucius, the practice of 恕 is imbued with "the total spectrum of social norms, customs, and mores, covering increasingly complicated relationships and institutions" (Hall and Ames, *Thinking Through Confucius* 86). It participates in a tradition of institutionalized human actions and procedures—that is, in "li" (禮, "ritual action," "ritualized living," or "observing ritual action"). Because there is no separating (consideration of) tradition or institutionalized relationships from putting oneself in the others' place at the right time and for the right purpose, 禮 becomes inherently tied to the practice of 恕.

When Yan Hui, his favorite student, asks about humaneness (仁), Confucius replies: "One becomes humane through self-discipline and ritualized living" (28, bk. 12, par. 1). Elsewhere Confucius asks rhetorically, "How can anyone who is not humane observe ritualized living?" (17, bk. 3, par. 3). It is clear that 禮 involves connecting to and internalizing specific and well-defined values, roles, and relationships within one's cultural milieu. The process of putting oneself in the others' place in this context is tantamount to how well one can enact these values, roles, and relationships which are filled with "echoes and reverberations" (Bakhtin, "Speech Genres" 91) of the tradition, and which in turn respond to and promote this tradition within the on-going contexts of speech events. To the extent that one succeeds in doing so, 禮 embodies a personalizing, and thus creative, process. As one shapes and measures one's conduct appropriate to this tradition, the individual also learns to dialogue with the tradition, to cultivate personal expression, and to develop one's own course of action. In the end, these performances enhance and enrich the very tradition that makes the practice of 恕 both possible and potentially transformative.

One can still ask: What exactly are these "well-defined roles, values, and relationships" with which the practice of 恕 is associated? And what exactly does Confucius say about the role of speech in the realization of 恕—especially considering that Confucius is said to be thinking of giving up speaking in the *Analects* (37, bk. 17, par. 19)? The discourse of 恕 is not complete, therefore, without some careful consideration of three more related terms. They are: "xiao" (孝, "filial piety"), "yan" (言, "speech"), and "xin" (信, "making good on what one says").

Whatever roles, values, and relationships one enacts by 恕 will not be sufficiently grounded until and unless they are being manifested and experienced within the immediate domain of the family. For Confucius, they can only be defined and explicated in terms of five cardinal relations or "wulun" (五倫). These five relationships are between parent and child; between ruler and subject; between husband and wife; between old and young; and between friends (King 58).[20] Of these five relations, three are familial in nature, and the other two are modeled after the familial. So, the relationship between ruler and subject is conceived in terms of emperor as father ("junfu," 君父) and subject as son ("zimin," 子民),[21] and the relationship between friends is understood in terms of elder brother ("wuxiong," 吾兄) and younger brother ("wudi," 吾弟). Further, this family model, in terms of complementary obligation, has been extended to explain nature and the world at large—no wonder the relationship between Chinese "tian" (天) or "qian" (乾) as "heaven" and "di" (地) or "kun" (坤) as "the earth" is defined as a "father and mother" relationship of familial obligation (Munro, "Family Network" 264–69).

Central to this familial system of relations are the father-son relationship—often characterized as "filial piety" (孝, "xiao")—and the elder brother-younger brother relationship known as "fraternal responsibility" (悌, "di"). Confucius sees (the realization of) these relationships as constituting the root of humane conduct (15, bk. 1, par. 2), and as instrumental to effecting good government (16, bk. 2, par. 21; 28, bk. 12, par. 11). If the family as a discursive model is fundamental and can be felt at both the micro (family) and macro (state) level, the roles, values, and relationships cannot but be familial, and they cannot but be hierarchical, reciprocal, and always in need of adjustment and modification. It is this familial model that serves as the immediate, indispensable framework determining the appropriateness and significance of the practice of 恕 and of the enacted roles, values, and relationships. As a result, one can put oneself in the others' place in terms of filial piety and fraternal responsibility, and one can establish and sustain an interpersonal relationship as part of an on-going process of becoming humane.

The practice of 恕 also needs 言 ("yan," speech) and 信 ("xin," making good on what one says). Contrary to some accounts that have portrayed Confucius as someone who favors silence over eloquence,[22] what the Master objects to is speech that has no chance of being "made good" (that is, 信). When speakers cannot live up to what they say, their speech becomes "glib talk" ("qiaoyan," 巧言) and shameful (20, bk. 5, par. 25). Such speech fails to comport with humane conduct (15, bk. 1; par. 3), and makes individuals unfit as humane persons (16, bk. 2; par. 22). By contrast, Confucius values 言 insofar as it does not supersede action (32, bk. 14, par. 27), and he sees this kind of language use as only befitting the humane person (21, bk. 7, par. 3). The Master has also made it quite clear that to understand others—an integral component of practicing 恕—depends on an understanding of 言 (39, bk. 20, par. 3), as long as one performs 言 with one's utmost effort or as long as one lives up to one's 言 (25, bk. 9, par. 25). And to be able to live up to one's 言 is 信—a character that consists of "person" (人, "ren") and "speech" (言, "yan"). The success of 恕 then depends on 信: to understand, to connect to, and to earn the trust of others, one has to be sincere in what one says to others, and one's 言 has to be substantiated by concrete actions and evaluated within the context of shifting, complementary relations.

It should be clear by now that the practice of 恕 seeks to establish a living or individualized relationship of interconnectedness and interdependence that echoes and resonates with a tradition of other such practices. This relationship is to be cultivated by 忠 (doing one's utmost for the others' interests), through 禮 (ritualized living), and with the help of 言 (speech) and 信 (making good on what one says). Once established, it realizes 仁 (humaneness). Further, the establishment of this relationship is grounded on familial terms, on 孝 (filial piety) and 悌 (fraternal responsibility). Differently stated, if the focal meaning of 恕 is the ability to infer and connect to others so as not to impose on them what you yourself do not want, one's understanding of how this ability can actually be put to action depends on 忠, 仁, 禮, 孝, 悌, 言, and 信. Both 恕 and these other "siblings" form a conceptual cluster, and together they give meaning and substance to what I call "the discourse of 恕," and to how individuals position themselves to realize and extend these reciprocal, ritualized, and humane relationships.

If what I have been developing here has merit, it becomes only appropriate to suggest that the discourse of 恕 be used in place of the discourse of deficiency or difference, and that its focus on interdependence and reciprocity, framed within the Chinese familial milieu, be duly recognized. More specifically, the discourse of 恕 should be called upon to assist in these well-meaning efforts to talk about and analyze how Chinese and Chinese Americans compose themselves at rhetorical borderlands. My basic claim is simply this: such discourse, as will be made clearer below, not only enables us to overcome the ideology of individualism which has underpinned much of our borderland conversation, but also points to a different space where self and other are irreducibly linked to each other in an ever-changing, every shifting circle of relations, and where the process of becoming is valued over the product of being.

I am certainly not surprised at all that Chinese rhetorical practices do not display or espouse the ideology of individualism. I am often at a loss, though, when its nonexistence in Chinese culture has contributed to a view that the latter is somehow deficient and that, because of its nonexistence, the latter is necessarily in want of something fundamental. I wonder why its nonexistence in Chinese culture has not inspired people to look for other discourses that convey a different body of knowledge, more suited to account for Chinese rhetorical practices in ways not constrained or handicapped by the discourse of deficiency or difference. I am no less puzzled by this apparent reluctance—especially in our field of rhetoric and composition—to look to Confucian ideology for a possible heuristic—one that can help us negotiate between these kinds of absences and/or differences.

The longevity of Confucian ideology is cause enough for us to reflect on its relevance to our own time. Just think for a moment of the kinds of challenges and attacks Confucian ideology has endured, ranging from the Hundred Schools of Thought at its inception, to Buddhism in the Han and Tang Dynasties, to Christianity in the sixteenth and seventeenth centuries, to the Communist Party's ideology in the twentieth century, to Western capitalistic democracies in the last twenty-five years (Rosemont, "Classical Confucian" 78). That it continues to generate intense responses—high praises or stinging criticisms or both—should lead us to consider "that there might be much in that tradition that speaks not merely to East Asians but perhaps to everyone. Not only in the past, but perhaps for all time" (Rosemont, "Classical Confucian" 78). In doing so, however, we have to be insistent on the distinction between the level of relevance we want to attribute to Confucian ideology *because of* our present rhetorical exigency and the level of relevance that accrued to Confucian ideology *because of* its own context and its own terms.

By developing this discourse of 恕, I am not proposing that such discourse be adopted in its entirety in order to intervene in cases where the ideology of individualism becomes the modus operandi. Rather, what I am proposing is, first and foremost, to demonstrate that there are terms such as 恕 and its other "siblings" that articulate a dynamic relation of interdependence and reciprocity in Chinese context.[23] Second,

in calling on the discourse of 恕 to play a viable role at rhetorical borderlands, I am focusing on its relevance not so much as a prominent
example of Confucian ideology, but as a constructive voice in our own
time and space. Third, while Confucius most likely didn't concern himself with some of the issues that are to follow in the rest of this chapter,
my effort is to foreground the relational, other-oriented characteristic
present in the discourse of 恕, in order to promote an interpersonal
praxis that necessarily calls for self to connect to others, and to create
and discern meaning through the others' eyes (or "I's").[24]

So far, I have been quite gender-conscious in developing the discourse
of 恕. I have been either gender-neutral or have so far used masculine
and feminine pronouns to include both the male and female gender
in my discussion, as in, for example, "one's ability (gender-neutral) to
infer and connect to the others" or "realizing his or her humaneness
(gender-specific) through ritualized living." In doing so, I am, in a way,
reflecting the semantic meanings of these Chinese characters (such as
恕, 忠, 仁, 禮, 孝, 悌, 言, and 信) because none of them morphologically
marks gender, number, or person. More specifically put, the practice of
恕 is morphologically open to both males and females, and its reciprocal
process does not discriminate against the female gender. The question
becomes this, Does the practice of 恕, like any other social-cultural activity, actually comply with the morphological features of these characters?
And does my gender-sensitive representation here fairly reflect what was
going on in Confucius' time? Does it mean that both men and women
in traditional China were equally capable of practicing 恕 and that they
were enjoying the same kind of opportunity to do so?

My answer is two-fold. On the one hand, my linguistic sensitivity to
gender equity shown here is *largely* misplaced because this apparent fit
between my pronoun choices and the morphological meanings of these
characters does not quite square with Confucian China. By way of this
"infelicitous" speech act, I want to dramatize a false sense of equity that
is embedded in these Chinese characters and to highlight a very gen-
der-biased or sexist context—Confucian China—where Chinese men
were normally the real referents, and where feminine pronouns were
linguistic anomalies as they did not have any real or immediate referents
to refer to.[25] In other words, this ever-expanding relation of interdependence and reciprocity was not gender-neutral or gender-inclusive:
it either excluded Chinese women or relegated them to a subordinate
position, and Chinese women were not as free as their male counterparts to practice 恕, however capable they might be.

As Wolf has demonstrated, it was Chinese boys, rather than Chinese girls, that were traditionally recognized as being an integral part of a larger whole, as being immediately capable of inferring and connecting to an ever-expanding circle of human relationships. As future fathers, grandfathers, and ancestors in China's patrilineal system, they were endowed with a sense of historical continuity, which linked them to both the past and the future (259–61), and which entitled them to the discourse of 恕 and to the right to participate in communal dialogues. In contrast, since Chinese girls were temporary residents in their parents' home, they were not considered to be a part of anyone's past or future—at least not until after they were married to some unknown family in some unknown place (Wolf 261–62). In order even to begin to contemplate practicing 恕, Chinese girls had to be relocated and integrated into their future husbands' community, where they could begin to construct and reconstruct relationships (Wolf 263–66)—upon which the development of their selves and the success of practicing 恕 very much depend. Therefore, any discussion about the ability, on the part of Chinese girls, to use self for analogy to infer and to connect is premature, and smacks of almost being fanciful when there is no self to speak of in the first place.

In short, the practice of 恕 in Confucian China was inevitably implicated by gender. Since Chinese girls were excluded from the community they were born into, they were deprived of the right to benefit from the participation of others in their parents' community. Whether or not they could become part of their husbands' community depended on how well they could construct their relationships with that community after marriage. Hence, the realization of 恕 and 仁 was at best once removed from, and at worst forever denied to, Chinese girls. Further, such realization, if and when it became possible, was fraught with additional uncertainties and risks entailed by their brand-new status in their husbands' community and by their domestic (and inferior) roles within the familial model (also see Wolf 265).

On the other hand, my linguistic sensitivity to gender equity also aims to suggest that the gendered practice of 恕 might not be inherent in Chinese culture, and the practice of 恕 might be accessible to women in both Warring States (479–221 BCE) and in the Han Dynasty (206 BCE-220 CE) before Confucian ideology became dominant as the prevailing social practice. According to Lisa Raphals, women in Warring States and Han narratives were represented as possessing the same virtues as valued by men; these virtues included "moral integrity, intellectual judgment, the ability to admonish a superior, courage, and chastity, in the sense of single-minded loyalty" ("Gendered Virtue" 236). These narratives, though compiled and redacted by men, suggest that virtue was not gendered at all times. Such narratives only gave way to "accounts of female chastity and widow suicide" after Confucianism was established as a hegemonic ideology from the Later Han (25–220) through the Qing Dynasty (1636–1911) (237). Elsewhere, Raphals asks:

> Can we assume, for example, that the readers, writers and audience of Chinese philosophical works (however defined), at all times, were all men? Can we assume that references to "people" (*ren* 人), including a range of "sages" and "developed individuals" inevitably referred to men? (*Sharing the Light* 3)

To the extent that women in early China were ethically virtuous, intellectually adroit, and rhetorically savvy, they may not have been completely denied the opportunities to practice 恕—however limited or challenging these opportunities may have been. In a word, my linguistic sensitivity is also gesturing toward an earlier moment in time when the practice of 恕 was perhaps more gender-neutral than gender-specific.

Just as reciprocity can only be found in situated actions where self and others are engaged with each other through a living relationship of interdependence, so the discourse of 恕 cannot help but dialogue with other voices at rhetorical borderlands. As a matter of fact, it realizes its discursive potential only when it enables us border residents to move beyond the ideology of individualism, to re-vision Chinese rhetorical practices, and to practice togetherness-in-difference.

It is perhaps worth emphasizing here that the discourse of 恕 is both constructive and limiting. It is constructive because it articulates a relation of interdependence and reciprocity, and it promotes a creative understanding of a social, interpersonal context. It is limiting because the discourse of 恕 does not dissolve or diminish the highly asymmetrical relations of power at rhetorical borderlands. Therefore, in order to have the discourse of 恕 fully participate in the borderland dialogue, we must recognize its limitations. And in order to make this discourse part of togetherness-in-difference in our classroom and beyond, we must not lose sight of its (Chinese) context of familial hierarchy. In so doing, we can in fact further cultivate the differences and diversity inherent in any borderland dialogue.

Attempting to illustrate the reciprocal relationship between the desire to assert (a unified) Asian American identity and the need to embrace diversity and even internal contradictions within such an identity, Lowe writes: "Just as the articulation of the desire for identity depends upon the existence of a fundamental horizon of differences, the articulation of differences dialectically depends upon a socially constructed and practiced notion of identity" (39). Drawing upon her insight, I submit that it is this newly articulated context of reciprocity and interdependence at rhetorical borderlands that enables us, dialectically, to recognize and cultivate our tensions and our asymmetries, and to bring about instances of heterogeneous resonance. To put it more succinctly, the knowledge of our interdependence permits us to articulate, with confidence and with connectedness, our differences.

In my Comparative Rhetoric seminar at my own school, I share with my students Chinese discursive examples, with the same purpose of developing borderland reflections that engage both Chinese and European American rhetorical practices. I discuss, among other issues, one characteristic that has often been cited to describe Chinese rhetorical practices. Namely, Chinese writers tend to conform to and convey a strong moral message, and they tend to use writing to create a sense of unity between self and others, and between one and many. Such practices are said "to preserve the general harmony and to promote social cohesion" (Matalene, "Contrastive Rhetoric" 795). One finds similar language in the current "General Guideline for High School Chinese Language Education." The goal of Chinese education, according to the Guideline, is to cultivate in students "healthy and noble temperament" and "socialist ideology, moral values and patriotism" (qtd. in Li 59). Model essays in high school writing textbooks are directly influenced by this language.

For example, the essay "On Diligence," the first in the textbook for the 2nd grade of senior high (grade 11 here) in Nanjing opens with the following two paragraphs:

> There is an old Chinese saying, "With diligence, nothing under the sun is too hard to crack." Han Yu, a great man-of-letters in the Tang Dynasty, once said, "Excellence is born out of diligence," which means, extensive knowledge and profound scholarship come from assiduous work.
>
> Diligence is a virtue for those who are eager to learn and eager to make progress. By diligence, we mean that people should cherish time, study diligently, think diligently, explore diligently, practice diligently, and sum up the experience diligently. On every page of the chronicles of all men with great accomplishment, in the past or present, in China or the world, is the giant character glistening with sweat: diligence. (qtd. in Li 71)

The same essay then proceeds to cite specific examples of these "giant characters" and their accomplishments.

High school students practice their writings on these model essays with the sole purpose of scoring good marks on the essay portion of the university entrance examination. They learn how to write a good essay or good "yiluwen" (议论文, "opinion writing") on an assigned (and morally-uplifting) topic during the examination (Li 62; 70–72). These writings, be they practice runs or the real deal, "must display knowledge rather than question received wisdom and produce texts that are inherently rule abiding and conformative" (Li 73).

This kind of characteristic, so goes the diagnosis at our rhetorical borderlands, is created by, and further contributes to, a lack of individualism. It privileges collective expression over individual voice and it adheres to the Confucian tradition whose objective it is to advance the dominant ideology of the time. The discourse of 恕, however, may provide a different diagnosis, and in fact it may gesture toward a different understanding of Chinese rhetorical practices.

To begin with, with the discourse of 恕 in place, we can now view this kind of characteristic as motivated by a time-honored disposition to connect to and negotiate with a tradition that features and celebrates such "moralistic" writings. Further, this kind of practice can also be seen as no more than trying to define oneself by way of nurturing a relationship of interdependence. If social harmony or cohesion depends on whether or not individuals can co-exist with each other and on whether or not they can enact humane relationships with each other, the discourse of 恕 becomes its biggest promoter and enforcer—because it focuses on how individuals conduct themselves through situated performances mediated by social norms and by localized re-alignments.

One may ask, as have my students, "So, is it still possible that the discourse of 恕 may hinder, if not stifle, creativity if it only aims to channel individual expressions to fit in with or to promote some larger social, cultural themes—in the same way that these ideology-heavy essays may hinder Chinese students' creativity?" As I have stated above, the discourse of 恕 indeed does not promote individual expression as uniquely distinctive or as possessing the ultimate value. On the other hand, within its own context, it does not deny the existence of the individual, nor does it necessarily hinder individual creativity.

We know by now that individual expression can be cultivated by appealing to the individual's own internal repertoire of thoughts, feelings, and actions—hence the ideology of individualism. We know, too, that individual expression can also be developed through a relationship that puts individuals in connection with each other, and that calls on individuals to situate their discursive performances within the context of "the total spectrum of social norms, customs, and mores, covering increasingly complicated relationships and institutions" (Hall and Ames, *Thinking Through Confucius* 86)—hence the discourse of 恕. Consequently, individual expression can be cultivated and experienced through a humane relationship between self and others, between one and many—in which there is no assumed assimilation of one by the other, but plenty of recognition that one's value stands only in relation to that of others. Similarly, moral messages or socially sanctioned codes of conduct are no more than what Fingarette calls "historically persistent forms of actual conduct" ("The Music of Humanity" 335) that are being experienced and realized through situated performances, through "making good on what one says."

It is also tempting, as some scholars have done, to attribute this tendency in Chinese writing to convey a moral message to a preference, if not reverence, for established discourse patterns or genres. As early as the 1970s, Robert Kaplan told us that essays written in English by his Chinese students showed such a preference, with some discernable traces of the Chinese "eight-legged essay" ("baguwen," 八股文)—the latter, to which I will return shortly, is known for its rigid structure and florid style (*Anatomy* 49–60). Professor Matalene has also told us that her Chinese college students almost invariably follow a fixed or standard pattern in their persuasive essays. This standard pattern usually consists of "an opening description of a specific incident, a look back at the usually unfortunate history of the issue or practice, an explanation of the current much improved state of affairs, and a concluding moral exhortation" ("Contrastive Rhetoric" 800). Her analysis at least leaves me, as well as many of my students, with the impression that there is not much room left for her students to develop and convey their own voices.

Without a doubt, the danger always remains for anyone to follow this standard structure too blindly, at the risk of silencing his or her own voice. Meanwhile, it is a mistake to equate this danger with the claim that this standard structure inherently hampers or stifles individual creativity. After all, any structure or genre has to be enacted by its users within a particular communicative context. And it is no less of a mistake, in my view, to equate this danger with another claim that such a structure is a tool of ideological control to be deployed by people in structures of power. Regardless, the discourse of 恕 sheds new light on how to address this danger, on how to negotiate this tension between (constraining) conventions and the creative space such conventions accord.

A productive analogy can be drawn between this preference for the standard structure and the carrying out of the discourse of 恕. As I have noted above, the discourse of 恕, to the extent that it is imbued with tradition, with 禮 ("li")-constituted conduct, has a normalizing, and thus potentially constraining, effect on its practitioners. The same can be said of the standard structure reported by Matalene or the genre of "opinion writing" reported by Li: either form can produce a constraining effect. At the same time, the discourse of 恕 also imbeds a social and creative dimension, because it nurtures a relationship of interdependence, and because it is predicated upon significations originating from or produced by interactions between self and others at the point of contact. In this regard, practicing the discourse of 恕 can entail a creative understanding of this interpersonal, social context. Similarly, the four-part standard structure or the genre of "opinion writing" is no less social. Not only because any form without individual creativity or situatedness is devoid of meaning, but also because any "preferred" structure or genre grows out of the lived experiences of other writers, and it is a link in the chain of other structures or genres, with its character being determined by their mutual reflections (Bahktin, "Problem" 91). Finally, just as the discourse of 恕 provides its practitioners with a life-long heuristic for their daily cultivation of humane relationships, so the knowledge of a "preferred" structure or genre allows individuals to respond to and construct recurring situations (Devitt 578, 580).

This standard structure reported by Matalene is in fact well known, and it has been encoded into four Chinese characters ("qi," "cheng," "zhuan," and "he," 起承轉合), almost forming a set phrase (Hsiung 50; Tsao 110). Each character in this phrase stands for a given substructure or function, and each substructure is related to the others within the overall structure. So, "qi" means "open" or "begin," signifying an opening of an argument or discourse; "cheng" can literally be translated as "support with one's palm" or "bear," and it marks and emphasizes a transition from introduction ("qi") to explanation; "zhuan" conveys the meaning of "turn," and subsequently of "turn to another viewpoint or perspective"; and "he" means "close" or "assemble," leading to the meaning of "to conclude" or "to pull everything together" (*Cihai*).[26] This four-character organizational structure finds its earliest expression in "jueju" (絶句). A particular type of classical Chinese poetry, "jueju" consists of four five-character or seven-character lines, and each line tends to correspond to each of the four substructures encoded in these four characters (Tsao 111).[27]

Seen through the lens of "qi, cheng, zhuan, and he" (起承轉合), this standard structure can then be characterized as embodying a mutually responsive and mutually entailing relationship. "Zhuan" (轉), the third character, can further provide individual writers with an important creative potential. In most cases, the "zhuan" substructure has to do with change or transformation, ranging from a change of mood to that of place, time, viewpoint, tone, or topic (Tsao 111). To bring about such a change, one is likely to make certain choices relative to specific situations, by, for example, relating the past (history) to the present (current state of affairs), old information to the new, and the personal (opinions) to the social (moral judgment). One not only responds to the immediate situation, but also enters into a dialogue with other writings that use the same four-character structure and that deal with similar themes or issues. In the process, the writer personalizes, and gives new meaning to, the structure, proving that he or she has the skills for variation, manipulation, and transformation—without necessarily having to violate anything (also see Devitt 580).

A word of caution has to be entered here. The discourse of 恕 does not in and of itself provide any guarantee for a life-long relationship of complementary reciprocity because it has to be realized by individuals who are willing to enter this relationship. Likewise, the "zhuan" structure is *not* a sure ticket to individual variation or innovation. Anyone could very well misuse this "zhuan" substructure or the entire four-character structure, either because of inexperience or zealousness. Should one decide to imitate, to a fault, those "zhuan" substructures embodied in ancient Chinese texts, one is likely to secure a formal, stylish "change" ("zhuan," 轉) without substance. These kinds of imitations could then be easily turned into some rigid, contentless writings associated with the "eight-legged essay."

An "eight-legged essay," according to the *Cihai*, consists of eight parts: (1) "po ti" ("breaking open the topic" with only two sentences, 破題); (2) "cheng ti" ("continuing the topic," 承題); (3) "qi jiang" ("initiating the explanation," 起讲); (4) "ru shou" ("transitioning from preliminary to formal explanation," 入手); (5) "qi gu" ("initial leg," 起股); (6) "zhong gu" ("center leg," 中股); (7) "hou gu" ("rear leg," 后股); and (8) "shu gu" ("mop-up leg," 束股). The first four parts represent an elaborate beginning. Each of the four legs in the next four parts includes two parallel statements or paragraphs, both in rhyme and in meaning—since "gu" (股) in Chinese means "parallel." There is a total of eight legs or parallels in the essay—hence the "eight-legged essay."

The "eight-legged essay" has often been singled out as the quintessential example of a structure or a form run amok, because of its association with those rigid, stereotyped essays in Chinese literary history. In our rush to critique, to condemn this form, several points often get overlooked. First, as Tu has demonstrated, there were, in Chinese literary history, plenty of "eight-legged" essays that were not rigid and did not lack imagination or originality (399–403). Second, not much recognition has been given to the fact that the "eight-legged essay" underwent several changes itself since it became the standard examination form in the Ming Dynasty (1368–1644) after the Imperial Civil Servant Examination was permanently established in 1385 (Tu 403). The fact that it did change suggests that the "eight-legged essay," almost like any other genre, was adaptive and reflective of the changing times.[28] Third, while the "eight-legged essay," if followed slavishly, could degenerate into a rigid or even an oppressive genre, we should resist the temptation to exaggerate the normalizing and constraining effect of a given structure on its users, and to assume that individual writers can be free and creative only by breaking out of—instead of working creatively within—such a generic structure (Devitt 574).[29]

I began this chapter in an effort to uncover an underlying ideology and to develop a discourse that challenges and moves away from polarizing dispositions. I intended to use this (new) discourse to recuperate a (Chinese) discursive tendency that espouses moral messages with a corresponding preference for a standard structure.[30] Now that I have completed these tasks, I realize that the discourse of 恕 also resonates, in a variety of ways, with "ethos" in European American rhetorical tradition—a topic that I now turn to for the remainder of this chapter.

Modern research abounds on ethos, a concept that is most often attributed to Aristotle and commonly defined as a means ("pistis") of persuasion employed by a speaker about how to create the most credible impression or character of him- or herself. A recent example is Baumlin and Baumlin's *Ethos: New Essays in Rhetorical and Critical Theory* (also see their selected bibliography 433–52).[31] Part of this fascination with ethos, in my view, comes from the etymological interplay encapsulated in the Greek word "ethos" about conceptions of self. It is an interplay between Greek "ἔθος" (ethos) as "habit," "custom," "institute," and Greek "ἦθος" (eethos) as "character" or "disposition," as well as "an accustomed place" (A. Miller 309–10). If the emphasis is on "habit" or "custom," ethos (ἔθος) seems to be describing a social, public self constructed on the basis of participation in realizing cultural norms and shared values. If the focus is on "character" or "disposition," ethos or eethos (ἦθος) appeals to a singular, private self whose attributes are grounded in the rhetor's actual character.[32] Incidentally, this interplay is reminiscent of a similar semantic intermingling, embedded in the word "persona," between a mask as an external, theatrical prop and an individual who is performing behind that very mask (Liddell and Scott). In the words of Mauss, it is an interplay between "the sense of what is the innermost nature of this 'person' (*personne*) and the sense of what is the 'role-player' (*personnage*)" (18).

In a series of essays spanning almost three decades, Halloran (1975, 1976, 1982, 1993) characterizes ethos in Western classical rhetoric as the living embodiment of the cultural heritage ("End of Rhetoric" 621), as the voice of cultural continuity ("Tradition and Theory" 235), or as "manifest[ing] the virtues most valued by the culture to and for which one speaks" ("Aristotle's Concept" 60). Under these definitions, ethos comes to represent communal wisdom rather than singular attributes; it epitomizes an ideal orator who internalizes all that is best in the tradition, in the shared world of speaker and audience ("End of Rhetoric" 627). This construction of ethos is based on previously established, shared knowledge as a foundation for rhetorical transactions, as a method of deciding questions of judgment or policy ("Further Thoughts" 112).

By associating ethos with the public rather than the private, the conventional rather than the singular, Halloran has identified, and thus sided with, the communal characteristic evidenced in ethos (or in ἔθος). Such a characteristic is perhaps a welcome corrective to a popular (over)dependence upon Aristotle's characterization, in the early part of the *Rhetoric*, of ethos as a persuasive means of appeal growing out of the character of the rhetor as artistically created in a speech (37–38, bk. 1, ch. 2, par. 2–4)—though Aristotle characterizes ethos, most of the time in the *Rhetoric*, as "moral character" that is deliberately created through speech and developed into a habit of mind. It further calls our attention to a necessary link between (the cultivation of) character and (the importance of) habit. It is clear that Halloran wants to remind us, through these discussions, of the necessary influence of a habitual gathering place on the shaping of a given character ("Aristotle's Concept" 60).

The influence of ἔθος upon ἦθος, or the significance of location in relation to the shaping of character, is not lost on feminist rhetoricians (Reynolds; Jarratt and Reynolds), who have also drawn upon this etymological interplay to demonstrate how character is being formed, both in sophistic rhetoric and in post-modern feminisms, through speaking to the interests of the community from a particular place in a particular social structure.[33] For Jarratt and Reynolds, ethos-building in sophistic rhetoric presumes not so much shared cultural knowledge as common interest in "kairos," in discovering provisional and probable truths. It focuses on heuristic processes where individual rhetors adjust to different standards of the community, and where they learn to "iden-tify contradictory propositions pertaining to the case at hand and work out arguments for each" (49). Through demonstrating how particular spaces contribute to the formation of self or character, Jarratt and Reynolds succeed in foregrounding the "kairos" in the shaping of char-acter, and in opening up new spaces for theorizing gendered subjects.

Originating in Confucian ideology and made viable at rhetorical borderlands, the discourse of 恕 provides a new perspective for this on-going dialogue over ethos. By focusing on the public and the habitual, Halloran sees ethos-building as based on shared knowledge or shared cultural heritage, to be exchanged in a habitual gathering place. In fact, this habitual gathering place has become, for Halloran, both a unified and unifying world to be articulated and reinforced, or "a common ground that is both its starting point and its goal" ("Further Thoughts" 116). This kind of characterization, to begin with, is at least a simplification or an idealization—to which Halloran has admitted ("Further Thoughts" 116). Further, I sense a subtle irony emanating from Halloran's project—an irony that has become more palpable with the discourse of 恕 now at its side. Here is how.

With an emphasis now being placed on the pre-existing values or norms in the shaping of character, self has become quite invisible, if not completely lost. It is almost overwhelmed by this need to conform, to be part of these values or norms. Embedded in Halloran's argument is this implicit, though perhaps unintended, anxiety to exorcise the ghost of the ideology of individualism, a move that I applaud. Unfortunately, though, this anxiety has perhaps begotten another. For fear of not being "right," Halloran may have "hypercorrected" himself—in the sense that the necessary recognition of, or appeal to, shared cultural values and norms has turned into a full-scale celebration, if not reification, at the expense of self or the role self may play in the shaping of character. By comparison, the discourse of 恕 does not make self disappear; nor does it make self stand over and above the surrounding social, cultural forces. Rather, it allows both self and others to cultivate a relationship of interdependence jointly. In this collaborative process, the emphasis is not so much on aligning oneself, habitually or otherwise, with pre-existing values or norms, as on taking cues from them to develop this relationship at every point of contact, in order to nurture a sense of complementary reciprocity appropriate to ongoing situations and unfolding speech events.

Any priority given to ethos (ἔθος) as "habit" may also have betrayed a desire to locate ethos in a safe, familiar space, where tensions or differences are minimized and where *shared* cultural knowledge and norms are exchanged safely and without much conflict.[34] Such space makes it possible for Halloran to postulate this (his) stable, unified, and thus idealized world in Western classical rhetoric—and one's habitual, virtuous performance in the shaping of character certainly reinforces such a world. Jarratt and Reynolds, as expected, do not subscribe to this stable, habitual space Halloran has envisioned. For them, ethos as the subject is always created at a particular point in time, fraught with the contingencies of history and imbued with a multitude of positions (Jarratt and Reynolds 47, 54–56). They no longer emphasize this cultural commonality because "*êthos* is the admission of a standpoint, with the understanding that other standpoints exist and that they change over time" (53).

The discourse of 恕 finds an affinity to this sophistic, feminist reconfiguring of ethos. The reason is obvious. The discourse of 恕 stresses a process in which the development of this relationship of interdependence does not revolve around a stable self that habituates a public place with the sole intention of immerseing oneself in shared cultural values or norms. And this relationship of interdependence is not an abstraction, much less a transcendence divorced from the discursive practices that produce its particular forms or manifestations. Differently stated, this relationship is inherently situated in each and every speech event, and it reacts, adjusts, and morphs in direct relation to the kinds of participants involved and to the kinds of participations inspired.

Reflective encounters of this kind at rhetorical borderlands will, in turn, recontextualize the discourse of 恕, and they will broaden its discursive sphere where new meanings and new alignments emerge. For example, any effort to realize the discourse of 恕 should now recognize that this relationship of interdependence or reciprocity does not make interpersonal differences go away. More importantly, the same effort should take into account how these differences beyond the familial milieu affect the production and consumption of particular manifestations of this relationship. Although Confucius recognizes interpersonal

differences, he conceptualizes them only in terms of a familial hierarchy—that is, in terms of parent and child, husband and wife, and old
and young. Once framed or contained within such a hierarchy, these
differences become predictable and easily manageable, thus preserving
the status quo and protecting the power imbalance. At our rhetorical
borderlands, differences cannot be contained within the family or the
community: they are necessarily spread out and located in the flow of
speech events and in the encounters of cultures. Inscribed in each and
every speech event, they are implicated in the positions self assumes
as he or she puts forth the utmost to connect with others. To allow
differences to make a difference thus creates space to foreground contingencies over habituation, and to face up to the complex, historically
determined relations of power, whose tensions and contestations further
complicate and problematize the discourse of 恕. Out of this process
thus emerge multiple acts of signification, be they intervening, transforming, or conflicting.

By engaging the discourse of 恕 and ethos in this borderland context,
I have no intention of discovering or arguing for points of commonality. For example, I do not seek to engineer some sort of rapprochement
between "ἔθος" as "habit" and "ἦθος" as "character." Nor do I want to
create a harmonious fusion between a feminist reconfiguring of ethos
and a 恕-oriented construction of self. In spite of such disclaimers that I
offer here and elsewhere in this chapter, I still harbor certain fears, and
I still nurse a sense of insecurity. In my heart of hearts, I wonder if others would still see this effort of mine as no more than a border resident
romanticizing Confucian ideology, ascribing some imaginary power to
an exotic discourse. Or would others accuse me of committing, to borrow a term from Hall and Ames, "cross-cultural anachronism" (*Thinking
Through Confucius* 7)? That is to say, the development of the discourse
of 恕 is made possible by an on-going, present-day debate originating
within Western rhetorical tradition—a debate that Confucius may not
have entertained at all in his own time. Or could my effort simply suffer
the normal perils of communicating at rhetorical borderlands, such as
miscomprehension or incomprehension?

Absent any immediate resolution of these misgivings, I want to plow
ahead. Not only because the discourse of 恕 helps recuperate Chinese
rhetorical practices at rhetorical borderlands, but also because it enables
me to arrive at a more complex understanding of self and others, of
place and character, and of the stable and the contingent. As I use the
discourse of 恕 to interrogate the ideology of individualism, to move

away from the discourse of deficiency or difference, and to enter a dialogue with ethos, I feel energized—because the knowledge that has been created out of these encounters has empowered me to move in and out of these situated, heterogeneous spaces with confidence and humility, with a discourse that creatively engages both Chinese and European American rhetorical traditions, and that exemplifies togetherness-in-difference through particular instances of communicative action.

5

FROM CLASSROOM TO COMMUNITY
Chinese American Rhetoric on the Ground

> What speaks is not the utterance, the language, but the whole
> social person . . . The *raison d'être* of a discourse is never to be
> found entirely in the speaker's specifically linguistic compe-
> tence; it is to be found in the socially defined site from which it
> is uttered . . .
> (Bourdieu, "Economics" 653, 657)

> At some point, on our way to a new consciousness, we will have
> to leave the opposite bank, the split between the two mortal
> combatants somehow healed so that we are on both shores at
> once, and at once, see through serpent and eagle eyes.
> (Anzaldúa 100)

Thus far, the making of Chinese American rhetoric has largely been
motivated and mobilized by my classroom practices and by my own experiences at rhetorical borderlands. As I continue to articulate Chinese
American rhetoric, and as I continue to reflect upon what it means to
promote an in-between subject position of comings-to-be, my thoughts
often turn to my fellow border residents: I wonder how they deal with,
consciously or subconsciously, this tension between the "structural
nostalgia" for the "ancestral culture" (JanMohamed 101) and the real
desire to be accepted as part of the American story—not as "innately
and irreversibly different from their fellow Americans" (Chang 389).[1] I
cannot help asking myself: How do my fellow border residents negotiate—through their use of language—between Chinese and European
American rhetorical traditions? How do they appropriate both traditions in their efforts to respond to social exigencies, to assemble[2] the
illocutionary force of the whole social person, and to bring about positive changes in the communities? To put it another way, I want to find
out how Chinese American rhetoric is being born and experienced on
the ground and through the mouths and pens of my fellow border residents. I want to know in what ways their use of language begins to accord

them a sense of a new identity, and in what ways it begins to validate and exemplify the rhetoric of togetherness-in-difference. Most directly put, I am anxious to take the making of Chinese American rhetoric to the street.[3]

On 3 October 2003, *CityBeat*, a Cincinnati news and entertainment weekly, published an article—titled "OTR Consultant: No Chinese Allowed"—that both angered and galvanized the local Chinese American community. According to this article, John Elkington, the Memphis redevelopment consultant, had told a group of local political and business leaders at an earlier Over-the-Rhine Chamber of Commerce luncheon that his years of experience in development had taught him "to never rent to a Chinese restaurant" (Dunlap, "No Chinese"). According to the same article, while he later characterized his own comment as "a joke," Mr. Elkington also stated explicitly that it was his policy not to rent to Chinese restaurants because "Chinese businessmen are hagglers" and "they use different math" (Dunlap, "No Chinese"). Mr. Elkington had been brought in by Cincinnati as a consultant as part of its efforts to revive and bring diversity to Over-the-Rhine ("OTR" for short)— Cincinnati's historical district which had been mired by racial tensions and shunned by investors and business owners. And the city was then considering awarding him a whopping $100,000 contract.

These racist remarks are blatantly offensive and deeply troubling. Not only because these remarks are aimed at openly disparaging and degrading one particular ethnic group, but also because they came from someone who was supposed to be doing just the opposite: to help ease the racial tensions and repair Cincinnati's image, which was severely, if not irreparably, damaged by the three-day race riots in Over-the-Rhine and other areas in the city in April 2001.[4] After these racist remarks came to light, thanks to *CityBeat*, the Chinese American community in Greater Cincinnati[5] rallied swiftly and forcefully in direct contrast to the city leadership's conspicuous silence and noncommittal stance.

First, the Chinese American community got together and quickly decided to form an ad hoc committee—the Chinese American Council—that consisted of seven local Chinese American organizations.[6] This committee was then charged with coordinating all the responses and communicating with fellow Chinese Americans in the area. The committee also made a conscientious effort to connect to other ethnic minority communities in the city, such as Jewish American and African American communities—because such offensive remarks, as they rightly concluded, should not be viewed as isolated, but as part of a larger discourse that persistently constructs the ethnic other as "deviant," as "undesirable." In pursuing these actions, the Chinese American community was in fact appropriating a rhetorical strategy used frequently by the dominant culture—that is, organizing and networking through grassroots actions.

Second, they wrote to Mayor Charlie Luken and other city leaders to express their outrage. and to demand that Mr. Elkington's racist remarks be unequivocally condemned and that he not be hired by the city. They also wrote to *CityBeat* and the *Cincinnati Inquirer*—the latter enjoys the largest circulation in the area—to express their anger and to mobilize the general public in support of their cause. Third, more than 100 Chinese Americans went to the City Council meeting on the afternoon of 15 October 2003, and a good number of Chinese Americans spoke to the entire Council prior to their business meeting, denouncing Mr. Elkington's racist remarks and demanding immediate actions from the City Council.[7]

These collective actions led the City Council to adopt a resolution at the meeting. The resolution, among other things, condemns Elkington's remarks, because they were "insensitive, without substance, and totally unacceptable to this community, now or at any time"; expresses regrets to those citizens who were offended by these remarks; recognizes the extraordinary contributions made by the Chinese American community to life in Cincinnati; and agrees to formally acknowledge the celebration of Chinese New Year the week of January 18, 2004 (see the entire resolution at the end of this chapter). The following day (16 October 2003), the *Cincinnati Inquirer* published "City Hall Assailed Over Chinese Slur," which summarized what went on inside City Hall and prior to the City Council's business meeting the day before (Korte).

Not by accident, these collective actions enacted by my fellow Chinese Americans bring up a discursive affinity to the rhetoric of protest or protest rhetoric. Protest rhetoric, traditionally defined as rhetoric "designed to effect change in the status quo through public confrontation" (Williams 20),[8] became openly evidenced, beginning in the 1960s, in the social movements associated with members of various minority groups (Jensen 28).[9] According to R. Gregg, protest rhetoric is self-directed, in the sense that it primarily appeals to the protestors themselves, "who feel the need for psychological refurbishing and affirmation" (74) and who thus fulfill what he calls "an ego-function" (74). More specifically, protest rhetoric takes three related postures to realize this ego-function. First, it recognizes and makes public that "one's ego is somehow ignored, or damaged, or disenfranchised." Second, it describes and extols "the strengths and virtues of the ego sought after." Third, it "decries and attacks the ignorance or malicious qualities of an enemy: a foreign ego which stands in dislogistic juxtaposition to the desired ego" (76).

What my fellow Chinese Americans did in the aftermath of Mr. Elkington's racist remarks manifests, to some extent, this ego-function. For example, they have pointed out unequivocally that such remarks, which portray them as "deviant" or "irrational," have marginalized and disenfranchised them. They have denounced Elkington or what he stands for, because he represents "a foreign ego" which stands in stark contrast to, and indeed threatens, the values and aspirations enshrined in our Constitution. At the same time, my fellow Chinese Americans have also performed something different. As I will be demonstrating shortly, they have also deployed a rhetoric that pronominally *both* excludes *and* includes the other—that is, the City Council and the Mayor—and that discursively straddles stinging criticism and constructive engagement. In the process, they not only have affirmed their collective identity, as Gregg has suggested for protest rhetoric, but also redefined the existing relations of power, contributing, as a result, to the emergence of an in-between subject position.[10]

In what follows, I will discuss how my fellow Chinese Americans used language to respond to this particular speech event, to reclaim their agency, and to redefine the existing relationship of power in a place of clashing cultures and conflicting ideologies. But before I proceed, it is perhaps necessary for me to examine first my own allegiances, to discuss how my own ideology guides and informs my analysis of their discursive behaviors.

From the publication of Dunlap's "No Chinese Allowed" on 3 October 2003 to that of Korte's "City Hall Assailed Over Chinese Slur" on 16 October 2003, I found myself negotiating between two positions. On the one hand, as I followed this unfolding situation closely, I felt I was aligning myself ever more closely with my Chinese American community, with a shared sense of mission to combat racism and to change our city for the better. I quickly became a participant, and I was anxious to see that our community be accepted and included, now or at any other time in the future. On the other hand, I also wanted to study my fellow Chinese Americans' rhetorical performances, and I wanted to investigate if these actions are examples of Chinese American rhetoric and if they represent the rhetoric of togetherness-in-difference. During this entire time, I also thought and acted like a researcher.

Since there was no wall separating one position from the other, these two positions quickly collapsed into one. Nevertheless, I felt, perhaps paradoxically, a sense of freedom and a rush of energy. I realized that it was now irrelevant, if not impossible, for me to claim a stance of absolute objectivity—one that anthropologists and ethnographers used to cherish, and that some of them may still be unwilling to abandon completely. What I did want to claim was that meanings are always imbued with their own historical precedents and with their own situational dynamics, and that, to appropriate Bourdieu, what speaks is "the whole social person" "in the socially defined site from which it [discourse] is uttered" ("Economics" 653, 657). To put it more succinctly, meanings become operative because of the occasion of use through both situated production and consumption. Further, "going native" took on new meanings for me: in this case, it meant participating in a discourse that rejects racial and rhetorical stereotypes and that fosters reflection and mutual understanding. Consequently, I found new relevance and inspiration in the kind of rhetoric I am articulating in this chapter, and throughout this book.

What are, then, some of the characteristics that can be discerned and assembled from the discursive performances of my fellow Chinese Americans? More specifically, in what ways do these practices help them negotiate between Chinese and European American face, between indirection and directness, and between their own community and the city leadership and good people of Cincinnati?

After the news about Mr. Elkington's remarks broke out, the seven local Chinese American organizations wrote an open letter to Mayor Luken and Councilman John Cranley. From the outset, the authors of the letter make a direct effort to situate Elkington's racist remarks within a historical context and to make the past an important part of this unfolding speech event. After expressing the Chinese American community's outrage at these racist remarks in the first paragraph, the authors use the second paragraph to link these remarks to a particular past in American history:

> It is incredible that Cincinnati is considering hiring a development consultant who still avows such disgraceful exclusionary policies which persecuted Chinese Americans during the 1800s and 1900s.

This is a past that saw widespread acts of violence and injustice visited upon the Chinese, culminating in the passage of the Chinese Exclusion Act of 1882, which was not repealed until 1943. By establishing this link, the authors make it quite clear that these remarks cannot be taken in isolation and that they must be seen as part of a larger social-cultural practice informed by racial hostility and by the asymmetrical relations of power. For Chinese Americans in particular, these remarks cannot escape all the other meanings with which they have been historically affiliated. In a way, they have already been framed or infected by them. As discourse analyst Gee rightly points out,

> Words have *histories*. They have been in other people's mouths and on other people's pens. They have circulated through other Discourses and within other institutions. They have been part of specific historical events and episodes. Words bring with them as *potential situated meanings* all the situated meanings they have picked up in history and in other settings and Discourses. (*Discourse Analysis* 54; emphasis original)[11]

Therefore, to describe Chinese restaurant owners as "hagglers" not only conveys the (usual) meaning about someone who makes it difficult to come to terms with an agreement to the point of mangling it, but also conjures up the historical, derogatory image of the Chinese as "deviant," as "unasssimilable." Similarly, by stating that Chinese Americans "use different math," Mr. Elkington contradicts our basic assumption about math—that is to say, mathematical rules and principles apply to everyone, irrespective of culture, race, or border. To suggest, then, that Chinese restaurant owners follow their own math amounts to accusing them of not playing by the same rules. And individuals who do not play by the same rules are at least "deviant," if not "inscrutable," and they must therefore be ruled out of order—much less renting restaurant space to them. To claim, as did Mr. Elkington, that these remarks were meant as "a joke" either reveals his own chutzpah that he can get away with uttering such remarks in public, or speaks to the significant challenges we border residents face as we try to promote co-presence and mutual understanding through the discourse of togetherness-in-difference.

Not only is the historical past highly relevant to our understanding of these remarks, but the present context is equally important, because it is the present that these offensive remarks are intended to impact and influence. In the third paragraph, the authors frame the present this way:

> Mr. Elkington's openly racist remarks stand in stark contrast to the objectives of diversity and inclusion promised for the proposed Over-the-Rhine development project. Given the recent racial tension in the City of Cincinnati, Mr. Elkington's openly anti-Chinese comments are an insult

to the progressive desires of the people of Cincinnati and the local business community.

As one can see, this paragraph presents an unmistakable contrast between Mr. Elkington's remarks, on the one hand, and the stated policies of diversity for the development of the Over-the-Rhine historical district and the people's desires for a racially inclusive community, on the other. Such contrast makes his derogatory remarks all the more insulting and downright unacceptable to both the Chinese American community and the people of Cincinnati. In so doing, this paragraph (the present) joins the preceding paragraph (the past) to further situate these remarks: they are anything but a joke.

The coupling of the past with the present in turn yields a new context for the future, one that would be very bleak if such remarks were allowed to go unchallenged. The next paragraph offers us a precise glimpse of such a future:

> If Mr. Elkington's policy of excluding Chinese businesses is allowed to stand, it will worsen the divided racial climate here. It will be detrimental to the economic success of the Main Street project and Over-the-Rhine businesses. It will reconfirm the negative national image of Cincinnati as a city that isn't open and welcoming to all ethnic groups.

Since none of these future consequences is acceptable to or compatible with the hopes and aspirations of the people of Cincinnati, Mr. Elkington's remarks must be categorically denounced and rejected, and redressive actions must be taken right away to heal the wounds inflicted by these remarks.

The move here to appeal to the past and the present bears a strong affinity to the Chinese applicant's statement of purpose that I have discussed in some detail in Chapter Two. Namely, in the case of the Chinese applicant, the past is intimately woven with the present, and they together help present a confident 脸 ("lian") and a presentable 面子 ("mianzi"), both of which are necessary to ensure a promising future for the applicant. For the Chinese applicant, therefore, to bring up her past is to help establish her 脸 and 面子 and, eventually, her personhood.

For the authors of the letter, representing the local Chinese American community, to bring up this particular historical past is to expose the pernicious nature of these remarks, and to ensure that such a past will neither be forgotten nor be repeated again. It is this past of exclusion and discrimination that has denied so many Chinese Americans the opportunity to establish their proper 脸 and 面子 in their adopted land and that has prevented their borderland experiences from being accepted as part of the American story. Differently put, only by rejecting such a past can the Chinese American community begin to reassert their 脸 and 面子, to articulate a different moment of relationship characterized not by bigotry and bias, but by inclusion and equality.

But unlike the Chinese applicant, the authors of the letter become quite *direct* when the time comes for them to convey their demands to the City Council. Drawing upon what I have been suggesting in the previous chapters, I characterize their appeal to the past and the present as an *indirect* criticism of the city leadership's failure to speak out forcefully, and of their blindness to the importance of the past; an indirect criticism minimizes the threat to the city leadership's positive face—its want to be liked and to be approved of. On the other hand, the ways in which the authors make their demands known are anything but indirect: they use a rhetorical strategy (of directness) that is perhaps most familiar to their intended audience. In the process, they help to secure and enhance a confident 脸 and 面子 for themselves and for their community. This direct, assertive approach is on full display in the remainder of the letter, as the authors move to articulate their demands:

> You need to immediately denounce Mr. Elkington's divisive insults and separate yourselves from his policies and from him. We ask you to take the following actions:
> 1. Make a clear public statement against Mr. Elkington's racist anti-Chinese policy as soon as possible. As leaders of the City of Cincinnati, you should not allow him to further divide our city.
> 2. Demand that Mr. Elkington make a clear public apology to the Cincinnati-area Chinese American community for his racially divisive comments.
> 3. Do not use Mr. Elkington's consulting service. After such self-confessed bias and long-time practice of excluding Chinese businesses, he should not even be considered for a development project that professes to be ethnically inclusive.
>
> The Chinese American Community appreciates your leadership to date in trying to create a racially inclusive community in Cincinnati where every hard-working American can be successful. Please do not compromise yourselves in this flagrant case of bias.

To begin with, the three numbered demands, as well as the last sentence, use the imperative mode, and they each also employ a transitive verb of action, thus leaving no doubt as to what actions need to be taken right away. The use of modal verbs such as "need to" and "should" creates what Fairclough calls a "relational modality," in which the authority of one participant is expressed and asserted in relation to others (105).[12] In this regard, "need to" and "should" signal obligation on the part of the subject in question. Further, "should"—here used with a "not," as in "you should not . . ." and "he should not . . ."—expresses the authors' determination to prevent the city from being further divided, and Mr. Elkington from being considered for the redevelopment project. Finally, the use of speech act verbs such as "allow," "demand," and "ask" actually produces such action-packed speech acts as granting permission, issuing a demand, asking a question, or their negative counterparts. Together, the imperative mood and the modal and speech act verbs enable the authors to claim a sense of moral authority and discursive agency over their addressees, in spite of the unequal relationship of power that exists between them. As a matter of fact, insofar as they are successful in performing these speech acts, they have redefined, at least discursively, this relationship.

To suggest, as I am doing now, that the authors have deployed a strategy of directness in this open letter is not to appeal to a hierarchical binary that pits directness against indirection and that privileges the former over the latter. As I have argued extensively in Chapter Three, the value of directness is parasitic upon that of indirection, and vice versa. Both directness and indirection always align themselves in relation to each and every situated encounter and both contribute to an ever-shifting relation of interdependence. Moreover, the values of directness and indirection are only made consequential by those who participate in such encounters, and by those who are in a position to bring their own discursive ideologies to bear on the process of consumption.

Consequently, the city leadership could view the direct, assertive style evidenced in this open letter as too direct, and thus too threatening to their negative face—its want to be left alone. And the penultimate sentence, intended to soothe the city leadership's positive face, would be seen as too little, too late. On the other hand, many enraged Chinese Americans could view the same approach as not direct enough for the city leadership, as not holding their feet close enough to the fire. And the same penultimate sentence would be seen as unnecessary, as giving credit where credit is not due. These respective positions are once again informed by the different social-cultural positions they occupy and by the kinds of social transformations or nontransformations they desire.

This discursive tendency to engage the past—either to embrace it, in the case of the Chinese applicant, or to critique it, as is seen in the open letter—resonates with Native American protest rhetoric or Red Power rhetoric. For example, the past is equally ever present in Native American protest rhetoric, not only because the past can never be separated from the present, but also because the past, or native "history," is always part of "an on-going tale of injustice" experienced by many Native Americans (Lake, "Between Myth and History" 125). This tendency to engage the past, evidenced in Native American protest rhetoric, is also motivated by a particular rhetorical exigency. According to Lake ("Between Myth and History"), the evolutionary or Euramerican narrative, by grounding itself in the linear metaphor of "time's arrow" (123), severs the link between the Native American past and contemporary life, thus "dissociating historical injustices from contemporary problems and protests" (128). Native American protest rhetoric, grounded in the circular metaphor of "time's cycle" (123), directly challenges this narrative so as to "renew the ties between the past and the present, and thereby to enact a future, by characterizing Red Power as the rebirth of traditional tribal life" (129). In short, the past becomes constitutive of contemporary Native American protest rhetoric as it connects to the present and to the inevitable victory in the future (137).

On the other hand, this discursive tendency to bring the past to the forefront stands in marked contrast to the 7 October 2003 editorial in the *Cincinnati Inquirer*. Titled "Inclusive Development: OTR Consultant; Chinese-Americans," the editorial seems to be taking the position of criticizing Mr. Elkington's remarks and promoting an inclusive environment, but it often ends up equivocating or sitting on the fence. For example, the editorial characterizes Mr. Elkington's remarks as "inept at best" and "offensive" at worst, but it fails to tell its readers what it really thinks. The readers are left wondering if these remarks are inept, offensive, or something in between. Similarly, the editorial states that "such stereotyping is contemptible," but this statement is immediately followed by Elkinton's denial: "but Elkington denies the quote." And the editorial further quotes Elkington as saying: "I would never say disparaging things about any racial group."[13] This kind of juxtaposition, which is perhaps in the name of being "fair and balanced," almost clears Elkington of the responsibility for having made these inflammatory remarks. By contrast, there is no Chinese American representative speaking in the editorial, and none is offered any space to refute Elkington's denial. The readers are left in the dark as to what Chinese Americans actually think of Mr. Elkington's racist remarks and of his denial.

What is most noteworthy is the fact that the editorial makes no reference at all to the historical context within which these remarks must be situated. Its silence about the past, or its failure to engage the past, either betrays its blindness or speaks to its own underlying ideology that chooses to contain these remarks within the framework of a misfired joke or personal ineptness. Either way, by ignoring, if not erasing, a past that has silenced the hopes and dreams of so many Chinese Americans, the editorial minimizes the seriousness of these racist remarks and sends a disturbing signal to both the Chinese American community and all the minority communities in the city.[14] Once again, words and utterances secure their uptake not necessarily because of how their users have characterized them, but because of the situational context they are in, and because of "all the situated meanings they have picked up in history and in other settings and Discourses" (Gee, *Discourse Analysis* 54).

On 15 October 2003, more than 100 Chinese Americans, together with other concerned citizens, including African Americans and Jewish Americans, went to City Hall to voice their anger and frustration and to demand action from the city leadership. A good number of Chinese Americans spoke before the City Council. According to City Council rules, speeches before the Council must be kept within two minutes. The following is the first speech delivered before the City Council by someone representing the Chinese American Council:

> Dear Vice Mayor Reece and Honorable Members of the Council,
>
> Good afternoon! My name is Jack Sheng.[15] I am here to represent the Chinese American Council, which is the organization in Cincinnati representing more than five thousand Chinese American families.
>
> We are truly offended and outraged by the recent racist and divisive remarks by Mr. John Elkington as reported by *CityBeat* last week. Mr. Elkington's derogatory remarks are not only an insult to the Chinese American community, but also to the great people of this great city at large. We believe his remarks are totally inconsistent with the diversity objectives of the OTR project and we believe also it is totally inconsistent with the dedication you have put to this great city for diversity and also for racial tolerance. We as a community respectfully put three action items for your consideration.
>
> 1. We urge Mr. John Elkington to publicly apologize to the Chinese American community and also to the great people of Cincinnati at large for his racist and divisive comments.

2. We urge this Honorable Council not to hire Mr. Elkington for the OTR project.
3. We also urge this Council to pass a resolution to celebrate Chinese culture in the week of the Chinese New Year.
   Thank you.

It is clear that our speaker is quite unequivocal in conveying the anger and outrage experienced by the Chinese American community toward Elkington's remarks. At the same time, he is careful not to criticize openly the City Council for its failure to speak out against these remarks in a clear, timely fashion. As a matter of fact, there is not a single harsh word or utterance directed at the City Council in this speech, and the speech is measured and polite, as can be seen in the use of the honorific "honorable" and in "We as a community respectfully put three action items for your consideration." In so doing, he succeeds in not threatening their positive face want too much, in order to ensure that his requests be satisfied immediately. To the extent that the City Council does satisfy these requests, the speaker will have boosted his own 脸 and 面子 and that of the Chinese American community he represents.

And the speaker does more. He reaches out and connects to both the people of Cincinnati and the City Council by trying to put himself in their position. They are, for now, almost just as much a victim to Elkington's racist remarks as are Chinese Americans, because these remarks are "totally inconsistent with" what they have built on and what they are aspiring to. The use of "you" in the second paragraph is revealing. It shows a visible attempt on the part of the speaker to bridge the gap between "you" (the City Council) and "we" (the Chinese American community). Because of the dedication the City Council (that is, "you") has shown so far, they (that is, "you" and "we") are now in this fight together—hence "we urge this Honorable Council" to take these actions. As a result, a relation of interdependence emerges where "we" and "you" become connected, and where Chinese 脸 and European American positive face can begin to look at each other not with recrimination, but with mutual understanding. Consequently, the two directives aimed at the Council—in the form of "We urge . . ."—no longer seem as threatening to the City Council's negative face want as they might otherwise be.[16]

This kind of discursive negotiation can also be found in the following speech delivered before the City Council:

Dear Cincinnati City Council:

My name is Chris Zhang; I represent the Cincinnati Contemporary Chinese School, a school with about 200 registered students and more than 150 households.

Mr. Elkington's racist remarks not only offended the Chinese American community and all conscience citizens, but also shed a huge shadow in our children's heart. They are deeply hurt by such openly racist comments. Our children have written to their teachers and to the board to express their sadness over this statement. They are also severely confused, why are they still judged by the color of their skin and not by the content of their character? Our children, no matter which school they are in, they are the hope of tomorrow. They are the tomorrow of America, our country. I cannot imagine what our country would be if our children grow up under such racist climate. I'm scared. Please, Mr. Mayor and the members of council, stand up with us to say NO to the racism and publicly appeal to all conscience citizens of Cincinnati to fight against any form of racism. We all have one common dream, which is to make this country stronger and richer for the families and the people who live here. Let's work together to keep this dream alive.

Like the open letter and Mr. Sheng's speech, Zhang's speech provides another example of how these Chinese Americans deploy different rhetorical strategies to negotiate some complex, historically determined relations of power and to create a confident, respectable 脸 for themselves and for the community. While Zhang must confront and denounce racism as directly as he can, he must not antagonize his intended audience—the City Council—too directly, and he must not make them feel that their positive face is being unfairly pressured.

After a quick self-introduction in the first paragraph, Mr. Zhang wastes no time in expressing the community's outrage. What is telling, though, is that he chooses, in the second and main paragraph, to focus on the damning consequences of Elkington's remarks, on how they have traumatized the children at the Chinese Language School. Namely, these children are deeply hurt and confused because such offensive remarks belie the kind of America they have been taught to love and to cherish, and because they have learned that they should be judged, invoking Dr. Martin Luther King, Jr., not by the color of their skin, but by the content of their character.

Further, similar to what we have seen in the other two examples, Zhang is also quite direct in appealing to the entire City Council—once again using the imperative mood—to stand up with the Chinese American community to denounce Elkington's remarks and say "No" to racism. By stating that the children at the Cincinnati Contemporary Chinese School "*are* the hope of tomorrow" and "*are* the tomorrow of America" (emphasis added), our speaker in fact issues two assertives, which "commit the speaker (in varying degrees) to something's being the case, to the truth of the expressed proposition" (Searle 12). The use of the simple present tense form "are" further reinforces the speaker's commitment to the representation of reality as categorically true, as the verb "to be" in its present tense form conveys what Fairclough calls "a categorical commitment" to the truth of the proposition (107). Moreover, such statements come quite close to assuming the force of a declaration, whose successful performance "brings about the correspondence between the propositional content and reality" or "guarantees that the propositional content corresponds to the world" (Searle 16–17).[17] That is to say, Zhang, by successfully performing these two speech acts, is not only committing himself to the truth of the expressed proposition, but also doing so in a manner that almost accords him the discursive force of bringing about an instantaneous fit between the word and the world. The ability to effect such a fit yields a sense of authority and authenticity, both of which lend 脸 and agency to the speaker and to the community he represents.

The direct approach adopted here by Zhang is also punctuated by some indirect criticisms in the speech. On the one hand, there is no direct criticism, in this paragraph or in his entire speech, of the City Council, in spite of the fact that the Council as a collective body has yet to denounce Mr. Elkington's remarks openly, and it has yet to rule out unequivocally any possibility of giving Elkington a city contract.[18] And the use of "please" in the only imperative sentence in this paragraph encodes a deferential gesture that will not be lost on his audience, because it lessens the imposition placed on their negative face by his direct appeal.

On the other hand, by stating that "We all have a common dream," our speaker is also reminding his audience, indirectly, that this common dream is not quite being shared by all yet, for then they would not need to gather here at all. And by urging them to work with Chinese American and other minority communities—"Let's work together to keep this dream alive," Zhang is guiding his audience to another unspoken, yet unmistaken, reality: they have yet to work together to address troubled race relationships in the city and to build a truly inclusive community.

In fact, because they have not worked together, the city now has to face up to Mr. Elkington's racist remarks while still trying to deal with the repercussions caused by the three-day race riots in April 2001.

There is more. The use of "our," "we," and "us"—as in "I cannot imagine what *our* country would be if *our* children grow up under such racist climate," "*We* all have one common dream," and "*Let's* work together to keep this dream alive" (emphasis added)—is inclusive in meaning, creating a sense of togetherness and unity between the two sides. At the same time, this kind of inclusive use also *challenges* the other side to "take possession" of these children and to meet its responsibility to protect them from getting further hurt and confused. And since the two sides are now united by *our* children, by *our* common dream, and by *our* working together, the other side has no other option but to stand up with Chinese American and other minority communities to denounce Elkington's remarks and to reject him as a candidate for the redevelopment job.

By arguing from consequences and by appealing directly to the City Council for immediate action, our speaker aligns himself with the Aristotelian "directness" paradigm. By restraining from faulting or criticizing his audience directly, our speaker projects a subject position that is indirect and imposition-conscious. This mixing of directness and indirection enables him to negotiate successfully between (Chinese) 脸 and (European American) positive face. His use of the inclusive "we" and of its "cognates" begins to establish a cooperative relationship, which is being enhanced by the image of "children"—an image that, as a synecdoche, invokes a series of other images such as innocence, hope, and the future of America. As our speaker's rhetorical performances help direct his audience to a particular course of action in the immediate future, they help him nurture and convey a new sense of identity—one that is constituted not so much by internal rhetorical coherence as by discursive practices that implicate both traditions, and that aim to subvert the existing structures of power.

It would miss the point altogether for anyone to think that these Chinese Americans are not capable of directly criticizing the city leadership for their failure to denounce Elkington's remarks swiftly and to create a more racially inclusive community in Cincinnati. As a matter of fact, a number of Chinese Americans were quite blunt in their speeches, laying the blame directly at the feet of the city leadership and the local business leaders. The following speech by a representative of Chinese American Association of Cincinnati is a good example of this directness:

Dear Cincinnati City Council:

   Mr. Elkington's racist remarks obviously offended the Chinese community and all citizens with a conscience. We are also very disappointed with
the climate of Cincinnati towards diversity. Elkington was invited by the
city officials and delivered his insensitive remarks and exclusive policy at
an OTR Chamber of Commerce luncheon where many local political and
business leaders were present; but none of them stood up and denounced
the act. I hope none of you were there. How backward this is? Did it
never occur to you and all the leaders there that this was wrong? It has
to take a lonely, small newspaper reporter with great courage to expose
the remarks and confront the racism. If these remarks were made against
other ethnic groups, the audience may have responded differently. This is
why we, the representatives of the greater Cincinnati Chinese community,
are here. We cannot be ignored any more. Enough is enough. You may
think us during the election time, but I want you to think us all the time,
all the year. We want to raise the consciousness of culture diversity in our
city, and we want our leaders including all councilmen and councilwomen
here to lead us for creating a truly inclusive climate for our people to live
and work here.

In comparison with our first two speakers, this speaker comes out
mincing no words. For example, he tells the City Council that the
Chinese American community is very disappointed at the city's racial
climate, not only because it was the city officials who brought Elkington
to the city, but also because those political and business leaders at the
luncheon failed to stand up and to denounce Elkington's remarks.
Their "backward" conduct sharply contrasts with the *CityBeat* reporter
who broke the story and brought attention to these racist remarks. His
rhetorical question—"Did it never occur to you and all the leaders there
that this was wrong?"—is tinged with sarcasm, and it further sharpens
his critical stance toward the city leadership. Namely, if the answer to
this question is affirmative, then our city leadership is really "backward"
because of their ignorance and/or bias. And if the answer is negative,
then it did occur to them that these remarks were wrong. It is equally
"backward," if not worse, for them not to speak out on the spot, not to
condemn these remarks openly and unequivocally.

His direct, in-your-face style culminates in these two short statements:
"We cannot be ignored any more. Enough is enough." The use of "any
more" presupposes that the Chinese American community has been
ignored in the past, and the tautological expression signals that the
Chinese American community won't put up with this kind of treatment

any longer, and that they will speak out against racism and exclusion on their own in the future if they have to. And statements like these two are, as I have pointed out in my discussion of Mr. Zhang's speech, assertives with the force of a declarative. That is to say, these statements not only commit our speaker to the truth of the expressed proposition, but also enable him to realize an instantaneous fit between the word and the world. In the process, our speaker exercises, both for himself and for the community he represents, discursive authority over his audience. And the use of the model verb "can," as in "We cannot be ignored any more," conveys a relational modality, further solidifying Zhang's authority claim and enhancing his confident 脸.

The palpable tension between "you" (the City Council) and "we" (the speaker and the Chinese American community) is evident from the get-go as "we" becomes increasingly critical of "you." Such tension is certainly less visible, to say the least, in the previous two speeches. At the same time, this tension or this relationship undergoes some subtle changes as the meanings of these pronouns shift in the speech. For example, the initial use of "you"—as in "I hope none of you , , ," and "Did it never occur to you . . ."—clearly associates the City Council with the other side, with those who have been conspicuously silent over Elkington's remarks. And the use of the exclusive "we" further heightens this tension, because it has become clear that "you"—the City Council—has failed to represent and speak for "we," the Chinese American community.

However, toward the end of the speech, our speaker initiates a pronominal shift. Namely, the use of "our" in the last sentence conveys an inclusive meaning because "our city" belongs to both "you" and "we." In addition, the speaker now characterizes the City Council members as "our leaders" who are now being invited to "lead us" for "our people." Here, "us" and "our people" could also be inclusive, referring to both the Chinese American community and "all citizens with a conscience." This emergent sense of inclusiveness signifies a shifting of positions. That is to say, by using the inclusive "our," the speaker is trying to bring the Chinese American community and the City Council together into a new relationship, where the discourse of mutual understanding and reciprocity can overcome the discourse of othering and bias.

The juxtaposition of "you" with "our leaders" within the same speech reveals, in a way, our speaker's own ambivalence and his own unsettled association: he is *both* highly critical of "you" *and* wants to transform "you" into "us," into "our leaders." Indeed, this kind of discursive straddling serves as an undercurrent for the other three texts (the open letter and the other two speeches) under discussion as well. It is a characteristic that is indicative of the discourse of togetherness-in-difference, and of the making of Chinese America rhetoric. It is a subject position that moves between the exile and the immigrant and that attempts to use a majority language (that is, English) to present a minority perspective, aiming to break down, in the process, the binary barriers of all kinds and to conjure up hope and aspiration for our children, for our future.

Limited and/or limiting as it might be, my analysis thus far aims to illustrate how my fellow Chinese Americans use language to respond to a particular speech event, and how their use of language draws upon and implicates both Chinese and European American rhetorical traditions. As I assemble and activate the meanings of their situated speech acts, it becomes abundantly clear to me that their communicative actions entail both symbolic and material consequences—symbolic because they serve to exemplify the making of Chinese American rhetoric on the ground, and material because they combat racism and push for positive changes in our communities. In the process, these rhetorical performances come to resemble, up to a point, protest rhetoric in general and Native American protest rhetoric in particular. While I have no intention of claiming uniqueness-qua-coherence for these rhetorical performances, I have become more encouraged by the opportunities rhetorical borderlands present, and by the positive transformations we border residents may be able to effect with our creative-ambiguous voices, with our emergent-ambivalent positions.

For my fellow Chinese Americans, as they confront Mr. Elkington's racist remarks and as they urge the city leadership to join them to take decisive actions against bigotry and racial hatred, they nurture and develop a rhetoric that grows out of two competing, often clashing, rhetorics—rhetorics that have circulated in different times and places and that have picked up different discursive, situational values along the way. This is a rhetoric that, situated in, and in direct response to, a particular speech event, juxtaposes Chinese 脸 and European American positive face; blends indirection with directness, not as a pair of hierarchical opposites, but as two interdependent strategies; and practices the discourse of 恕 ("shu") by connecting to the city leadership, to the people of Cincinnati.

To the extent that they are successful in persuading the city leadership to denounce Elkington's remarks and to move toward promoting cultural understanding and exchange, they will begin to cultivate a new consciousness, one that rejects the binary discourse severing the past from the present and that initiates "a change in the way we perceive reality, the way we see ourselves, and the ways we behave" (Anzaldúa 102). They will also begin to bring about—thanks to their assertives with the force of a declarative—a different kind of reality, where racism in any shape or form will not be tolerated and where different cultures will be able to speak to each other with understanding and reflection, but without the fear of being exoticized or silenced.

A caveat, though. As I have argued in previous chapters, while the making of Chinese American rhetoric is a phenomenon of rhetorical borderlands, it is not a guaranteed phenomenon. Because it is always tied to particularizing contexts and to unequal relations of power, Chinese American rhetoric could be easily misunderstood or not understood at all. Or it could be quickly appropriated by the dominant culture as "the new kid on the block." Either outcome fails Chinese American rhetoric miserably. Then, there are these instances of ambiguity and ambivalence that we border residents experience as we practice Chinese American rhetoric, and as we try to be, to quote Anzaldúa again, "on both shores at once, and at once, see through serpent and eagle eyes" (100).

What, then, does all this mean? How can we best represent ourselves between moments of articulated relationships and moments of uncertainty and unsettled feelings? And how can we best pursue the rhetoric of togetherness-in-difference as we move forward to communicate, to persuade, and to adjust?

First, as we try to assert our agency, and to establish our residency in a space inhabited by competing rhetorical traditions and dominated by unequal relations of power, we, consciously or subconsciously, engender a discourse that implicates Chinese and European American rhetorical traditions. Since our discursive experiences will not be automatically understood and embraced on their own terms, we have to speak out more openly about these experiences, about these reflective encounters. We should do so not by touting uniqueness or incommensurability, but by highlighting how our own subject positions call for and enact the rhetoric of togetherness-in-difference in situated contexts, and how such rhetoric in turn helps rename and transform our cultural and discursive reality.

Second, as we practice and promote this rhetoric of togetherness-in-difference, we need to learn how to place ourselves in the others' position and how to "word" the world through the others' eyes or "I's." For example, when we contemplate enhancing 脸 and 面子, we should learn to think about how it can unsettle and recast positive and negative face. When we characterize certain discursive experiences as examples of indirection or directness, we should call upon ourselves to remember that they are part of an ever-shifting circle of complementary contrasts, where the value of one is never complete without that of the other. And when we practice the discourse of 恕 ("shu"), we have to teach ourselves and our interlocutors that our mission is not to banish or impoverish self, but to incorporate both self and other into a relationship of interdependence and interconnectedness.

Third, part of our challenge in the making of Chinese American rhetoric lies in how we border residents can best reconnect to our own rhetorical history, and in how we can best represent it or transform the other's representations of it. To do so—it cannot be emphasized enough—is not to get bogged down by such history, but to use it to lay claim to the present, and to reclaim our agency and our identity—not only because such history inevitably influences or implicates our ongoing production and consumption of Chinese American rhetoric, but also because it enables us to resist both the discourse of assimilation and the discourse of deficiency or difference. Moreover, this turn toward history gives us another reason to initiate and assemble a different way of speaking: it injects new meanings into our understanding of Chinese and European American rhetorical traditions, and it further reconfigures the relationship that both traditions cannot help but enter and share—a relationship whose complicated entanglement is both indicative of a hybrid rhetoric at rhetorical borderlands, and generative of hope and potential for the future.

RESOLUTION NO. **117** - 2003

EXPRESSING the City Council of Cincinnati's strong condemnation of the recent comments made by Mr. John Elkington relating to "renting to Chinese restaurants."

WHEREAS, the comments made by Mr. John Elkington at a recent Over the Rhine Chamber of Commerce luncheon was insensitive, without substance, and totally unacceptable to this community, now or at any time; and

WHEREAS, City Council greatly regrets that any of our citizens were offended as a result of this incident, and welcomes the opportunity to acknowledge the extraordinary contribution of people of Chinese ancestry to the quality of life in Cincinnati; and

WHEREAS, City Council would like to formally acknowledge the celebration of Chinese New Year, which will take place during the week of January 18, 2004. The New Year is the most important focal point of Chinese culture and is a celebration for members of the community to enjoy; now, therefore

BE IT RESOLVED by the Council of the City of Cincinnati, State of Ohio:

That the Council condemns the racially insensitive comments made by Mr. John Elkington and regrets that any of our citizens were offended as a result of this incident.

That the City Council would like to formally acknowledge the celebration of the Chinese New Year, which will take place the week of January 18, 2004.

That a copy of this resolution be spread upon the minutes of the Council and a copy be sent to the Chinese American Council, which represents numerous Chinese American organizations.

Passed _October 15_, 2003

_____
Mayor

Attest _____
Clerk

Submitted by Councilmember Jim Tarbell

6

CLOSING COMMENT
Chinese Fortune Cookie as a Topic Again

En unas pocas centurias, *the future will belong to the* mestiza.
Because the future depends on the breaking down of paradigms, it
depends on the straddling of two or more cultures.

(Anzaldúa 102)

As the title of this concluding chapter indicates, I am now coming to a
close, and I will be using the Chinese fortune cookie again as my central topic in this chapter. In so doing, I not only want to signal that I
have now come full circle, but I also want to use this nifty image of the
Chinese fortune cookie to extend what I have developed so far and to
flush out further the significances and implications of this project.

Structurally speaking, I see this chapter as a fitting conclusion, too.
As one may recall, in Chapter Three I discussed the topic-comment
structure in the Chinese language in order to illustrate this language's
structural disposition toward discursive interdependence as part of my
effort to re-conceptualize Chinese indirection and European American
directness. Now I want to compare my entire project to this topic-comment structure, imagining it as one single Chinese utterance informed
by this structure, by this relational focus. More plainly put, I see my
Introduction and my first five chapters as consisting of a series of "topics," which ranges from my musings over Chinese fortune cookies at
rhetorical borderlands, to face dynamics, to the yin-yang of indirection
and directness, to reciprocity and individualism, to the rhetorical performances of my fellow Chinese Americans.

These topics, interconnected and wide-ranging, aim to present several
clusters of contingent conditions and interdependent relationships, and
they seek to constitute an elaborate, but no less situated, context filled
with local histories, present-day face-to-face encounters, and reflections
not of harmony, but of togetherness-in-difference. In a way, these topics—almost like the "yinwei" (因为, "because") part in the Chinese connective pair "yinwei ...... suoyi ......" (因为 ....所以 ......, "because ...
so ...")—establish a "causal" framework necessary for this chapter—the

comment-like "suoyi" ("so") part—to emerge, to complete the "utterance"[1] (read as this project) started by these "topics." In other words, this chapter fills in the second part of this topic-comment structure, as it represents a necessary outcome (or "so," 所以) emerging out of these "causes" (or "becauses," 因为). Neither "delayed" nor "dispreferred," this chapter in particular seeks to spotlight those hidden dissimilarities between the Chinese fortune cookie and Chinese American rhetoric and to open up more opportunities, more moments of articulation, as I press forward to continue practicing Chinese American rhetoric.

Productive vagueness is particularly at work when one uses analogies or metaphors to develop connections between events and/or things that otherwise may not embody any shared essence or identity. My effort in this book to use the Chinese fortune cookie as a generative analogy to articulate the making of Chinese American rhetoric is no exception. It is only fitting that I now come back to the Chinese fortune cookie, to tease out these instances of productive vagueness and to bring these interconnected conditions and relationships into a sharper focus, into another related "topic"—so that my fellow border residents, as well as my European American interlocutors, can develop their own comments on this topic and complete, from their perspectives, this "yet-to-be-completed" utterance of mine.

Born of two competing traditions and made viable in a border zone, the Chinese fortune cookie is real and identifiable. On the other hand, Chinese American rhetoric, as I have so far developed it, may not be as easily identifiable, and it may not be as quickly reducible to a list of traits or features. How do I then account for this apparent difference?

First, like the Chinese fortune cookie, Chinese American rhetoric is a hybrid, too: it is born of two competing traditions at rhetorical borderlands. However, it becomes visible and viable not by securing a logical or unified order, but by participating in a process of becoming, where meanings are distributed in a flow of events and/or things and where significations are predicated upon each and every particular experience. In this process of becoming, Chinese American rhetoric is not to be had either by abstraction or by anyone searching for fixed features. Rather, the making of Chinese American rhetoric lies in reflective encounters, and it finds its markings or moorings through re-visioned histories, emergent alignments, and even unsettled associations. Otherwise stated, in a land of border zones, meanings are not necessarily to be calculated in terms of orders, patterns, or expected outcomes. Instead, they are defined and determined in terms of our distributed experiences and our negotiated positions. As a result, there may not be any generalizable patterns to the kinds of reflective encounters I present in this book.

For example, I may not be able to ascribe my classroom experiences and my reflections of Chinese practices, linearly and unequivocally, to the calling of "lian" (脸) and "mianzi" (面子), and my students' experiences and reflections to that of positive and negative face. Nor can Min-Zhan Lu tie her cravings for a cup of good coffee to her being Chinese, to her being Chinese American, or to her being an American Chinese immigrant (*Shanghai Quartet* 243). And nor can I really point to any recurring pattern behind the rhetorical performances of my fellow Chinese Americans and say, "That's it! That's Chinese American rhetoric right there!" What has collectively emerged out of these encounters, however, is a hybrid rhetoric, marked by an in-between subject position and realized through particularizing instances of communicative activity. At times ambivalent and unsettling, these kinds of encounters can be no less enabling and energizing.

Therefore, both my students and I begin to see what lies beyond our own face needs, and to learn how to negotiate tensions and conflicts each time we face up in the classroom and at our life's crossings. We do so by deploying a rhetoric that rejects dualism, and that engages both Chinese and European American rhetorical traditions. Similarly, because of such encounters, Lu can begin figuring out "new ways of seeing and talking about" the question "Do the Chinese drink coffee?" (*Shanghai Quartet* 230). With growing confidence, I can respond to "Where are you from?" with an answer that not only "messes up" the boundary between indirection and directness, but also enables us—my interlocutors and myself—to see what each wants from the other and to envision what opportunities and challenges await both of us. In this regard, the making of Chinese American rhetoric becomes quite specific—to the extent that each and every one of our encounters is informed and marked by these reflections and by these negotiations; to the extent that each and every one of these encounters enriches this web of interdependence, in spite of our own ambivalences and apprehensions.

Second, for both border residents and European Americans, reading fortunes and eating fortune cookies have probably become a welcome indulgence at the end of every Chinese meal here in America. We share our fortunes with comforting laughs or loud protestations or both, and we then go on with our lives without necessarily thinking about the need to modify our behavior in relation to the predictions or injunctions conveyed in those fortunes. In other words, while there may be a lot of illocution or uptake in such an event, there is, most likely, not much perlocution as a result of it (Austin, *How to Do Things* 116–19). That is to say, whatever "auspicious" readings we like to claim or embrace from our fortunes, in spite of the sneaking suspicion to the contrary, we hardly act on such readings beyond the confines of the restaurant.

On the other hand, when Chinese and European American rhetorical traditions come in contact face to face, and when we are engaged in nurturing togetherness-in-difference, both illocution and perlocution are a must. Namely, our experiences at rhetorical borderlands will inevitably call for and lead to changes in our behavior, in our views about ourselves and the other, and in our visions for the future—changes that Anzaldúa refers to as "a new mythos" (101). For us border residents, then, this new mythos is not *just* centered upon illuminating our own 脸 and 面子, upon making indirection mean more than innuendos or allusions, or upon moving away from the ideology of individualism as our modus operandi. Rather, it has to be enriched and constituted by our on-going experiences, in which we border residents engage the other not to apply a "reverse orientalist" logic, but to develop a different discourse, and to effect positive changes in how we talk about the world, as well as about ourselves. And as these experiences command their own context, and as they bring about their own web of interdependence, they create for us a new sense of identity and authority—one that can be indeterminate or ambiguous, but one that can never be not intensely rich in associations and significations.

Third, the Chinese fortune cookie, to all intents and purposes, has become a natural part of eating a Chinese meal in America, even though, as I have suggested in Chapter One, it could be considered a gastronomical contradiction par excellence. In comparison, there is nothing natural at all about articulating and practicing the making of Chinese American rhetoric. While it is a fact of life that Chinese and European American cultures are now forever entangled, we border residents do face several choices.

We Chinese and Chinese Americans can reject or silence our "authentic" selves in order to be "a full-fledged subject of the new society" (JanMohamed 101) and in order to write direct, transparent English equipped with subheadings and other transitional phrases—almost in the same way as Shen did soon after he came to America (460–61). Or we could remain on the margin, like the exile, nursing this longing for our ancestral culture while forever switching between 脸 and 面子 and positive and negative face, between indirection and directness, and between the discourse of 怒 and the ideology of individualism. Such practices remind us of how Lu juggled between her (Western humanistic) home discourse and her (Marxist) school discourse as she was growing up in Shanghai ("From Silence to Words" 438; *Shanghai Quartet* 254–64). Or we could practice a hybrid rhetoric by engaging the representation by the dominant of ourselves (read as our 脸 and 面子, our indirection, and our lack of individualism), by negotiating our borderland residency between the exile and the immigrant, and by claiming both "the ghostly otherness" and America at the same time—even though the latter is "so thick with ghosts," too (Kingston, *The Woman Warrior* 113).

Not only does each choice entail its own communicative and material consequences, but, more importantly, each choice reveals an individual's shifting allegiance(s), and it bespeaks an individual's desire to use language to represent his or her borderland experiences. Speaking for myself, the decision to nurture and enact Chinese American rhetoric is very much grounded in my own desire to challenge binary paradigms, to nurture an in-between subject position, and to seek resonances not only with my ancestral culture, but also with other rhetorics, with other emerging voices. Differently stated, my on-going alignments at rhetorical borderlands are never divorced from these voices, which are forever implicated in, and continuously impress themselves upon, my communicative actions and my rhetorical choices. Therefore, unless I take the time to open up, as I have done in this book, the Chinese fortune cookie, it will most likely remain a "harmonious" constituent of a Chinese meal on this side of the Pacific. By contrast, unless I get to the bottom of things, and unless I call a spade a spade, the making of Chinese American rhetoric will probably be seen as incoherent, as unnatural, or as unspecific.

Finally, there seems to be an equilibrium born of the Chinese fortune cookie. Without exception, since its inception, each and every fortune cookie continues to represent both traditions well—one tradition uses message-stuffed pastry as a means of communication, and the other serves desert at the end of a meal. I am afraid there is no equilibrium yet in the making of Chinese American rhetoric.

For one thing, it is still English—not Chinese or some other, third language—that serves as the means of representation. The use of English in this endeavor of mine obviously has consequences. To be brutally direct—though with fear of injuring my face perhaps beyond redemption, it favors European American rhetoric, because it helps European American rhetoric stay as the unmarked or "exnominated" norm. On the other hand, Chinese rhetorical tradition may continue to be seen as marked, and on the outside looking in. Until there is, ideally, a different language—a rhetorical creole of sorts—emerging to serve as the code for Chinese American rhetoric, we border residents will have to acknowledge and deal with this phenomenon here and now. That is to say, we need to ask ourselves: How can we use English in such a way that promotes other voices and that incorporates other modes of doing things with words? More specifically put, how can we represent Chinese face, indirectness, and personhood in a discourse whose undergirding ideology espouses something very different, and whose discursive authority is almost being challenged by such representations? Or how can we, to use Eoyang's words, "embody in a majority language the strangeness of a minority culture, and manage to make that strangeness accessible to the reader" (23) and, I might add, to the user?

For another, the making of Chinese American rhetoric on this side of the Pacific will be inflected, for the foreseeable future at least, by these historically complex, highly imbalanced relationships of power that have depended on European American ways of speaking for representation and for consolidation. To challenge these relationships and to redress this imbalance, we border residents have to interrogate and bring to the fore those conditions or forces that have helped make the representation of these relationships so dominating and controlling, without them having to justify themselves. In so doing, we can begin to blur the boundaries, to foster differing voices, and to cultivate resonances as we engage, reflect, and persuade. Without such interrogations, on the other hand, we may end up either generating an oppositional discourse on the margin or constructing Chinese American rhetoric in ways that are reminiscent of the dominant paradigms and their unmarked modalities.

And there is another challenge facing Chinese American rhetoric. On the one hand, Chinese American rhetoric, because of its newly emergent characteristics, risks being put on display and/or being appropriated by (dominant) European American rhetoric. The more it gets appropriated, the more likely it is that it will begin to lose its creative, transformative potential. On the other hand, future practitioners of Chinese American rhetoric—for example, young Chinese and Chinese Americans—may choose either to further mix their Chinese American ways of speaking and writing with the rhetorical repertoire of another group of color, or to speak like mainstream European Americans in some specific situational contexts. Consequently, togetherness-in-difference will take on a different set of associations and significances.

The response to this kind of challenge will be contingent upon a number of forces. For example, to what extent will orientalist logic continue to exert its subtle influence upon what we say and how we say it? Will young Chinese and Chinese Americans feel so accepted by their European American counterparts that there will be no need for them to deploy this hybrid rhetoric in order to speak out their rhetorical and cultural identity? Or will they continue to feel "recognized," and will they want to appeal to other ethnic rhetorics to empower themselves and to enhance their rhetorical expressiveness? Will Chinese American rhetoric then begin to signify a togetherness-in-difference that embraces Chinese rhetoric, European American rhetoric, and other rhetorics of color?

Because of these unequal relationships, and because of these uncertain discursive dynamics, I could very well get discouraged or even silenced as I continue to practice Chinese American rhetoric. Should this ever come to pass, I would stop at my favorite local Chinese restaurant to order a Chinese meal with a bowl and a pair of chopsticks, and to wait to enjoy a Chinese fortune cookie at the end of the meal. Not that I necessarily trust the healing power of the "good fortune" in any fortune cookie, but because I can use the occasion to reflect upon the meaning of the Chinese fortune cookie again, and to remind myself and my interlocutors that it is viable and vital to practice and promote Chinese American rhetoric, just as it is now commonplace to enjoy a fortune cookie at the end of every Chinese meal in America—uncertainties and ambivalences notwithstanding. After all, if I can echo Anzaldúa, quoted in my epigraph for this chapter, the future belongs to us border residents straddling two or more cultures, to those of us who learn to cultivate and speak out our in-between subject positions, and who learn to practice the discourse of hybridity through the making of Chinese American rhetoric and/or other ethnic rhetorics. In a word, it belongs to those of us who learn to read a Chinese fortune cookie with a sense of history and with a disposition toward nurturing togetherness-in-difference at every situated-distributive turn imaginable.

ENDNOTES

INTRODUCTION
THINKING THROUGH PARADOXES

1. McLuhan, in *The Gutenberg Galaxy*, returns to the metaphor of "global village." He writes, "But certainly the electro-magnetic discoveries have recreated the simultaneous 'field' in all human affairs so that the human family now exists under conditions of a 'global village'" (31). The term "global village," as Susan Herring aptly points out, is an appealing example of an oxymoron: a village is typically of a small size whereas the globe is vast (vii). And in the words of the *New York Times'* columnist Thomas Friedman, globalization has made our world "flat."

2. The use of the word "resonance" also aims to evoke a way of thinking where different phenomena or things come to interact with and influence each other, not necessarily by some shared essence, but by association, by complementary opposition. For example, drawing upon Donald Munro's work (*The Concept of Man*), social psychologist Richard Nisbett argues that the ancient Chinese classified things not necessarily according to their shared attributes. Rather, things were put into different classes based on whether or not they could influence each other through resonance (138; also see 27–28, and note 28 of Chapter One).

3. I am borrowing this phrase from Hall and Ames (*Anticipating China* xxii). They use this phrase to characterize one of the tendencies in the West to rationalize the (imperfection of the) circle, to render it "in some formulaic manner that more closely approximates the demands of exactness and certitude" (xxii).

4. The text that bears his name and is attributed to him is generally regarded as one of the classic Daoist texts in Chinese history. Not much is known about Zhuangzi and about his background. Therefore, (the use of) Zhuangzi represents, for many, less of a specific individual known to us through history than of the mind or minds embodied in the text called *Zhuangzi* (Watson, "Introduction" 3; Combs 16–17). I am here using Watson's translation. Throughout this book I will be using the pinyin system for the romanization of Chinese characters, and I will include, if called for, the Wade-Giles system in parentheses.

5. This is exactly what Humpty Dumpty does in Lewis Carroll's *Through the Looking-Glass*. As we all probably remember, Humpty Dumpty chooses to use "an un-birthday present" to mean "a present given when it isn't your birthday" (162) and "glory" to mean "there's a nice knock-down argument for you" (163). Such practices utterly confuse Alice, drawing repeated objections from her.

6. On the other hand, the colonialist and the anthropologist "apprehend the new culture, not as a field of subjectivity, but rather as an object of and for their gaze" (102). For the colonialist, his success lies in not "going native," not getting contaminated by the new culture. And for the anthropologist who may be obliged to learn the native language and culture, he or she cannot afford to "go native" all the way—to do so would mean "the loss of an 'objectivity' essential to professional status" (102). In short, the main difference between the two is that the gaze of the colonialist is "military, administrative, and economic," whereas the gaze of the (traditional) anthropologist is "epistemological and organizational" (102).

7. For Bakhtin, such understanding can be achieved only if the person "understands to be *located outside* the object of his or her creative understanding—in time, in space, in culture" ("Response" 7; emphasis original).

CHAPTER ONE
OPENING TOPICS: READING CHINESE FORTUNE COOKIE

1. Kennedy's work on comparative rhetoric is a good example—where Kennedy anchors his discussions of other cultures' rhetorical traditions, quite explicitly, within the Western rhetorical paradigm of logos, ethos, and pathos. As a result, Chinese American rhetoric can become more visible, more viable insofar as it can measure up to the unmarked norm of this dominant tradition.

2. The term "order of discourse" is evidently Michel Foucault's. It refers to a social space structured and indeed constituted by different types of discourse, and it is where knowledge is formed and produced. Because discursive rules and categories are both constitutive of discourse and knowledge and controlled by exclusionary, prohibitive procedures, they remain invisible and thus natural, making it virtually impossible to think independently of them.

3. See, for example, Schroeder et al. and Gilyard and Nunley.

4. I am appropriating Pierre Bourdieu here, largely to highlight, with the use of "cultural capital," how cultural acquisitions, including knowledge, skills, and other resources, impose themselves with authority and in an unequal fashion. For more on this concept and on its link to other forms of capital such as symbolic capital, see Bourdieu ("Forms;" *Outline* 171–83).

5. For a related point, see my discussion of multicultural rhetorics toward the end of this chapter.

6. The term "distributed" was initially used by Roy Pea and David Perkins to describe how a person's knowledge is not just banked in one's head, but "in the notes that one has put into accessible notebooks, in the books with underlined passages on one's shelves, in the handbooks one has learned how to consult, in the information sources one has hitched up to the computer, in the friends one can call up to get a reference or a 'steer,' and so on almost endlessly" (Bruner 106)—hence this situated-distributive nature of knowledge. My appropriation of their term here aims to claim this situated-distributive perspective for the making of Chinese American rhetoric.

7. In the year 1353 peasant leader Zhu Yuanzhang, who became the founding emperor of the Ming Dynasty (1368–1644), had hidden inside the moon-cakes the message about the time and place of the rebellion against the Mongols of the Yuan Dynasty (1206–1368), and the moon-cakes were then distributed to the villagers on the day of the Mid-Autumn Festival (Stepanchuk and Wong 55; Dorothy Perkins 21).

8. According to Dorothy Perkins, the fortune cookie was invented in the 1920s by a worker in the Kay Heong Noodle Factory in San Francisco (167). But another legend has it that the fortune cookie was first introduced as a variation of the Japanese rice cracker in the Japanese Tea Garden in San Francisco's Golden Gate Park to accompany the tea (Driscoll). Still another legend states that it was invented between 1918 and 1919 in Los Angeles by David Jung, founder of the Hong Kong Noodle Company (Driscoll). So, the dispute continues over who "owns" the idea of creating fortune cookies on this side of the Pacific.

9. Ang also invokes the image of *nyonya* food, one of the culinary attractions in Malaysia developed by people of Chinese descent out of their encounter with local, Malay spices and ingredients. And she further recounts the experience of seeing a young man of Chinese descent who grew up in Surinam performing the best salsa dance at a Caribbean party in Amsterdam (35).

10. Malea Powell, a mixed-blood of Indiana Miami, Eastern Shawnee, and Euro-American ancestry, uses the word "survivance"—a blend of "survival" and "resistance"—to characterize the language used by Sarah Winnemucca Hopkins and Charles Alexander Eastman, two nineteenth-century American Indian intellectuals.

She suggests that it is this language that allowed them "to reimagine and, literally, refigure 'the Indian'" and to transform "their object-status within colonial discourse into a subject-status, a presence instead of an absence" (400).

11. One such example Pratt provides was the letter which, written in 1613 in a mixture of Quechua and ungrammatical Spanish by American Indian Guaman Poma to King Philip III of Spain, consisted of twelve hundred pages of both written text and elaborate line drawings with explanatory captions. It was discovered in 1908 in the Copenhagen library, though no one knew how it got there or how long it had been there, and no one bothered to read it—in part because Quechua was not known as a written language in 1908. It was not until the late 1970s that Western scholars began to read Guaman Poma's text as "the extraordinary intercultural tour de force" (Pratt, "Contact Zone" 34; also see her *Imperial Eyes* 3–4).

12. The term "transculturation" was originally coined by Cuban sociologist Fernando Ortiz in the 1940s. It seems, though, that Pratt is, perhaps by oversight, focusing only on the subordinated groups' use and appropriation of materials transmitted by a dominant culture (also see *Imperial Eyes* 6) without stressing enough how this creative process also embodies local experiences and local idioms—in the same way that autoethnographical texts do. Ortiz writes, "the word 'transculturation' better expresses the different phases of the process of transition from one culture to another because this does not consist merely in acquiring another culture, which is what the English word 'acculturation' really implies, but the process also necessarily involves the loss or uprooting of a previous culture, which could be defined as a deculturation. In addition, it carries the idea of the consequent creation of new cultural phenomena, which could be called neoculturation" (103).

13. See Chapter Three for a related discussion.

14. Contact language, though, doesn't have to be improvised all the time. It could be a language native to one group. For example, French might be described as a contact language for speakers of English right after the Norman Conquest in 1066 (*The Concise Oxford Dictionary of Linguistics*).

15. In the same essay Hall and Rosner point out that the metaphor of contact zone "turns on a troubling contradiction." They specifically argue that while the image of contact "suggests a benign or even genial relationship," Pratt's definition of contact zone entails violence and battle (107). Obviously this suggestion chooses to ignore Pratt's own explanation about the meaning of "contact" in the metaphor, and about what she aims to foreground with the borrowed term (*Imperial Eyes* 6–7). In addition, it fails to take into account how the term "contact language" is used in linguistics—where, briefly, its use connotes no "benign" or "genial" relationship, but halting, chaotic, though no less interlocking, communication, often, to use Pratt's words again, "within radically asymmetrical relations of power" (*Imperial Eyes* 7). Brown also sees Pratt's "contact zone" as an agonistic, rather than a benign, trope; in fact, "contact" for him conveys violence in a variety of linguistic contexts (114–15). His critique of Pratt is not that her explication of "contact zone" lacks relevance to resistance pedagogy, but that it "proves more agonistic in theory than in practice" (116).

16. Let me be more specific here. In *Imperial Eyes,* which came out in 1992, Pratt characterizes "contact zone" as "the space in which peoples geographically and historically separated come into contact with each other and establish ongoing relations, usually involving conditions of coercion, radical inequality, and intractable conflict" (6). This characterization is not much different from what she offers in "Arts of the Contact Zone." In "Criticism in the Contact Zone," an essay that was published a year later (1993), Pratt proposes a "contact perspective" in order to expose the fallacy of the homogeneous speech community and to foreground the socially and historically structured co-presence of those marginalized or invisible groups (88). In other words, the emphasis here is not so much on conflicts, clashes, or hierarchies—

which are assumed and very much present—as on the presence of the invisible other. Pratt further defines borderlands as "sites of ongoing critical and *inventive interaction* with the dominant culture, as permeable contact zones across which significations move in many directions" ("Criticism" 89; emphasis added). Hall and Rosner see the insertion of "inventive interaction" in the definition as evidence of revision on Pratt's part, but I see that as a reaffirmation of how the subordinated groups at contact zones are necessarily *in dialogue with* or *select and invent from* the representations of them by the dominant culture (Pratt, "Contact Zone" 35, 36).

17.   This line of reasoning is in part informed by Eckert and McConnell-Ginet's insight that gender and language studies suffer from "abstracting gender and language from the social practices that produce their particular forms in given communities" (484). For them, our understanding of gender and language has to be rooted "in the everyday social practices of particular local communities" and in how they are "jointly constructed in those practices" (486).

18.   Incidentally, Chinese martial arts are an example of hybridity: they originated from the teachings of Bodhidharma at the Shaolin Temple (a Buddhist monastery) when he visited China in the sixthcentury, and they were further enriched by various Chinese philosophies after they were introduced.

19.   "Common sense" assumptions are examples of ideology insofar as they are in support of existing power structures—though they may not appear to be ideological because they are so "commonsensical" now (Fairclough 88–89). And this effort to denaturalize what has been taken for granted or what has been considered "common sense" reminds me of ordinary language philosopher J. L. Austin's not so ordinary plea against our tendency to treat words as transparent, as facts or things. He writes: "we need therefore to prise them [words] off the world, to hold them apart from and against it, so that we can realize their inadequacies and arbitrariness, and can relook at the world without blinkers" ("A Plea for Excuses" 182).

20.   Critical discourse analysis is not without its critics. For example, Tyrwhitt-Drake argues that much of critical discourse analysis is flawed because it is based on "partial description and political commitment rather than on rigorous analysis and open-minded enquiry" (1082). For me, though, partiality evidenced in critical discourse analysis is not due to any absence of rigorous analysis, but due to a self-acknowledged presence of political commitment. For a rebuttal of Tyrwhitt-Drake's critique, see Flowerdew.

21.   For example, eighteenth-century Britain witnessed the need to standardize, to codify English to ensure minimum variation in form. Further, English uniformity was promoted in the interests of the newly created union (read as the dominant class). For more on this, see Crowley.

22.   Fairclough distinguishes between three types of value any linguistic form may embody: "experiential," "relational," and "expressive." Experiential value represents the text producer's experience of the natural or social world, focusing on contents, knowledge, and beliefs. Relational value refers to the social relationships enacted in the text. And expressive value refers to subjects and social identities (93–94). Obviously, Fairclough's classification here is reminiscent of Halliday's semantic system that consists of ideational, interpersonal, and textual components (128–33) though Fairclough does not explicitly mention this connection.

23.   I will have a lot to say on this point in Chapter Four when I engage individualism and 恕 (Chinese reciprocity).

24.   For Said, it is a vacillation between the West's "delight in—or fear of—novelty" of Islam and its "contempt for what is familiar" (59). Such vacillation results from adopting "a method of controlling what seems to be a threat to some established view of things" (59).

25.   Halliday characterizes one type of oppositional discourse as "antilanguage." An antilanguage is created as "a conscious alternative" to the dominant or established

discourse(s) (164). Examples include the language of the criminal underworld or the coded language of the slaves.

26.   I am here drawing upon Gee's work in literacy studies. Gee distinguishes between discourse, which refers to "connected stretches of language that make sense" (*Social Linguistics* 127), and Discourse, which is "composed of ways of talking, listening, (often, too, reading and writing), acting, interacting, believing, valuing, and using tools and objects, in particular settings at specific times, so as to display and recognize a particular social identity" (128). Therefore, a primary Discourse constitutes our first social identity, and it serves as a framework for how we are going to acquire and learn other Discourses later in life (*Social Linguistics* 137–45).

27.   According to Geertz, the distinction between "experience-near" and "experience-distant" concepts was originally formulated by psychoanalyst Heinz Kohut (57). Experience-near concepts are concepts that the natives might naturally and effortlessly use to define what they or their fellows see, feel, think, or imagine. On the other hand, experience-distant concepts are those that specialists use to "forward their scientific, philosophic, or practical aims" (57). Geertz makes it quite clear that the distinction here is more of a matter of degree than of polar opposition. For him, the real question is "what roles the two sorts of concepts play in anthropological analysis" (57). For me, though, the real question becomes this: What happens when experience-near and experience-distant concepts face up to each other at rhetorical borderlands? And what roles do such encounters play in the making of Chinese American rhetoric, as well as in the transformation of these two different sets of concepts—especially when experience-distant concepts have already been abstracted from the conditions of the present?

28.   Commenting on the Chinese language, which Hall and Ames characterize as the "language of deference" that recognizes "mutual resonances among instances of communicative activity" (*Anticipating China* 229), they write: "There is no referencing beyond these acts of communication as they resonate with one another and with the entertained meanings of the models from the tradition" (*Anticipating China* 229). Of course, such characterization should not be taken to mean that acts of communication in such a language do not refer to reality, true or imaginary—because reality is always being reflected, selected, and deflected in the process (Burke, *Language* 45). On the other hand, I am far less inclined to subscribe to their claim that the Chinese language lays no emphasis on the grammar and syntax that one finds in the more rationalistic languages of the West (229).

CHAPTER TWO
FACE TO FACE: CHINESE AND EUROPEAN AMERICAN

1.   As a matter of fact, communication scholar Jia has gone so far as to suggest that face "may define the true nature of Chinese communication, Chinese culture, and the Chinese character and may indicate the route to social and cultural change in China" (2). Related to the concept of face is the term "renqing" (人情, "human feelings"), which connotes how one should conduct oneself in social relationships, and which also refers to obligations of reciprocity shaped by social networks and emotional attachment. For more on the dynamics of "renqing" and its connection to "guanxi" (关系, "relationships"), see Yang (67–70) and Hwang.

2.   It is clear that Brown and Levinson's intent is to offer a universal concept of face that can transcend spatial-temporal boundaries. For a detailed discussion of the untenable nature of their claim, see, for example, Matsumoto.

3.   The Chinese character "mian" (面) was first found on oracle bone inscriptions ("jiaguwen," 甲骨文) in the late Shang Dynasty (circa 1200 BCE), and the character "lian" (脸) originated in the Yuan Dynasty (1206–1368) (Jia 17). And according to Zhongtian Yi, 面子 may have come from "mianju" (面具) meaning "mask" or "face tool," which was used to communicate with the deities or spirits in ancient China (qtd. in Jia 17).

4.   In fact, Cheng further argues that Chinese face (both 脸 and 面子) is deeply rooted in or directly based upon three principles of Confucian social and moral philosophy, which aim to articulate how self should cultivate him- or herself in relation to others, to larger familial, social relationships. For more on the link between Chinese face and Confucian ideology, see "The Concept of Face" (338–44).

5.   Occasionally, "lianmian" (脸面) is used to refer to either 脸 or 面子, though it is a more formal variant.

6.   For more on their dynamics and their contextual dependence, see Mao ("Beyond Politeness Theory").

7.   The Chinese expression "si yao mianzi huo shouzui" (死要面子活受罪, "suffer mightily to gain 面子"), vividly identifies the danger of pursuing 面子 at any cost. Should this happen, the amount of 面子 one gains loses its value, and in fact whatever one gains is tainted with negative connotations, with vanity and shallowness. Similarly, "da zhong lian chong pangzi" (打肿脸充胖子) literally means to beat one's face swollen so that it makes one look big. Metaphorically speaking, this expression mocks at those individuals who would pay any price to gain face ("yao lian," 要脸).

8.   In the same essay, Yum traces this discursive tendency back to Confucian ideology, to its emphasis on humaneness and reciprocity. See Chapter Four for a more detailed discussion on Confucian ideology and on the discourse of reciprocity.

9.   See note 27 from Chapter One.

10.   For more on the use of citations by Chinese writers, and on their rhetorical and social contexts, see Bloch and Chi.

11.   For example, de Kadt shows that face in the Zulu language is oriented more toward what is socially correct than toward what one should do for one's own needs (181–84). She also points out that the view of the generalized other plays an important role in the shaping of self in Zulu culture (178–79).

12.   In articulating this contrast between Chinese and European American face, I have no intention whatsoever of idealizing Chinese face. As I have indicated above, if pursued at any cost, Chinese face (脸 and 面子) could lead to undesirable consequences, upsetting this reciprocal balance between self and the public. Cheng writes, "But in so far personal ambition and self-interest become the motive force for applying face, *face* becomes a disguise and cover-up of intrigue, conspiracy, arbitrariness, willfulness, and personal self-assertion at the expense of public good, as well as true virtue and law" ("The Concept of Face" 341).

13.   I will draw on *Shanghai Quartet* again in Chapter Three when I discuss the complementary relationship between indirection and directness.

14.   For R. Lakoff, to issue an apology is to perform an emotionally charged speech act because it changes "the world for participants in terms of their relative status and their future relationship" (23). She further suggests that what counts most is the form of an apology, or simply the fact that an apology has been made and delivered, rather than the sincerity of an apology (31).

15.   There are many layers of irony in the film, ranging from winning because of a broken rib, not because of "being kicked where it counts," to detaining the Chief only after he has saved Qiu Ju's and her baby boy's life, to the Chinese justice system that fails Qiu Ju even though the perpetrator is being punished. According to Silbergeld, the main reason that the film has left American audiences and critics disappointed has to do with the fact that "they missed the ironic tone, lodged in small, comic moments, that animates the film" (122). Another reason why this film has disappointed American audiences, while it was voted the Hundred Flowers' most popular film of the year inside China (1992), is its quasi-documentary style, through which everything in the film looks just like it really happened (Silbergeld 126–27). For me, though, their disappointment may also have come from their failure to appreciate the intricacies of Chinese face, to read Chinese face on its own terms.

16. A word or two should perhaps be said here about my use of Kagan and Kristol. While Kagan and Kristol, extremely conservative and blatantly ethnocentric, may or may not represent the Bush administration in this cross-cultural confrontation, their general views about the "irrational," face-obsessive behavior by the Chinese leadership are not that atypical. For example, Richard Cohen, writing in the *Washington Post* the day after this diplomatic crisis was resolved, characterizes Beijing's behavior as "irrational," "nuts," "unpredictable," and just plan "weird." Joseph Bosco, who teaches at Georgetown University's School of Foreign Service, writing in the *Los Angeles Times* a day before the resolution of the crisis, blames the Chinese communist leadership for the revived negative images of China in the American public. He characterizes its behavior as "cutting off its nose to spite its face"—a kind of conduct that is anything but rational. Titled "Work for Safeguards with China," the editorial in the *Los Angeles Times*, commenting on the resolution the day after, also concludes that China's handling of the incident is a blow to the political trust that is necessary to maintaining the economic ties between the two countries. On the other hand, Butterfield, writing in the *New York Times*, attempts to contextualize China's demand for an apology by tracing Chinese face-saving culture all the way back to Confucian ideology, to its value system that stresses conformity over individuality, and collective ethos over personal responsibility. In a word, there seems to be a tendency in the major national newspapers to characterize the behavior of the Chinese leadership, in varying degrees of intensity, as "irrational," i.e., the very antithesis of European American rationality.

CHAPTER THREE
INDIRECTION VERSUS DIRECTNESS: A RELATION OF COMPLEMENTARITY

1. For example, Arthur Smith observes that it is impossible for a foreigner to tell what a Chinese means from merely hearing what the same individual says. The reason is that "the speaker did not express what he had in mind, but something else more or less cognate to it, from which he wished his meaning or a part of it to be inferred" (66). For Smith's observation of Chinese face, see Chapter Two.

2. Of course, I suspect there are perhaps as many Chinese who can be just as direct in situations such as in taxis, train ticket sales, and banks. Scollon and Scollon suggest that these "exceptions" are due to the fact that "the participants are and remain strangers to each other" ("Face Parameters" 135).

3. On the other hand, Tan's negotiation does not entirely hinge upon her ability to speak and/or write in Chinese, because what she is negotiating can simply be between two cultural, rather than ontological, realities shaped and promoted by our discourses about assertiveness and about wishy-washiness. I have more to say about this point shortly.

4. Pennycook reports a different kind of disconnect. One of his Chinese students told him that she actually found English writing to be circuitous, going round and round and round, with its introductions, conclusions, and topic sentences. By contrast, she felt that the opposite was true of Chinese, and that "Chinese was written in a straight, clear line" (161). To accentuate her point, the student drew the two textual patterns in the air—patterns that were, Pennycook tells us, so reminiscent of Robert Kaplan's influential diagrams of English and Oriental cultural thought patterns ("Cultural Thought Patterns"). However, this time the diagrams were being formed almost perfectly in reverse (Pennycook 161).

5. By "reify," I am referring to how European American directness has been treated as "a fixed, idealized entity removed from the vagaries of time, place, and use"—an entity, though, "that is always in process, located in and subject to ongoing and varying material practice" (Horner and Trimbur 596).

6.   See Chapter One for a related discussion of the perceived stability or homogeneity of European American rhetoric.

7.   According to Hall and Ames, the notion of correlative thinking may be traced back to Marcel Granet's *La pensée chinoise*, written in 1934, where "correlativity is taken to be a characteristic of the 'Chinese mind'" (*Anticipating China* 295). On the other hand, in 1938 Professor Chang Tung-sun published an essay in Chinese, which was independent of Granet's thesis and which later was translated into English (1959). In this essay Chang suggests that Chinese culture is informed by what he calls "correlation logic" (316)—a logic that focuses exclusively on "the correlational implications between different signs" (312) and that relies on "nonexclusive classification, analogical definition" (316).

8.   There are different legends behind the origin of the twelve animals of Chinese astrology. According to one legend, the dying Buddha asked all the animals in creation to visit him on New Year's Day to bid him farewell before he departed his life on earth, but only twelve animals came. The Buddha thus rewarded each of the twelve who came with a year bearing its personality traits (Dorothy Perkins 630).

9.   The Chinese further associate each cycle with one of the Five Processes—Wood, Fire, Soil, Metal, and Water—to form a sixty-year cycle. Each of the Five Processes is then associated with several other aspects, such as "yin" and "yang" (Graham, *Disputers* 325–34; Dorothy Perkins 630). In this sense, the world, according to the Chinese, is one of correlation, both expansive and unlimited.

10.   So, in a scheme of twos that features "king, men," "lion, beasts," "king, throne," and "chairman, chair," by metaphor the lion is the king of beasts, and the king is a lion among men. By metonymy, the monarchy is the throne and the chairmanship is the chair (Bodde 88).

11.   This characterization is widely shared. In discussing the yin-yang system, Graham states that "China tends to treat opposites as complementary, the West as conflicting" (*Disputers* 331). Similarly, Hall and Ames argue that the correlative explanation of various processes in terms of "complementary contrasts" is "fundamental to the Chinese tradition" (*Anticipating China* 130).

12.   The other four "qi" are: wind, rain, dark, and light (Raphals, *Sharing the Light* 146).

13.   For example, "yin" is associated with earth, moon, north, below, squareness, darkness, cold, wetness, softness, quiescence, femininity, and much else; whereas "yang" is associated with heaven, sun, south, above, roundness, brightness, heat, dryness, hardness, activity, masculinity, and much else (Bodde 100).

14.   Roland Barthes describes the process—where the dominant group in society becomes normalized and thus invisible—as one of "exnomination," and he sees the bourgeoisie as an exnominated group that "has obliterated its name in passing from reality to representation" (qtd. in Lakoff 53). As Lakoff explains, "They just *are*. Their rules become the rules" (54; emphasis original).

15.   Of course, Chinese also has a subject-verb construction, just as English has a topic-comment construction, which is often marked by "as to," "in regard to," or "you know." On the other hand, a topic in Chinese can be separated from the comment by a pause or by one of the pause particles (Li and Thompson, *Mandarin Chinese* 86). And regardless of how topics are marked in different languages, to quote Li and Thompson, "some languages can be more insightfully described by taking the concept of topic to be basic, while others can be more insightfully described by taking the notion of subject as basic" ("Subject and Topic" 460).

16.   Kirkpatrick has argued that Modern Standard Chinese should not be characterized, across the board, as following the topic-comment structure, and that there is a difference between "topic" that concerns what the sentence is all about and "topic" that sets the frame within which the sentence is presented ("Topic-Comment"

95). He has suggested, therefore, that sentences that follow the latter meaning of "topic" should be characterized as examples, not of the topic-comment structure, but of the modifier-modified structure ("Topic-Comment" 107–10). Either characterization, incidentally, reinforces the discursive interdependence I am trying to highlight in this part of my discussion.

17. For more on these connective pairs, see Li and Thompson (*Mandarin Chinese* 635–40).

18. Interestingly enough, the English word "thing" is "dong-xi" (东西) in Chinese, which literally means "east-west" and which expresses "a nonsubstantive relationship" (Ames and Rosemont, "Introduction" 22). On the other hand, the popular news program on NPR (National Public Radio) is called "All Things Considered," but not "All Events Considered"—a not-insignificant choice of word, in my view.

19. This kind of characterization certainly qualifies as another myth about Chinese (see Tong 37–39 for other myths about Chinese from a historical perspective). But this much needs to be said here: Becker's characterization about Chinese should not be mistaken for skepticism toward language as a medium of representation in Chinese intellectual tradition (Tong 34; also see the discussion toward the end of my Introduction).

20. Ames and Rosemont have argued that the classical written Chinese is a distinct, visually oriented medium of communication independent of the spoken language. For a detailed analysis of their reasoning, see their *The Analects of Confucius* (285–300). For a similar perspective, see P. Chen (65–90). On the other hand, Robert Wardy has offered a scathing critique of such characterization (30–34).

21. There are, of course, instances where Chinese indirection misfires, and where unnecessary repetitions and superfluous appeals get ahead of effective parallels and appropriate invocations. But we should no more use such misfires to condemn Chinese indirection than we should use similar abuses of European American directness to reject the latter.

22. Another example of this "othering" can be found through the myths about the Chinese language. Namely, the non-phonetic character of the Chinese language has been frequently cited as an example of a culture that is totally different from Western culture. And for Derrida, it embodies a "testimony of powerful movement of civilization developing outside of all logocentrism" (qtd. in Tong 30). As a result, Chinese represents a sharp contrast to logocentrism. But as Tong tells us, such a reading of Chinese is in fact a misread, because it is derived from glorifying ideographic Chinese characters as a "perfect" medium of poetic representation. Therefore, any assertion of Chinese as a direct challenge to logocentrism should be called into question (30).

23. I thank Professor Jan Swearingen for alerting me to this connection—though I am solely responsible for what is being developed here.

24. Not to mention the fact that Frank Chin, her fellow Asian American writer, accuses her of faking Asian literature and lore in history, and of pandering to the Christian stereotypes about Asians, about the Chinese (3, 8, 50).

25. I am using the pinyin system here, and in parentheses is the Wade-Giles system that Kingston uses. Also see note 4 from the Introduction.

26. For a complete English translation of "Eighteen Songs of a Nomad Flute" and Cai Yan's brief biographical note (both by Dore Levy), see Chang and Saussy (22–30). I thank Professor Wilt Idema for the reference.

27. Take, for example, Professor Ien Ang, who was born in Indonesia of Chinese ancestry, educated in the Netherlands, and now lives and works in Australia. She was often asked, when traveling on holiday in Spain, Italy, or Poland, "Where are you from?" Her interlocutors, after hearing, almost with disbelief, that she was from Holland, would usually follow with this: "No, where are you *really* from?" Her standard answer to this question is "I was born in Indonesia but my ancestors were from China" (Ang 29).

CHAPTER FOUR
TERMS OF CONTACT RECONFIGURED: 恕 ("SHU" OR "RECIPROCITY") ENCOUNTERING INDIVIDUALISM

1. Foss defines ideology as "a pattern or set of ideas, assumptions, beliefs, values, or interpretations of the world by which a culture or group operates" (291)—a definition that I am drawing upon here and elsewhere in this book.

2. According to the *Oxford English Dictionary* (2nd ed.), the word "individualism" first occurred in English in 1835 in the English translation by Henry Reeve of Alexis de Tocqueville's *Democracy in America.* And its first uses in its French form, "individualisme," grew out of the general European reaction to the French Revolution and the Enlightenment (Lukes 3). On the other hand, the genesis of individualism can be traced back to philosophical activities carried out by generations of thinkers, including Hellenistic teachers. Rosemont has also offered a succinct account of why individualism is culture-specific, and why it is "the ideological child of the Age of the Enlightenment" ("Classical Confucian" 69, 68–70).

3. Collaborative overlapping or back-channeling is not considered an interruption, though. And by contrast, in Japanese culture, conversation is viewed as a collective work between interlocutors, and it is accomplished by "response words" or by Japanese "aizuchi," which conjures up the image of two swordsmiths hammering on a blade in turn (Wierzbicke 80–82).

4. The prominent sociologist Erving Goffman has also viewed self as a social construct, as a complex script of learned roles or socially engineered performances. In much the same spirit, social constructionists see self as "enmeshed in a net of others" who are complicit "in our narratives and our Self-constructions" (Bruner 114). Bruner characterizes this shift as the "narrative turn" (114).

5. According to mainland Chinese linguists Gao Mingkai and Liu Zhengtan, of 1,266 onetime neologisms that now are part of modern Chinese, 459 compounds were borrowed from Japanese *kanji* (Chinese characters), which were translations of European, mainly English, words (qtd. in L. Liu 17–18, 32). The rest either came directly from the West or from Russian. For a compelling discussion of how such neologisms reflect linguistic and rhetorical tensions between Chinese and English, and of their unprecedented scope and influence, see L. Liu (27–42; also see Bodde 284–86).

6. This kind of ambivalence is also evident in how children in China are being brought up. For example, Chinese children are being taught to be selfless and deferential toward social norms. Meanwhile, they are also expected to bring honor to themselves and their family through individual accomplishments (Pye 21). Such educational practices once again reveal a similar tension between the need to conform and the desire to establish one's identity through one's own action.

7. Other terms like "agency," "autonomy," "duty," and "obligation" did exist in classical Chinese, but were reintroduced into modern Chinese at the turn of the twentieth century via Japanese, which used *kanji* (Chinese characters) to translate modern European words. These loanwords are called "return graphic loans" because they are classical Chinese-character compounds used by the Japanese to translate European words, and then re-imported by the Chinese. In the process, these words acquired new meanings that didn't exist in classical Chinese (L. Liu 259–63, 302–42).

8. The establishment of equivalence of meaning remains a complex issue, because the historical conditions under which such equivalences of meaning were established and became naturalized, say between Chinese and English, are contingent upon what L. Liu calls "the politics of translingual practice" (8). Not to mention, of course, the deconstructionist's desire to prove that equivalents do not exist (L. Liu 15–16).

9. "Shou" (說) and "shui" (說) are homographs in Chinese; homographs were quite common in classical Chinese.

10. For example, Hall and Ames, in *Thinking Through Confucius,* view Confucius not merely as a repository of cultural values in classical China, but as a potential participant, because of his vision, in present philosophic conversation (6). I must add, though, as will become clear in my subsequent discussion, that Confucius is no less of a participant in our present-day rhetorical conversations, too. On the other hand, there are critics out there who view Confucius as representing a negative force in Chinese culture, as someone who degraded women (*Four Books* 37, bk. 17, par. 25) and who impeded social progress (Louie).

11. See Ames and Rosemont for a more detailed discussion of its textual history ("Introduction" 7–10).

12. The *Four Books* are: the *Analects,* the *Great Learning,* the *Doctrine of the Mean,* and the *Mencius.* The *Great Learning* was compiled by Zengzi, one of Confucius' disciples, and the *Doctrine of the Mean* was attributed to Zisi, Zengzi's student and Confucius' grandson (483–402 BCE). These four books became fully canonized and known as the *Four Books* after they were complied and annotated by Zhu Xi (1130–1200 CE), the famed Southern Song scholar-philosopher, who played a pivotal role in the development of what has come to be known as neo-Confucianism.

13. Their proposal finds a ready echo in Hansen's study of classical Chinese language and logic. Hansen suggests that classical Chinese nouns constitute a more mass-like part/whole, rather than one-many, picture. Instead of making some abstract reference to classes, to species, and to universals, they make reference to stuff or bits of stuff scattered in space-time (34). As he puts it, "[M]a 'horse' in term position might refer to the entire mereological object—the concrete species, or to some part, specific herd, team, or an individual horse, depending on the context" (36). In this sense, part is whole, and one is all (see also L. Young 42). While Harbsmeier challenges this mass noun hypothesis, Graham observes that it is this part/whole interpretation, rather than specifically the hypothesis, that constitutes Hansen's contribution ("Reflections and Replies" 277–78).

14. Unless otherwise indicated, all translations here and elsewhere in this chapter are mine, and I have benefited from consulting other translations by Ames and Rosemont (*The Analects of Confucius*), Dawson (*Confucius: The Analects*), and Lau (*Confucius: The Analects*). All the references are to *Four Books and Five Classics.*

15. While what I develop here concerning the discourse of 恕 is in part inspired by Hall and Ames' analysis of 恕 (283–90), I do not characterize 恕, as they do, as "a *methodology* that brings coherence and meaning to his philosophical reflections" (284; emphasis added). Rather, I see 恕, as will become more evident shortly, as a central concept whose significations are to be realized and made complete by its discursive siblings in the *Analects.*

16. 仁 ("ren") has seen many English translations, including "benevolence," "humanity," "human-heartedness," and "perfect virtue." For Hall and Rosemont, the use of "benevolence" psychologizes "ren"—a practice that does not comport well with the Chinese tradition; whereas "humanity" suggests "a shared, essential condition of being human owned by all members of the species"—a condition that "ren" does not necessarily abide by ("Introduction" 49). They have instead used "authoritative person" as their translation of "ren" because "ren" refers to one's entire person, to "one's cognitive, aesthetic, moral, and religious sensibilities" ("Introduction" 49). And the adjective "authoritative" conveys "authority," which is the reward of becoming "ren," of "embodying in oneself the values and customs of one's tradition" (50; also see Hall and Ames, *Thinking Through Confucius* 110–14). I have opted for "humaneness," partly because it is more accessible than "authoritative." But more importantly, in my view, "humaneness" accentuates the important link between the practice of "ren" and the process of becoming a person. After all, "ren" (仁)

is made of "person" (人) and the numeral "two" (二), conveying, etymologically, that one cannot be "ren" without the involvement of some other human being or beings. Similarly, "humaneness" is characterized by behavior toward others as befits becoming a person, and such behavior, I might add, is not determined by one's inner psyche, but by an on-going process of approximation and adjustment.

17.   In this sense 恕 becomes linked to "kairos": it depends on "temporality of the situation," and on the "impetus for discourse, the tension in situation" (Poulakos 39–41).

18.   Confucian "dao" is more about a way of becoming a humane person within the context of internalizing the golden tradition and doing one's utmost as one practices 恕, carries out ritual action, and conducts oneself in terms of familial relations. On the other hand, "dao" in *Daodejing* is more about a way of becoming a humane person within the context of nature, and by transcending conventions and societal impositions. Also see Combs (19–21).

19.   忠 ("zhong") should not be translated here as "loyalty." Lau states that such a translation fails to recognize that the meaning of the word as "loyalty" was a later development ("Introduction" xvi).

20.   In the *Mencius*, Mencius sees the centrality of such relationships to teaching and nurturing people: they are of "love between father and son, loyalty between ruler and subject, distinction between husband and wife, deference from the young to the old, and trust between friends" (*Four Books* 55, bk. 3A, par. 4).

21.   Again Mencius, in the *Mencius*, sees the family as the very model upon which the state should be based. "Mencius said, 'The root of the empire is in the state, the root of the state is in the family, and the root of the family is in the self'" (*Four Books* 60, bk. 4A, par. 4).

22.   For example, Xu suggests, in "The Use of Eloquence," that Confucius opposes eloquence in favor of silence—a position that, in my view, is formed by mistakenly equating Confucius' objection of eloquence (read as "glib talk") with his objection of speech. Again, what Confucius shuns and objects to is eloquent speech that does not deliver or that puts itself ahead of action (*Four Books* 16, bk. 2, par. 13).

23.   "Shu" and its focal meaning of "putting oneself in the others' place" continue to circulate in contemporary Chinese—as can be seen in such compounds as "shu-mian" (恕免, "forgive" or "pardon"), "shusi" (恕思, "think in the manner of 'shu'"), and "shuci" (恕辞, words used to seek forgiveness). I thank Professor Qi Feng for providing these examples.

24.   There is a family resemblance between the discourse of 恕 and de Bary's "Confucian personalism." For de Bary, Confucian personalism sees "the individual as fulfilling himself through the social process and a moral and spiritual communion with others" (332), and it emphasizes the importance of the individual's physical and social environment since the latter "stimulates him and defines his worth" (332). In the same essay, though, de Bary argues that this Confucian personalism was rearticulated by Neo-Confucianism in the Sung Dynasty, and it was "marked now by individualistic tendencies typical of the Sung period" (349; also see 334). Similarly, since the discourse of 恕 is predicated upon an on-going dialogue between self and others, it relates to Vygotsky's concept of "the zone of proximal development," where a child's spontaneous concepts interact with and are enriched by an adult's scientific concepts. And this kind of interaction between the child (like self) and the adult (like other) eventually becomes an integral part of the child's own reasoning (187, 193–94).

25.   My ironic use of masculine and feminine pronouns should call our attention to an almost identical phenomenon in discussions of Western classical rhetoric—where masculine pronouns are often used even though social positions and rhetorical practices were clearly gendered. Without a doubt, there is a lack of fit between the world (women and feminine roles) and words (masculine pronouns) in such a context.

26. Tsao has translated "cheng" literally as "hook up" and derivationally as "elucidation of topic" (110). Hsiung defines "cheng" as "lateral elaboration" (50)—a translation that seems to have been adopted by others (Erbaugh 24). However, "cheng" does not exactly convey the meaning of "elucidation of topic" derivationally. What it does convey, in this context, is "move from introduction to elucidation," and its focus is upon proper transition, which leads to proper elucidation of the topic. L. Chen, on the other hand, adds one more sub-structure "jie" (结), which means "end" or "conclusion," but he also acknowledges that "he" and "jie" may be "one and the same thing" (206).

27. "Jueju" was first developed in the Southern and Northern Dynasty (420–589), and it came to full maturity in the Tang Dynasty (617–907) (*Cihai*). Hinds identifies a similar pattern in Japanese expository writing known as "ki-shoo-tenketsu"— though he does not link it to "jueju" (149–50). L. Young also indicates that this four-character organizational structure is used in Chinese classical poetry (94). For a similar discussion of the link between "jueju" and this four-character structure, see Kirkpatrick ("Chinese Text Structures" 229–31).

28. In addition, there is still disagreement over whether or not the "eight-legged essay" has influenced contemporary Chinese writing. Kirkpatrick cites three reasons why it is unlikely for such a form to have an impact in contemporary China ("Chinese Text Structures" 235–37). X. Li, though, argues just the opposite: by analyzing model essays in contemporary Chinese high school writing textbooks and the two student essays, she concludes that the influence of the "eight-legged essay" is far from being over (70–71).

29. Elsewhere in the same essay, Devitt writes: "Working within existing genres as well, individuals choose and create: even the most rigid genre requires some choices, and the more common genres contain substantial flexibility within their bounds" (580). On the other hand, there are times when individual writers may not be able either to work creatively within a given genre or break out of it because their lives are in the balance. For example, during the Cultural Revolution in China (1966–76), didactic moralizing and mimicking of party lines permeated literary discourse, and any expressive attempt that appeared to deviate in the slightest from the party doctrine would be courting disaster.

30. In fact, I also see how this effort of mine can be extended to developing a more balanced understanding of the conventional American English "five-paragraph essay" formula: while recognizing its constraining and normalizing effect, we should not turn a blind eye to its embedded creative, interpersonal potential. As Devitt points out, "genre is a dynamic response to and construction of recurring situation, one that changes historically and in different social groups, that adapts and grows as the social context changes" (580).

31. In "Aristotle's *Rhetoric:* A Guide to the Scholarship," Walzer et al. have also provided a helpful summary of the recent scholarship on the concept of êthos (194–95).

32. Brinton, in "Ēthotic Argument," explicitly leans on ethos or $\acute{\varepsilon}\theta$ os (eethos) as character imbued with moral commitments. By contrast, A. Miller sees a "basic consubstantiality" between $\acute{\varepsilon}\theta$ os (ethos) as "habit" and $\acute{\eta}\theta$ os (eethos) as "character."

33. Drawing on Liddell and Scott, Jarratt and Reynolds further suggest that both $\acute{\varepsilon}\theta$ os and $\acute{\eta}\theta$ os are related to "êthea," a plural noun meaning "haunts" or "hangouts" (48).

34. It would be strange, to say the least, if the public place one habituates should turn out to be unsettling, riddled with tensions. According to A. Miller, the most basic meaning of $\acute{\eta}\theta$ os (eethos) is not "character," but "an accustomed place" (310).

CHAPTER FIVE
FROM CLASSROOM TO COMMUNITY: CHINESE AMERICAN RHETORIC ON THE GROUND

1. In *The Chinese in America: A Narrative History,* Iris Chang chronicles the journey, both past and present, of the Chinese in America with a fervent hope that the story

she tells of her people is recognized "not as a foreign story, but a quintessentially American one" (389). Part of the objective in writing this chapter is not only to write the rhetorical experiences of my fellow border residents into this American story, but also to show that their story or our story is one of situated hybridity, through which we overcome silence and bigotry both to establish our 脸 ("lian") and 面子 ("mianzi") and to achieve our agency and interconnectedness within relationships of unequal power.

2.   I am borrowing this verb from Gee to emphasize the situatedness or contingency of meaning in the sense that meanings emerge "on the spot" and as we speak, listen, consume, and act (*Discourse Analysis* 46). And my use of "assemble" is also intended to echo my discussion of indirection in Chapter Three, of how our utterances are filled with meaning surplus, with richly vague significance.

3.   In writing this chapter I have benefited a great deal from Charlie Zhang and Barbara Chin, who have kindly made available many documents necessary for my research. It is no exaggeration to state that I would not have been able to write this chapter without their help. I am solely responsible, however, for the analysis I present in this chapter.

4.   The three-day race riots in Cincinnati began shortly after the police fatally shot unarmed Timothy Thomas on 7 April 2001 in Over-the-Rhine as he tried to run away from the police. Thomas, an African American, had been wanted for a series of minor traffic violations. The riots were among the worst since the 1992 Rodney King riots in Los Angeles.

5.   It generally refers to the city of Cincinnati, its suburbs, northern Kentucky, and southern Indiana.

6.   They are: Chinese American Association of Cincinnati (CAAC), Cincinnati Contemporary Chinese School (CCCS), Greater Cincinnati Chinese Music Society (GCCMS), Cincinnati Chinese Culture Learning Association (CCCLA), Cincinnati Chinese Friendship Association (CCFA), Chinese American Business Association (CABA), and Chinese Senior Association (CSA).

7.   Other speakers included two European American mothers representing Families with Children from China, two speakers from the African American community, and one speaker from the Jewish American community. After the speakers finished their two-minute speeches and before the Council started its business meeting, Councilman John Cranley spoke briefly. He thanked the speakers and condemned the statements made by Mr. Elkington at the Over-the-Rhine Chamber of Commerce luncheon. He also indicated that no contract for Elkington was under consideration by the city.

8.   Williams challenges and complicates such a definition. By analyzing three quilts created by American women to communicate their dissatisfaction with the status quo of their times (two were created in the nineteenth century and the other in the late 1980s), she argues that the emphasis on confrontation encoded in such a traditional definition of protest rhetoric has excluded "alternative strategies of protest, including non-confrontational strategies" (21). Drawing upon her own analysis of these three quilts, she advocates a reconceptualization of protest rhetoric based on a feminist perspective (35–40).

9.   For more on the study of social protest from a rhetorical perspective, see Morris and Browne, who have put together a volume of thirty previously published essays from the rhetorical tradition of social protest and social movement scholarship. The volume is divided into three sections: "theoretical foundations," "competing perspectives," and "critical touchstones." For a review of this collection, see Steiner.

10.   Randall Lake characterizes Native American protest rhetoric, or Red Power rhetoric, as "a form of ritual self-address" ("Enacting Red Power" 141)—a characterization that corroborates Gregg's general thesis. Riding on the strength of his analysis,

Lake also points out that such rhetoric is not confined only to this need "for psychological refurbishing and affirmation" (Gregg 74) and that it is also mobilized by "the demands of an entire *weltanschauung*" (141). In fact, Red Power rhetoric becomes what Gresson calls the "rhetoric of creation" (qtd. in Lake 141).

11.   This is almost another way of saying that our utterances always enjoy a surplus of meaning to be realized by participating interlocutors within specific instances of communicative activity, and that such realizations further instantiate new meanings, new richly vague significances. See Chapters One and Three for a related discussion.

12.   "Relational modality" is one of the two dimensions to modality in English. The other is what Fairclough calls "expressive modality," which is "a matter of the speaker or writer's authority with respect to the truth or probability of a representation of reality" (105). So, the use of "may" conveys relational modality in "You may come in," and expressive modality in "It may rain soon."

13.   His denial came from the letter he wrote to Mayor Luken on 6 October 2003. In the letter, he stated that he had never made any such comments to *CityBeat* (Dunlap, "Occidental Slip").

14.   And to suggest, as does the editorial, that Elkington's remarks have offended only Chinese Americans seems to be perpetuating this binary discourse that continues to depict Chinese Americans as different, as the other. The reason is simple: one doesn't have to be Chinese American to be offended by these kinds of derogatory remarks.

15.   Speeches delivered before the City Council are recorded and kept as public record. Audio tapes of these speeches are available for purchase with a nominal fee. I want to thank the three speakers who have also personally allowed me to use their speeches in this chapter. To preserve their anonymity, I have substituted fictitious names for their real names.

16.   According to Searle, directives are attempts, in varying degrees of intensity, to get the interlocutor to do something (13). And such attempts directly interfere with his or her want to be left alone.

17.   Examples of a declarative provided by Searle include: marriage pronouncement by a minister, the act of declaring a state of war, say, by the Congress, and the issuing of a sentence by a judge (17). What makes a declarative noteworthy is not so much about the individual who issues the utterance as about the institution that confers the power and authority upon the individual who almost serves as its conduit, so to speak.

18.   For example, Mayor Luken appeared to be quite noncommittal in his public statements prior to the City Council meeting on 15 October 2003. On the one hand, he told Dunlap that if Elkington said these derogatory remarks, he would be disqualified for the city contract. On the other hand, the Mayor also said that he had told Elkington that he must return to Cincinnati to meet with the offended parties and to address the issue of diversity (Dunlap, "Occidental Slip"). Even the resolution passed by the City Council on 15 October 2003 fails to rule out this possibility, even though not hiring Elkington is one of the demands made explicitly by the Chinese American community and by every speaker before the Council.

CHAPTER SIX
CLOSING COMMENT: CHINESE FORTUNE COOKIE AS A TOPIC AGAIN

1.   In a way, my use of "utterance" here, and indeed throughout this entire book, finds resonance with Bakhtin, with his insight that utterances are never isolated or self-contained. Utterance, for him, "always presupposes utterances that precede and follow it. No one utterance can be either the first or the last. Each is only a link in the chain, and none can be studied outside this chain" ("From Notes" 136). Elsewhere

in the same essay, he writes: "Therefore, there can be neither a first nor a last meaning; it always exists among other meanings as a link in the chain of meaning, which in its totality is the only thing that can be real" (146).

REFERENCES

Ames, Roger T. and David L. Hall, trans. *Daodejing: "Making This Life Significant"; A Philosophical Translation*. New York: Ballantine, 2003.

Ames, Roger T., and Henry Rosemont, Jr., trans. *The Analects of Confucius: A Philosophical Translation*. New York: Ballantine, 1998.

———. Introduction. Ames and Rosemont, *Analects of Confucius* 1–70.

Ang, Ien. *On Not Speaking Chinese: Living between Asia and the West*. London: Routledge, 2001.

Anzaldúa, Gloria. *Borderlands/La Frontera: The New Mestiza*. 2nd ed. San Francisco: Aunt Lute, 1999.

Aristotle. *Aristotle on Rhetoric*. Trans. George A. Kennedy. New York: Oxford UP, 1991.

Austin, J. L. *How to Do Things with Words*. Ed. J. O. Urmson and Marina Sbisá. 2nd ed. Cambridge: Harvard UP, 1962.

———. "A Plea for Excuses." *Philosophical Papers*. Ed. J. O. Urmson and G. J. Warnock. 3rd ed. Oxford: Oxford UP, 1979. 175–204.

"Baguwen" (八股文). *Cihai* (*The Encyclopedic Dictionary of the Chinese Language*, 辞海).

Bakhtin, M. M. "From Notes Made in 1970–71." In Bakhtin. *Speech Genres and Other Late Essays*. Trans. Vern W. McGee. Austin: U of Texas P, 1986. 132–58.

———. "The Problem of Speech Genres." In *Speech Genres and Other Late Essays* 60–102.

———. "The Problem of the Text in Linguistics, Philology, and the Human Sciences: An Experiment in Philosophical Analysis." In *Speech Genres and Other Late Essays* 103–31.

———. "Response to a Question from the *Novy Mir* Editorial Staff." In *Speech Genres and Other Late Essays* 1–9.

Barber, Benjamin. "Jihad vs. McWorld." *Atlantic Monthly* Mar. 1992: 53–63.

Baumlin, James S., and Tita French Baumlin, eds. *Ethos: New Essays in Rhetorical and Critical Theory*. Dallas: Southern Methodist UP, 1994.

Becker, Carl B. "Reasons for the Lack of Argumentation and Debate in the Far East." *International Journal of Intercultural Relations* 10 (1986): 75–92.

Bernstein, Basil. *Theoretical Studies towards a Sociology of Language*. London: Routledge, 1971. Vol. 1 of *Class, Codes and Control*. 4 vols. 1971–75.

Bhabha, Homi. "The Third Space." *Identity: Community, Culture, Difference*. Ed. Jonathan Rutherford. London: Lawrence, 1990. 207–21.

———. *The Location of Culture*. London: Routledge, 1994.

Bizzell, Patricia. "Basic Writing and the Issue of Correctness, or, What to Do with 'Mixed' Forms of Academic Discourse." *Journal of Basic Writing* 19 (2000): 4–12.

———. "The Intellectual Work of 'Mixed' Forms of Academic Discourses." Schroeder, Fox, and Bizzell 1–10.

Bloch, Joel, and Lan Chi. "A Comparison of the Use of Citations in Chinese and English Academic Discourse." *Academic Writing in a Second Language: Essays on Research and Pedagogy*. Ed. Diane Belcher and George Braine. Norwood, NJ: Ablex, 1995. 231–74.

Bodde, Derk. *Chinese Thought, Society, and Science: The Intellectual and Social Background of Science and Technology in Pre-Modern China*. Honolulu: U of Hawaii P, 1991.

Bosco, Joseph A. "Foes of Trade Gain Strength as China Delays Solution." *Los Angeles Times* 11 Apr. 2001: B9.

Bourdieu, Pierre. "The Economics of Linguistic Exchanges." *Social Science Information* 16 (1977): 645–68.

———. "The Forms of Capital." *Education: Culture, Economy, and Society*. Ed. A. H. Halsey, Hugh Lauder, Phillip Brown, and Amy Stuart Wells. Oxford: Oxford UP, 1997. 46–56.

———. *Outline of a Theory of Practice*. Trans. Richard Nice. Cambridge: Cambridge UP, 1977.

Brinton, Alan. "Ēthotic Argument." *History of Philosophy Quarterly* 3 (1986): 245–58.

Brown, Stephen Gilbert. *Words in the Wilderness: Critical Literacy in the Borderlands*. Albany: State U of New York P, 2000.

Bruner, Jerome. *Acts of Meaning*. Cambridge: Harvard UP, 1990.

Burke, Kenneth. *A Grammar of Motives*. Berkeley: U of California P, 1962.

———. *Language as Symbolic Action: Essays on Life, Literature, and Method*. Berkeley: U of California P, 1968.

Butterfield, Fox. "China's Demand for Apology Is Rooted in Tradition." *New York Times* 7 Apr. 2001, natl. ed.: A6.

Carpenter, Edmund, and Marshall McLuhan. Introduction. *Explorations in Communication: An Anthology*. Ed. Carpenter and McLuhan. Boston: Beacon, 1960. ix-xii.

Carroll, Lewis. *Through the Looking-Glass*. In Carroll. *Alice in Wonderland*. New York: Norton, 1971. 101–209.

Chang, Iris. *The Chinese in America: A Narrative History*. New York: Viking, 2003.

Chang, Kang-I Sun, and Haun Saussy, eds. *Women Writers of Traditional China: An Anthology of Poetry and Criticism*. Stanford: Stanford UP, 1999.

Chang, Tung-sun. "A Chinese Philosopher's Theory of Knowledge." *Our Language and Our World*. Ed. S. I. Hayakawa. New York: Harper, 1959. 299–324.

Chen, Liu Ming. "Qĭ, Chéng, Zhuăn, Hé, Jié: The Discourse Pattern of a Chinese Text of Literary Criticism." *La Trobe University Working Papers in Linguistics* 2 (1989): 205–26.

Chen, Ping. *Modern Chinese: History and Sociolinguistics*. Cambridge: Cambridge UP, 1999.

Chen, Victoria. "(De)hyphenated Identity: The Double Voice in *The Woman Warrior*." *Our Voices: Essays in Culture, Ethnicity, and Communication: An Intercultural Anthology*. Ed. Alberto González, Marsha Houston, and Victoria Chen. Los Angeles: Roxbury, 1994. 3–11.

Cheng, Chung-Ying. "Chinese Philosophy and Contemporary Human Communication Theory." Kincaid 23–43.

———. "The Concept of Face and Its Confucian Roots." *Journal of Chinese Philosophy* 13 (1986): 329–48.

Chin, Frank. "Come All Ye Asian American Writers of the Real and the Fake." *The Big Aiiieeeee!: An Anthology of Chinese American and Japanese American Literature*. Ed. Jeffery Paul Chan, Frank Chin, Lawson Fusao Inada, and Shawn Wong. New York: Meridian, 1991. 1–92.

Cihai (*The Encyclopedic Dictionary of the Chinese Language*, 辞海). Shanghai: Shanghai Dictionary Publishing House, 1979.

Cohen, Richard. "A War of Words." *Washington Post* 12 Apr. 2001: A31.

Combs, Steven C. *The Dao of Rhetoric*. Albany: State U of New York P, 2005.

"Contact Language." *The Concise Oxford Dictionary of Linguistics*. Ed. P. H. Matthews. Oxford: Oxford UP, 1997.

Crowley, Tony. "Wars of Words: The Roles of Language in Eighteenth-Century Britain." In Crowley. *Language in History: Theories and Texts*. London: Routledge, 1996. 54–98.

Cushman, Donald P., and D. Lawrence Kincaid. "Introduction and Initial Insights." Kincaid 1–10.

Dawson, Raymond, trans. *Confucius: The Analects*. Oxford: Oxford UP, 1993.

———. "Western Conceptions of Chinese Civilization." *The Legacy of China*. Ed. Raymond Dawson. Oxford: Clarendon, 1964. 1–27.

de Bary, Wm. Theodore. "Neo-Confucian Individualism and Holism." Munro, *Individualism and Holism* 331–58.

de Kadt, Elizabeth. "The Concept of Face and Its Applicability to the Zulu Language." *Journal of Pragmatics* 29 (1998): 173–91.

Devitt, Amy J. "Generalizing about Genre: New Conceptions of an Old Concept." *College Composition and Communication* 44 (1993): 573–86.

Dobrin, Sidney I. "A Problem with Writing (about) 'Alternative' Discourse." Schroeder, Fox, and Bizzell 45–56.

Driscoll, Melissa. "San Francisco's Claim to Fortune Fame." *Prism Online* Nov. 1995 <http://www.journalism.sfsu.edu/www/pubs/prism/nov95/30.html>.

Dunlap, Stephanie. "Occidental Slip: OTR Consultant's Remarks Enrage Chinese Americans." *CityBeat* 15–21 Oct. 2003: 13+.

———. "OTR Consultant: No Chinese Allowed." *CityBeat* 1–7 Oct. 2003: 11–12.

Eckert, Penelope, and Sally McConnell-Ginet. "Communities of Practice: Where Language, Gender, and Power All Live." *Language and Gender: A Reader.* Ed. Jennifer Coates. Oxford: Blackwell, 1998. 484–94.

Emerson, Ralph Waldo. "Self-Reliance." *Emerson's Prose and Poetry: Authoritative Texts, Contexts, Criticism.* Ed. Joel Porte and Saundra Morris. New York: Norton, 2001. 120–37.

Eoyang, Eugene Chen. "English as a Postcolonial Tool." *English Today* 76 (2003): 23–29.

Erbaugh, Mary S. "Taking Advantage of China's Literary Practices in Teaching Chinese Students." *Modern Language Journal* 74 (1990): 15–27.

Fairclough, Norman. *Language and Power.* 2nd ed. London: Longman, 2001.

Fingarette, Herbert. "Following the 'One Thread' of the *Analects.*" *Journal of the American Academy of Religion* Thematic Issue 47.3 Thematic Issue S (September 1980): 373–405.

———. "The Music of Humanity in the Conversations of Confucius." *Journal of Chinese Philosophy* 10 (1983): 331–56.

Flowerdew, John. "Description and Interpretation in Critical Discourse Analysis." *Journal of Pragmatics* 31 (1999): 1089–99.

Foss, Sonja K. *Rhetorical Criticism: Exploration and Practice.* 2nd ed. Prospect Heights, IL: Waveland, 1996.

Foucault, Michel. "The Order of Discourse." *Untying the Text: A Post-Structuralist Reader.* Ed. Robert Young. Boston: Routledge, 1981. 48–78.

Four Books and Five Classics (四書五經, *Sishuwujin*). Wulumuqi, PRC: Xingjiang People's P, 1996.

Fox, Helen. *Listening to the World: Cultural Issues in Academic Writing.* Urbana, IL: NCTE, 1994.

Friedman, Thomas L. *The World Is Flat: A Brief History of the Twenty-First Century.* New York: Farrar, 2005.

Garrett, Mary M. "Asian Challenge." *Contemporary Perspectives on Rhetoric.* Ed. Sonja Foss, Karen A. Foss, and Robert Trapp. 2nd ed. Prospect Heights, IL: Waveland, 1991. 293–314.

———. "Classical Chinese Conceptions of Argumentation and Persuasion." *Argumentation and Advocacy* 29 (1993): 105–15.

———. "Some Elementary Methodological Reflections on the Study of the Chinese Rhetorical Tradition." *International and Intercultural Communication Annual* 22 (1999): 53–63.

Gee, James Paul. *An Introduction to Discourse Analysis: Theory and Method.* London: Routledge, 1999.

———. *Social Linguistics and Literacies: Ideology in Discourses.* 2nd ed. London: Taylor, 1996.

Geertz, Clifford. "'From the Native's Point of View': On the Nature of Anthropological Understanding." In Geertz. *Local Knowledge: Further Essays in Interpretive Anthropology.* New York: Basic, 1983. 51–70.

Gilligan, Carol. *In a Different Voice: Psychological Theory and Women's Development.* Cambridge: Harvard UP, 1982.

Gilyard, Keith, and Vorris Nunley, eds. *Rhetoric and Ethnicity.* Portsmouth, NH: Boynton-Cook, 2004.

Giroux, Henry. "Resisting Difference: Cultural Studies and the Discourse of Critical Pedagogy." *Cultural Studies.* Ed. Nelson C. Grossberg and P. Treichler. New York: Routledge, 1992. 199–211.

Glenn, Cheryl. *Rhetoric Retold: Regendering the Tradition from Antiquity through the Renaissance.* Carbondale: Southern Illinois UP, 1997.

Goffman, Erving. *Frame Analysis: An Essay on the Organization of Experience.* 1974. Boston: Northeastern UP, 1986.

———. "On Face-Work." In Goffman. *Interaction Ritual: Essays in Face-to-Face Behavior.* New York: Pantheon, 1967. 5–45.

———. *The Presentation of Self in Everyday Life.* New York: Doubleday, 1959.

Graham, A. C. *Disputers of the Dao: Philosophical Argument in Ancient China.* La Salle, IL: Open Court, 1989.

———. "Reflections and Replies." Rosemont, *Chinese Texts* 274–78.

———. *Yin-Yang and the Nature of Correlative Thinking.* Singapore: Natl. U of Singapore, 1986.

Gray-Rosendale, Laura, and Sibylle Gruber. "Introduction: Moving beyond Traditions; Exploring the Need for 'Alternative Rhetorics.'" *Alternative Rhetorics: Challenges to the Rhetorical Tradition.* Ed. Laura Gray-Rosendale and Sibylle Gruber. Albany: State U of New York P, 2001. 1–13.

Gregg, Joan. "Comments on Bernard A. Mohan and Winnie Au-Yeung Lo's 'Academic Writing and Chinese Students: Transfer and Developmental Factors.'" *TESOL Quarterly* 20 (1986): 354–58.

Gregg, Richard B. "The Ego-Function of the Rhetoric of Protest." *Philosophy and Rhetoric* 4 (1971): 71–91.

Grice, Paul. *Studies in the Way of Words.* Cambridge: Harvard UP, 1989.

Gries, Peter Hays, and Kaiping Peng. "Culture Clash? Apologies East and West." *Journal of Contemporary China* 11 (2002): 173–78.

Gumperz, John J. *Discourse Strategies.* Cambridge, Cambridge UP, 1982.

Hall, David L., and Roger T. Ames. *Anticipating China: Thinking through the Narratives of Chinese and Western Culture.* Albany: State U of New York P, 1995.

———. *Thinking from the Han: Self, Truth, and Transcendence in Chinese and Western Culture.* Albany: State U of New York P, 1998.

———. *Thinking through Confucius.* Albany: State U of New York P, 1987.

Hall, Edward. *Beyond Culture.* Garden City, NY: Anchor, 1976.

Hall, R. Mark, and Mary Rosner. "Pratt and Pratfalls: Revisioning Contact Zones." *Crossing Borderlands: Composition and Postcolonial Studies.* Ed. Andrea A. Lunsford and Lahoucine Ouzgane. Pittsburgh: U of Pittsburgh P, 2004. 95–109.

Halliday, M. A. K. *Language as Social Semiotic: The Social Interpretation of Language and Meaning.* London: Arnold, 1978.

Halloran, S. Michael. "Aristotle's Concept of *Ethos,* or if Not His, Somebody Else's." *Rhetoric Review* 1 (1982): 58–63.

———. "Further Thoughts on the End of Rhetoric." *Defining the New Rhetorics.* Ed. Theresa Enos and Stuart C. Brown. Newbury Park, CA: Sage, 1993. 109–19.

———."On the End of Rhetoric, Classical and Modern." *College English* 36 (1975): 621–31. Rpt. in *Professing the New Rhetorics: A Sourcebook.* Ed. Theresa Enos and Stuart C. Brown. Englewood Cliffs, NJ: Prentice Hall, 1994. 331–41.

———. "Tradition and Theory in Rhetoric." *Quarterly Journal of Speech* 62 (1976): 234–41.

Hansen, Chad. *Language and Logic in Ancient China.* Ann Arbor: U of Michigan P, 1983.

Harbsmeier, Christopher. "The Mass Noun Hypothesis and the Part-Whole Analysis of the White Horse Dialogue." Rosemont, *Chinese Texts* 49–66.

Herring, Susan C. Foreword. *Culture, Technology, Communication: Towards an Intercultural Global Village.* Ed. Charles Ess. Albany: State U of New York P, 2001. vii-x.

Hinds, John. "Reader versus Writer Responsibility: A New Typology." *Writing across Languages: Analysis of L2 Text.* Ed. Ulla Connor and Robert B. Kaplan. Reading, MA: Addison-Wesley, 1987. 141–52.

Ho, David Yau-fai. "On the Concept of Face." *American Journal of Sociology* 81 (1975): 867–84

Horner, Bruce, and John Trimbur. "English Only and U.S. College Composition." *College Composition and Communication* 53 (2002): 594–629.

Hsiung, James C. "Chinese Ways of Thinking and Chinese Language." *Journal of the Chinese Language Teachers Association* 4 (1969): 41–54.

Hu, Hsien Chin. "On the Concept of Chinese Face." *American Journal of Sociology* 46 (1944): 45–64.

Hwang, Kwang-kuo. "Face and Favor: The Chinese Power Game." *American Journal of Sociology* 92 (1987): 944–74.

Ikas, Karin. Interview. Anzaldúa 227–46.

"Inclusive Development: OTR Consultant; Chinese-Americans." Editorial. *Cincinnati Inquirer* 7 Oct. 2003: C10.

JanMohamed, Abdul R. "Worldliness-without-World, Homelessness-as-Home: Toward a Definition of the Specular Border Intellectual." *Edward Said: A Critical Reader.* Ed. Michael Sprinker. Oxford: Blackwell, 1992. 96–120.

JanMohamed, Abdul R., and David Lloyd. "Introduction: Toward a Theory of Minority Discourse; What Is to Be Done?" JanMohamed and Lloyd, *Nature and Context 1–16.*

———, eds. *The Nature and Context of Minority Discourse.* New York: Oxford UP, 1990.

Jarratt, Susan C., and Nedra Reynolds. "The Splitting Image: Contemporary Feminisms and the Ethics of Êthos." Baumlin and Baumlin 37–63.

Jarratt, Susan C., Elizabeth Losh, and David Puente. "Transnational Identifications: Biliterate Writers in a First-Year Humanities Course." Unpublished essay, 2004. 1–31.

Jensen, Richard J. "Evolving Protest Rhetoric: From the 1960s to the 1990s." *Rhetoric Review* 20 (2001): 28–32.

Jia, Wenshan. *The Remaking of the Chinese Character and Identity in the 21st Century: The Chinese Face Practices.* Westport, CT: Ablex, 2001.

Johnson, Frank. "The Western Concept of Self." *Culture and Self: Asian and Western Perspectives.* Ed. Anthony J. Marsella, George DeVos, and Francis L. K. Hsu. New York: Tavistock, 1985. 91–138.

Jolliffe, David A. "Writers and Their Subjects: Ethnologic and Chinese Composition." *A Rhetoric of Doing: Essays on Written Discourse in Honor of James L. Kinneavy.* Ed. Stephen P. Witte, Neil Nakadate, and Roger D. Cherry. Carbondale: Southern Illinois UP, 1992. 261–75.

"Jueju" (绝句). *Cihai* (*The Encyclopedic Dictionary of the Chinese Language,* 辞海).

Kagan, Robert, and William Kristol. "A National Humiliation." Editorial. *Weekly Standard* 16 Apr. 2001: 11–16.

Kaplan, Robert B. *The Anatomy of Rhetoric: Prolegomena to a Functional Theory of Rhetoric; Essays for Teachers.* Philadelphia: Center for Currilum Development, 1972.

———. "Cultural Thought Patterns in Inter-Cultural Education." *Language Learning* 16 (1966): 1–20.

Kennedy, George A. *Comparative Rhetoric: An Historical and Cross-Cultural Introduction.* New York: Oxford UP, 1998.

Kim, Elaine H. "Defining Asian American Realities through Literature." JanMohamed and Lloyd, *Nature and Context* 146–70.

Kincaid, D. Lawrence, ed. *Communication Theory: Eastern and Western Perspectives.* San Diego: Academic, 1987.

King, Ambrose Y. C. "The Individual and Group in Confucianism: A Relational Perspective." Munro, *Individualism and Holism* 57–84.

Kingston, Maxine Hong. "Cultural Mis-Readings by American Reviewers." *Asian and Western Writers in Dialogue: New Cultural Identities.* Ed. Guy Amirthanayagam. London: Macmillan, 1982. 55–65.

———. *The Woman Warrior: Memoirs of a Girlhood among Ghosts.* New York: Vintage, 1977.

Kirkpatrick, Andy. "Topic-Comment or Modifier-Modified?: Information Structure in Modern Standard Chinese." *Studies in Language* 20 (1996): 93–113.

———. "Traditional Chinese Text Structures and Their Influence on the Writing in Chinese and English of Contemporary Mainland Chinese Students." *Journal of Second Language Writing* 6 (1997): 223–44.

Korte, Gregory. "City Hall Assailed over Chinese Slur." *Cincinnati Inquirer.* 16 Oct. 2003: C1.

Kress, Gunther. "Critical Discourse Analysis." *Annual Review of Applied Linguistics* 11 (1990): 84–99.

Kwok, Man-ho. *Dog.* Scarborough, ON: Prentice, 1994.

Lake, Randall A. "Between Myth and History: Enacting Time in Native American Protest Rhetoric." *The Quarterly Journal of Speech* (77) 1991: 123–51.

———."Enacting Red Power: The Consummatory Function in Native American Protest Rhetoric." *Quarterly Journal of Speech* 69 (1983): 127–42.

Lakoff, George, and Mark Johnson. *Metaphors We Live By.* Chicago: U of Chicago P, 1980.

Lakoff, Robin Tolmach. *The Language War.* Berkeley: U of California P, 2000.

Lau, D. C. *Confucius: The Analects.* 2nd ed. Sha Tin, Hong Kong: Chinese UP, 1992.

"Let Patriotism Become the Force of Modernization." Editorial. *People's Daily* 11 Apr. 2001: 1.

Levinas, Emmanuel. *Totality and Infinity: An Essay on Exteriority.* Trans. Alphonso Lingis. Pittsburgh: Duquesne UP, 1969.

Li, Charles N., and Sandra A. Thompson. *Mandarin Chinese: Functional Reference Grammar.* Berkeley: U of California P, 1981.

———. "Subject and Topic: A New Typology of Language." *Subject and Topic.* Ed. Charles N. Li. New York: Academic, 1976. 457–89.

Li, Xiao-ming. "'Track (Dis)Connecting': Chinese High School and University Writing in a Time of Change." *Writing and Learning in Cross-National Perspective: Transitions from Secondary to Higher Education.* Ed. David Foster and David R. Russell. Urbana, IL: NCTE, 1999. 49–87.

Liddell, Henry George, and Robert Scott, comps. *A Greek-English Lexicon.* Rev. ed. Oxford: Clarendon, 1961.

Lipson, Carol S. and Roberta A. Binkley, eds. *Rhetoric before and beyond the Greeks.* Albany: State U of New York P, 2004.

Liu, Lydia H. *Translingual Practice: Literature, National Culture, and Translated Modernity— China, 1900–1937.* Stanford: Stanford UP, 1995.

Liu, Yameng. "'Nothing Can Be Accomplished If the Speech Does Not Sound Agreeable': Rhetoric and the Invention of Classical Chinese Discourse." Lipson and Binkley 147–64.

———. "To Capture the Essence of Chinese Rhetoric: An Anatomy of a Paradigm in Comparative Rhetoric." *Rhetoric Review* 14.2 (1996): 318–35.

Lloyd, G. E. R. *Adversaries and Authorities: Investigations into Ancient Greek and Chinese Science.* Cambridge: Cambridge UP, 1996.

Louie, Kam. *Critiques of Confucius in Contemporary China.* New York: St. Martin's, 1980.

Lowe, Lisa. "Heterogeneity, Hybridity, Multiplicity: Marking Asian American Differences." *Diaspora* 1 (1991): 24–44.

Lowry, Richard J., ed. *Dominance, Self-Esteem, Self-Actualization: Germinal Papers of A. H. Maslow.* Monterey, CA: Brooks-Cole, 1973.

Lu, Min-zhan. "Conflict and Struggle: The Enemies or Preconditions of Basic Writing." *College English* 54 (1992): 887–913.

———. "From Silence to Words: Writing as Struggle." *College English* 49 (1987): 437–48.

———. *Shanghai Quartet: The Crossings of Four Women of China.* Pittsburgh: Duquesne UP, 2001.

Lu, Xing. *Rhetoric in Ancient China, Fifth to Third Century B.C.E.: A Comparison with Classical Greek Rhetoric.* Columbia: U of South Carolina, 1998.

Luke, Steven. *Individualism.* Oxford: Blackwell, 1973.

Lyons, Scott. "A Captivity Narrative: Indians, Mixedbloods, and 'White' Academe." *Outbursts in Academe: Multiculturalism and Other Sources of Conflict.* Ed. Kathleen Dixon. Portsmouth, NH: Boynton-Cook, 1998. 87–108.

Mao, LuMing. "Beyond Politeness Theory: 'Face' Revisited and Renewed." *Journal of Pragmatics* 21 (1994): 451–86.

———. "Re-Clustering Traditional Academic Discourse: Alternating with Confucian Discourse." Schroeder, Fox, and Bizzell 112–25.

———. "Reflective Encounters: Illustrating Comparative Rhetoric." *Style* 37 (2003): 401–25.

Markus, Hazel Rose, and Shinobu Kitayama. "Culture and the Self: Implications for Cognition, Emotion, and Motivation." *Psychological Review* 98 (1991): 224–53.

Massey, Doreen. "A Global Sense of Place." In Massey. *Space, Place, and Gender*. Minneapolis: U of Minnesota P, 1994. 146–56.

Matalene, Carolyn. "Contrastive Rhetoric: An American Writing Teacher in China." *College English* 47 (1985): 789–808.

———. "East and West: Identity and Difference." *Rhetoric Review* 16 (1997): 162–63.

Matsumoto, Yoshiko. "Reexamination of the Universality of Face: Politeness Phenomena in Japan." *Journal of Pragmatics* 12 (1988): 403–26.

Mauss, Marcel. "A Category of the Human Mind: The Notion of Person; the Notion of Self." *The Category of the Person: Anthropology, Philosophy, History*. Ed. Michael Carrithers, Steven Collins, and Steven Lukes. Cambridge: Cambridge UP, 1985. 1–25.

McLuhan, Marshall. *The Gutenberg Galaxy: The Making of Typographic Man*. Toronto: U of Toronto P, 1962.

Mead, George H. *Mind, Self and Society: From the Standpoint of a Social Behaviorist*. Chicago: U of Chicago P, 1934.

Miller, Arthur B. "Aristotle on Habit (ἔθος) and Character (ἦθος): Implications for the *Rhetoric*." *Speech Monographs* 41 (1974): 308–16.

Miller, Richard E. "Fault Lines in the Contact Zone." *College English* 56 (1994): 389–408.

Morris, Charles E., III, and Stephen H. Browne, eds. *Readings on the Rhetoric of Social Protest*. State College, PA: Strata, 2001.

Munro, Donald J. *The Concept of Man in Contemporary China*. Ann Arbor: U of Michigan P, 1977.

———. "The Family Network, the Stream of Water, and the Plant." Munro, *Individualism and Holism* 259–91.

———, ed. *Individualism and Holism: Studies in Confucian and Taoist Values*. Ann Arbor: Center for Chinese Studies, 1985.

Nisbett, Richard E. *The Geography of Thought: How Asians and Westerners Think Differently . . . and Why*. New York: Free P, 2003.

Ogulnick, Karen, ed. *Language Crossings: Negotiating the Self in a Multicultural World*. New York: Teachers College P, 2000.

Oliver, Robert T. *Communication and Culture in Ancient India and China*. Syracuse: Syracuse UP, 1971.

Ortiz, Fernando. *Cuban Counterpoint: Tobacco and Sugar*. Trans. Harriet de Onis. New York: Knopf, 1947.

Pea, Roy D. "Practices of Distributed Intelligence and Designs for Education." Salomon 47–87.

Pennycook, Alastair. *English and the Discourses of Colonialism*. London: Routledge, 1998.

Perkins, David N. "Person-Plus: A Distributed View of Thinking and Learning." Salomon 88–110.

Perkins, Dorothy. *Encyclopedia of China: The Essential Reference to China, Its History and Culture*. New York: Roundtable P, 1999.

Peters, John Durham. "John Locke, the Individual, and the Origin of Communication." *Quarterly Journal of Speech* 75 (1989): 387–99.

Poulakos, John. "Toward a Sophistic Definition of Rhetoric." *Philosophy and Rhetoric* 16 (1983): 35–48.

Powell, Malea. "Rhetorics of Survivance: How American Indians *Use* Writing." *College Composition and Communication* 53 (2002): 396–434.

Pratt, Mary Louise. "Arts of the Contact Zone." *Profession 91*. New York: MLA, 1991. 33–40.

———. "Criticism in the Contact Zone: Decentering Community and Nation." *Critical Theory, Cultural Politics, and Latin American Narrative*. Ed. Seven M. Bell, Albert H. LeMay, and Leonard Orr. Notre Dame: U of Notre Dame P, 1993. 83–102.

———. *Imperial Eyes: Travel Writing and Transculturation*. London: Routledge, 1992.

Prueher, Joseph W. "Letter from Ambassador Prueher to Chinese Minister of Foreign Affairs Tang." <http://www.whitehouse.gov/news/releases/2001/04/20010411-1.html>.

Pye, Lucian W. "The State and the Individual: An Overview Interpretation." *The Individual and the State in China*. Ed. Brian Hook. Oxford: Clarendon P, 1996. 16–42.

"Qichengzhuanhe" (起承轉合). *Cihai (The Encyclopedic Dictionary of the Chinese Language*, 辞海).

Raphals, Lisa. "Gendered Virtue Reconsidered: Notes from the Warring States and Han." *The Sage and the Second Sex: Confucianism, Ethics, and Gender*. Ed. Chenyang Li. Chicago: Open Court, 2000. 223–47.

———. *Sharing the Light: Representations of Women and Virtue in Early China*. Albany: State U of New York P, 1998.

"Ren" (仁). *Shuowenjiezi (Shuowen Lexicon*, 説文解字).

Reynolds, Nedra. "*Ethos* as Location: New Sites for Understanding Discursive Authority." *Rhetoric Review* 11 (1993): 325–38.

Rosaldo, Renato. *Culture and Truth: The Remaking of Social Analysis*. Boston: Beacon, 1989.

Rosemont, Henry, Jr. "Against Relativism." *Interpreting across Boundaries*. Ed. Gerald James Larson and Eliot Deutsch. Princeton: Princeton UP, 1988. 36–70.

———, ed. *Chinese Texts and Philosophical Contexts: Essays Dedicated to Angus C. Graham*. LaSalle, IL: Open Court, 1991.

———. "Classical Confucian and Contemporary Feminist Perspectives on the Self: Some Parallels and Their Implications." *Culture and Self: Philosophical and Religious Perspectives, East and West*. Ed. Douglas Allen. Boulder: Westview P, 1997. 63–82.

Roskelly, Hephzibah, and Kate Ronald. *Reason to Believe: Romanticism, Pragmatism, and the Possibility of Teaching*. Albany: State U of New York P, 1998.

Said, Edward. *Orientalism*. New York: Vintage, 1979.

Salomon, Gavriel, ed. *Distributed Cognitions: Psychological and Educational Considerations*. Cambridge: Cambridge UP, 1993.

Sanger, David E. "Powell Sees No Need for Apology: Bush Again Urges Return of Crew." *New York Times* 4 Apr. 2001, natl. ed.: A1.

Schroeder, Christopher, Helen Fox, and Patricia Bizzell, eds. *ALT DIS: Alternative Discourses and the Academy*. Portsmouth, NH: Boynton-Cook, 2002.

Scollon, Ron, and Susanne B. K. Scollon. "Face Parameters in East-West Discourse." *The Challenge of Facework: Cross-Cultural and Interpersonal Issues*. Ed. Stella Ting-Toomey. Albany: State U of New York P, 1994. 133–57.

———. *Narrative, Literacy and Face in Interethnic Communication*. Norwood, NJ: Ablex, 1981.

———. "Topic Confusion in English-Asian Discourse." *World Englishes* 10 (1991): 113–25.

Searle, John. "A Taxonomy of Illocutionary Acts." In Serle. *Expression and Meaning: Studies in the Theory of Speech Acts*. Cambridge: Cambridge UP, 1979. 1–29.

Shen, Fan. "The Classroom and the Wider Culture: Identity as a Key to Learning English Composition." *College Composition and Communication* 40 (1989): 459–66.

Shohat, Ella. "Notes on the 'Post-Colonial.'" *Social Text* 31/32 (1992): 99–113.

Shuowenjiezi (Shuowen Lexicon, 説文解字). Comp. Xushen. Ed. Quhua Chui and Zhongwei He. Beijing: Beijing Normal UP, 2000.

Silbergeld, Jerome. *China into Film: Frames of Reference in Contemporary Chinese Cinema*. London: Reaktion, 1999.

Smith, Arthur H. *Chinese Characteristics*. Rev. ed. New York: Fleming, 1894.

Steiner, Mark Allan. "Remembering the Rhetorical Tradition of Social Protest Scholarship." *The Review of Communication* 2.2 (2002): 192–95.

Stepanchuk, Carol, and Charles Wong. *Mooncakes and Hungry Ghosts: Festivals of China.* San Francisco: China Books, 1991.

Tai, James H. Y. "Temporal Sequence and Chinese Word Order." *Principles and Prediction: The Analysis of Natural Language.* Ed. John Haiman. Amsterdam: Benjamins, 1985. 49–72.

Tan, Amy. "The Language of Discretion." *Encountering Cultures: Reading and Writing in a Changing World.* Ed. Richard Holeton. Englewood Cliffs, NJ: Prentice, 1992. 61–68.

———. "Mother Tongue." *The Best American Essays 1991.* Ed. Joyce Carol Oates. New York: Ticknor, 1991. 198–202.

Tannen, Deborah. *You Just Don't Understand: Women and Men in Conversation.* New York: Morrow, 1990.

Tong, Q. S. "Myths about the Chinese Language." *Canadian Review of Comparative Literature* March–June (1993): 29–47.

Tsao, Feng-Fu. "Linguistics and Written Discourse in Particular Languages: Contrastive Studies; English and Chinese (Mandarin)." *Annual Review of Applied Linguistics.* Ed. Robert B. Kaplan. Rowley, MA: Newbury, 1982. 99–117.

Tu, Ching-I. "The Chinese Examination Essay: Some Literary Considerations." *Monumenta Serica* 31 (1974–75): 393–406.

Tyrwhitt-Drake, Hugh. "Resisting the Discourse of Critical Discourse Analysis: Reopening a Hong Kong Case Study." *Journal of Pragmatics* 31 (1999): 1081–88.

Vygotsky, Lev. *Thought and Language.* Trans. and ed. Alex Kozulin. Cambridge: MIT, 1986.

Walzer, Arthur E., Michael Tiffany, and Alan G. Gross. "Aristotle's *Rhetoric:* A Guide to the Scholarship." *Rereading Aristotle's Rhetoric.* Ed. Alan G. Gross and Arthur E. Walzer. Carbondale: Southern Illinois UP, 2000. 185–203.

Wardy, Robert. *Aristotle in China: Language, Categories and Translation.* Cambridge: Cambridge UP, 2000.

Watson, Burton. Introduction. Zhuangzi 1–28.

Wierzbicka, Anna. *Cross-Cultural Pragmatics: The Semantics of Human Interaction.* 2nd ed. Berlin: Mouton, 2003.

Williams, Mary Rose. "A Reconceptualization of Protest Rhetoric: Women's Quilts as Rhetorical Forms." *Women's Studies in Communication* 17 (1994): 20–44.

Wolf, Margery. "Beyond the Patrilineal Self: Constructing Gender in China." *Self as Person in Asian Theory and Practice.* Ed. Roger T. Ames, Wimal Dissanayake, and Thomas P. Kasulis. Albany: State U of New York P, 1994. 251–67.

"Work for Safeguards with China." Editorial. *Los Angeles Times* 12 Apr. 2001: B10.

Xu, George. "The Use of Eloquence: The Confucian Perspective." Lipson and Binkley 115–29.

Yang, Mayfair Mei-hui. *Gifts, Favors, and Banquets: The Art of Social Relationships in China.* Ithaca: Cornell UP, 1994.

Young, Linda W. L. *Crosstalk and Culture in Sino-American Communication.* Cambridge: Cambridge UP, 1994.

Young, Robert J. C. *Colonial Desire: Hybridity in Theory, Culture and Race.* London: Routledge, 1995.

Yum, June Ock. "The Impact of Confucianism on Interpersonal Relationships and Communication Patterns in East Asia." *Communication Monographs* 55 (1988): 374–88.

Zhang, Longxi, "The Myth of the Other: China in the Eyes of the West." *Critical Inquiry* 15 (1988): 108–131.

Zhu, Xi. *Notes on the Analects.* Jinan, PRC: Qiru P, 1992.

Zhuangzi. *The Complete Works of Zhuangzi (Chuang Tzu).* Trans. Burton Watson. New York: Columbia UP, 1986.

INDEX

LuMing Mao is Associate Professor and Director of Graduate Studies in the Department of English at Miami University. He teaches and researches Chinese and European American rhetorical traditions, Chinese American rhetoric, linguistics, pragmatics, and writing in multi-cultural spaces. He is co-editor, with Robert Hariman, Susan Jarratt, Andrea Lunsford, and Jacqueline Jones Royster, of the upcoming *Norton Anthology of Rhetoric and Writing*. He is also collaborating with Morris Young on an edited collection, titled *Representations: Doing Asian American Rhetoric*.